"*Wholly Different* is a moving and fascinating experience of Darwish's discovery of Biblical values. This precious account of a courageous woman confronting the trauma of discovering and revising her past life's dilemmas in total conflict with Western values describes her final liberation from the past into values of truth and love. A most enlightening and well-analyzed book that should be widely read."

—BAT YE'OR, author of *Eurabia*, *The Dhimmi*, and *Islam and Dhimmitude*

WHOLLY DIFFERENT

WHOLLY
DIFFERENT

Why I Chose Biblical Values
Over Islamic Values

NONIE DARWISH

REGNERY
FAITH

Regnery Faith™ is a trademark of Salem Communications Holding Corporation; Regnery® is a registered trademark of Salem Communications Holding Corporation

Cataloging-in-Publication data on file with the Library of Congress

ISBN 978-1-62157-578-8

Published in the United States by
Regnery Faith
An imprint of Regnery Publishing
A Division of Salem Media Group
300 New Jersey Ave NW
Washington, DC 20001
www.RegneryFaith.com

Manufactured in the United States of America

10 9 8 7 6 5 4 3 2 1

Books are available in quantity for promotional or premium use. For information on discounts and terms, please visit our website: www.Regnery.com.

Distributed to the trade by
Perseus Distribution
www.perseusdistribution.com

To my pastor and his wife,
Jim and Alice Tolle

CONTENTS

INTRODUCTION

Recently there has been a push to replace the term "Judeo-Christian" with the term "Abrahamic"—so as to include Islam in the roll of religions that are the source of our common values. Westerners are eager to show good will toward Muslims, ready to make a real effort to settle the cultural differences that have divided people from different religious backgrounds. Thus it seems to make sense to unite Islam with Christianity and Judaism as an Abrahamic faith, to tout it as preaching more or less the same principles and values. Some interfaith groups have even started referring to certain confluence between Christianity and Islam as Chrislam.

In fact, attempts to reconcile and unite Islam with Christianity are as old as Islam itself. But such attempts have always failed. A primary reason for that failure is that Islam's moral values are diametrically opposed to Biblical moral values. Many Muslims deny this fact—particularly when communicating with Westerners. In private, in mosques, and in Islamic books, Muslims see Jews and Christians as their enemies.

It is true that Islam, like the Bible, originated in the same area of the world, the Middle East, and some call Arabs and Jews "cousins." But close proximity and blood relations are no guarantees to harmony or compatibility. In fact some of the deadliest and most toxic relationships could stem from within the same family. Islam's position on the Bible was the original Mideast cultural clash in which Islam charged into a bloody reversal of where Middle East Biblical values were heading. At its core, Islam came to preserve and re-assert Arabian Peninsula culture.

Islam's opposition to Biblical and Western values explains why, wherever Muslims go, Muslim leaders stand against assimilation. Islamic doctrine absolutely rejects the Western idea of the melting pot. Muslims are inculcated with contempt for Christians, Christian values, and the Western civilization they built.

Supporters of incorporating Islam into Western culture don't understand that co-existence as equals with other religions is prohibited under Islam. The West is only now, after decades of trying to assimilate millions of Muslim refugees and immigrants, discovering the impossibility of incorporating Islam.

Most people are unaware of the context in which Islam was born. Islam was created six hundred years after Christianity not to affirm the Bible, but to discredit it; not to co-exist with "the people of the book,"—Jews and Christians—but to replace them.

Despite Islam's doctrine of non-assimilation, a large number of Muslim immigrants in the West have chosen to assimilate. That was my choice, as a Muslim immigrant to the United States. But many Muslim immigrants who are more faithful to the teachings of Islam refuse to assimilate and work hard against the assimilation of other

Muslims. Muslim leaders frequently speak out against assimilation, as when London's Muslim mayor Sadiq Khan said in a speech when visiting the U.S. that immigrants shouldn't have to assimilate into American culture. The mayor did not say why assimilation was a bad idea.[1]

Consider that it takes more effort on the part of an individual not to assimilate than to assimilate to the society he or she lives in. To intentionally refuse assimilation is not the norm; it requires a great effort and runs against the grain of human nature, which tends to acclimate and adapt to new environments. This is how human beings are wired, and this is what I chose to do when I moved to the U.S. I assimilated because it came naturally.

The refusal to assimilate to the West by a religion or ideology should be a clear red flag. Particularly if that refusal is motivated by hostility and contempt for Western values.

But for their own reasons, liberals in the West tend to agree with Mayor Khan. Progressives share the same negative views of the melting pot as faithful Muslims. The Left's celebration of "multiculturalism" works in tandem with Islamic teachings regarding assimilation to preserve the cultural identity, customs, and moral values of Muslim immigrants.

Neither Islamic leaders nor Western liberals talk about the end game of non-assimilation. In fact the refusal to assimilate means separation of immigrant groups and division in society—then, perhaps, if the wishes of the truly hardcore Muslims are fulfilled, Islamic dominance could be the end game.

Islam's Goals

The strategic goals of those faithful Muslims in North America are no real secret. They can be found in Islamic books, heard in mosque sermons, garnered from the speeches of Muslim politicians, heard at Islamic conferences and on Arab media. They were summarized in a document used as evidence in the 2008 Holy Land Foundation terror-funding trial. Below is a partial English translation of the document:

> Enablement of Islam in North America, meaning: establishing an effective and a stable Islamic Movement led by the Muslim Brotherhood which adopts Muslims' causes domestically and globally, and which works to expand the observant Muslim base, aims at unifying and directing Muslims' efforts, presents Islam as a civilization alternative, and supports the global Islamic State wherever it is.... the Movement must plan and struggle to obtain "the keys" and the tools of this process in carry out [sic] this grand mission as a 'Civilization Jihadist' responsibility ... The process of settlement is a 'Civilization-Jihadist Process' with all the word means. The Ikhwan [Muslim Brotherhood] must understand that their work in America is a kind of grand jihad in eliminating and destroying the Western civilization from within and "sabotaging" its miserable house by their hands and the hands of the believers.... [emphasis added][2]

Those, plain and simple, are the values I grew up with. All the resources and energy of Islamic culture are dedicated to conquering the land of the "kafirs" (the unbelievers, meaning non-Muslims), which is described as a miserable house. Islam regards a society based on Biblical values as a miserable abomination. Muslims must never live in such a society without the goal of rebelling against it.

The goals of Islam are not religious goals. Or at least they are not religious in the sense that Christians tend to understand religion. The aim of faithful Muslims is the submission of the whole world to Islam. In fact, submission is exactly what "Islam" means.

The existential threat that Islam poses to Western civilization is no longer the old-fashioned one of Islamic armies standing at the gates of Vienna or Spain. The conquest is being attempted again, but today it's through immigration and by taking advantage of the Western values of inclusion and tolerance.

In the modern era, Islamic armies are weaker than Western armies. So in our day Islam has chosen conquest from within through immigration. And so far, the West has been a willing participant in its own invasion, by way of a one-sided open door policy.

While Muslim refugees and other immigrants have been welcomed into Europe and America, flooding Western cities and little towns, the Islamic nations have never reciprocated. In fact the few remaining traces of Christian and Jewish presence in the Middle East are being systematically liquidated and ethnically cleansed.

The subject of Islam and its moral values is uncomfortable to most people, and scary to many. Scared and uncomfortable is exactly how I felt when I started this project to delve into why I chose to live by Biblical values rather than Islamic values. But fear and denial are what Islam counts on to keep the West uninformed about the bold goals of Islam—and its many weaknesses. The Muslims who aim for eventual Islamic domination over Western society live in fear of exposure, but Islam thrives on other people's human decency and fear of terror, and on human beings' ability to compromise against their best interest in order to survive. That was how I survived life in the Islamic world for thirty years.

My life under Islam was a constant struggle to survive and placate a system that was unforgiving and unaccepting of anything less than total surrender of my humanity, dignity, and privacy—in other words, my life, liberty, and pursuit of happiness.

Every Islamic terror attack on the West sends a message: *Islamic values, morality, and way of life must replace those of the West whether you like it or not.* With every stabbing and beheading by Muslims chanting "Allahu Akbar" that is proudly posted on the internet, the message is *Allah's law must replace Western laws.*

Islam is very competitive. Muslims constantly compare their own society with the West. Terrorism is a symptom of a culture unable to co-exist and immersed in frustration at not measuring up.

Even though, as we shall see, Islamic moral values are the antithesis of those of the West, Muslims in the West are desperately trying to convince everyone here that Islam, Judaism, and Christianity are all basically one and the same Abrahamic faith. But that is an intentional lie, the opposite of everything preached in mosques.

The Koran is predominantly a book about the kafirs, or non-Muslims, rather than a book about Muslims. Sixty-four percent of the Koran speaks about non-Muslims, the kafirs, who include Jews and Christians. The Islamic God, Allah, requires his followers to dedicate their lives to change, fix, convert, or kill the evil kafirs, whom Allah calls his enemies. That, in a nutshell, is the holy mission of a Muslim if he is to please his God and go to heaven.

A Religion with No Faith in Itself

What is written in the Koran about non-Muslims should alarm the West. Islam's focus on changing others by force has produced a system that is destructive to everyone, including Muslims themselves.

Conversion by force is necessary in Islam because Muslim leaders believe that if humanity is allowed freedom whether or not to choose life under Islamic values, Islam will disappear. In February of 2013, on Al Jazeera TV network, Sheikh Yusuf al-Qaradawi stated that the application of the death penalty for those who leave Islam is a necessity because without such severe punishments no one would choose to live under Islam. These were his exact words: "If they had gotten rid of the apostasy punishment Islam wouldn't exist today."[3]

Since its inception and up to today, Islam lacks confidence in itself. Muslims do not believe that their religion will be chosen without the use of force. Muslims' frustrations and insecurity about Islam's inability to compete with the West and its Biblical values have led them to adopt attitudes, actions, and customs unique to the Islamic community—ranging from being easily offended and avoiding honest debate to the use of threats, fear, government coercion, and terrorism to enforce Islamic "sharia" law.

The mere existence of a freely chosen competing faith threatens Islam at its very core and undermines its ability to produce the kind of society it envisions.

Thus the Bible has become the number one threat to Islam's ability to prevail and create its worldwide caliphate.

How Multiculturalism Fails Muslims

Islam absolutely rejects Biblical values, but the multicultural Left in the West has a more complicated relationship with them. Multiculturalism means giving mutual respect and freedom to other religions and cultures. Ironically, for multiculturalism to succeed, all parties would have to share such values: co-existence, respect for other cultures, freedom of the individual, and human rights. But unfortunately that is not the reality in our world, where values are often incompatible and at odds with one another. The truth is that the freedom and mutual respect that multiculturalism is based on are ultimately Biblical values. The Golden Rule and "Love your neighbor as yourself," which can seem obviously true and universal to those of us who live in the West, are straight from the Bible. The concept of the Golden Rule—"Do unto others as you would have them do unto you"—is totally alien to Islam. Nothing like love and tolerance to other human beings just because they are human exists in Islam, but only between Muslims of the same sect.

If the ethics of Islam were based on the Golden Rule and generally on the ethics of the Bible, the world today would not have an Arab-Israeli conflict or a fourteen-hundred-year-old Shiite-Sunni vendetta, still going strong. Nor would we be seeing the mass flight and expulsion of Christians from the Middle East. But the brotherhood of humanity does not exist in Islam, period.

Promoters of multiculturalism have ignored the deep roots of predatory ideologies, particularly the supremacist religion of Islam. Islam is the only religion whose fundamental objective is the subjugation of all other religions and all non-Muslims to live under its own law (sharia) even if they don't believe in it or want to. For that reason force, terrorism, humiliation, deception, and financial extortion (jizya)—all tools to make Islam supreme—are values in Islam.

Interfaith dialogue is only practiced in the West and almost always initiated by Jewish or Christian groups. To discuss religion openly with non-Muslims in a friendly atmosphere and on equal terms is an alien and uncomfortable idea to most Muslims.

Since its inception, Islam has never tolerated being compared to the Bible and its values. Islam simply doesn't stand up well to the comparison. One way the Koran avoids being judged in light of the Bible is the claim—in the Koran itself—that Jews and Christians don't even have the original Bible, because they corrupted it. Muslims believe that there are major discrepancies between what was originally revealed in the Bible and what the Bible says today—which the Koran came to correct.

That goes some distance to explaining why it is a stressful experience for Muslims to discuss their religion openly with Christians and

Jews. In addition, there is the uncomfortable feeling Muslims have when they follow their obligation under Islamic law to lie if necessary to protect Islam. Questions about the concepts of "jihad" (mandatory war against non-Muslims), "taqiyya" (holy deception), and the "kafir" (despised unbelievers) do necessitate lying if the discussion is to be kept civil. Dialogue between Muslims and non-Muslims could also bring Muslims face to face with the destructive values of their own religion, which prohibits questioning.

Christians and Jews in the Middle East, who are scorned and oppressed, would welcome any opportunity to express their concerns and fears, but they never get a chance to dialogue with Muslims. Christians who make any attempt at what we in the West call inter-faith dialogue are called troublemakers and disrespectful to Islam. Sometimes they are arrested and punished. And Muslims who reach out to learn about other faiths risk being branded apostates—who are at risk of the death penalty in many Islamic countries. Although friendships between Muslims and non-Muslims do exist, they are usually kept quiet in Muslim countries, where non-Muslims are not equal with Muslims in the eyes of the law.

For centuries Muslims have been forbidden to question, analyze, or critique their own scriptures, let alone to read those of other faiths. But today it only takes an airplane flight from the Muslim world to the West for a Muslim to suddenly be told that dialoguing with Jews and Christians is a virtue.

As a former Muslim who lived in the Muslim world up to age thirty, I never heard a discussion about why Muhammad married a six-year-old girl. No one around me questioned why, and neither did I. It was only when I moved to the West and encountered Biblical val-ues that I started evaluating the norms and values that I grew up with.

There are various defenses Muslims raise against having to answer the difficult questions about Islam that are raised by comparing it to other religions. We have all heard Muslims defend radical Islam by putting down Christianity and Judaism as not any better, or by saying that all religions have a radical side or all religions have terrorists. Such generalizations are not true; they are simply meant to end the discussion.

Multiculturalism gives Muslims permission not to reconsider Islamic values in the light of the Biblical values that have shaped the West. As an immigrant myself, I know firsthand that the message many of us heard from multiculturalists was *Please don't change. We love you and want you to stay just the way you are.* This message is unhealthy for everyone involved. It only encourages Muslim immigrants who live in the West to put their efforts into remaining loyal to the old culture. This stunts the natural growth of immigrants in their new— much freer, healthier, and all-around better—environment.

Multiculturalism only tightens the taboos against questioning Islam and prolongs the ignorance that props up that religion.

The Threat Is Not Just ISIS

The threat of Islam is of course obvious in the continual terror attacks all over the world. But Islam also poses a hidden threat to the West, one that most are unaware of: the danger of the erosion of Biblical values.

I had to write this book to uncover the full scope of this threat from Islam—something that the West desperately needs to be aware of. Islamic values versus Biblical values is a bloody collision waiting to happen. The West must be warned. But I am also writing this book for Muslim immigrants who think they can be devout Muslims and at the same time good American citizens with respect for their new country's values and Constitution. Any Muslim who is aware of Islamic doctrine should be honest with him or her self and admit that Islamic values are fundamentally incompatible with Western values, the U.S. Constitution, and the American way of life.

Mazin AbdulAdhim, a Muslim imam in Canada who is affiliated with the radical Islamic global movement of Hizb ut-Tahrir, points out that "Islam and democracy are contradictory and absolutely incompatible." He has "called on Canadian Muslims to stick to the Islamic law, reject secularism, work together to spread Islam, re-establish the Islamic State [the caliphate] and implement" sharia law.[4]

This sheikh is not committing acts of terror, but nonetheless he is doing jihad in the open and asking Muslims in Canada to do the same: to fight democracy and Biblical values, to defy the Canadian system of government and law, and to establish an Islamic state instead. All Western countries have hundreds and thousands of Muslim leaders and individuals who think the same way.

ISIS terrorists have already infiltrated the refugee population. But that population contains many more Muslims who are not terrorists—and yet want Islam to take over their new homes, replacing Biblical values with Koranic values. That's ironic, considering the reason refugees from all over the Middle East are flocking to the West in the first place. The Muslim world does not have a shortage of land for its citizens. In fact the size of the Muslim world and its natural resources are larger than those of Europe. What the Muslim world lacks are stable governments, respect for human and women's rights, equal gender and religious rights under the law, stability, and a good foundation of laws upon which citizens can build their lives and thrive. If Muslim immigrants eventually succeed in replacing Western laws and traditions and Biblical values with sharia, the very conditions that drew them to the West in the first place will have vanished.

Of course there are also Muslims among the refugees who do not want to impose sharia on the United States. But their immigration contributes to the problem in another way. The West prides itself on having a big heart, but it will not solve the problem of Islam by continuing to absorb refugees who are supposedly the moderate ones that don't want to live under ISIS. By absorbing all the "good guys" the West is emptying Syria, Iraq, and many other hot spots in the Middle East of those who should resist the likes of ISIS. And if no one resists ISIS, Al Qaeda, and their ilk, then how will Islamic culture ever reform? The West is simply making it easier for ISIS to prevail without any resistance.

Daily, I encounter Westerners who have no clue as to what is at stake when it comes to Islam. A Jewish woman at one of my talks asked, "But how come Muslims in my interfaith group tell me that they love peace and friendship with Jews and Christians and if it wasn't for Islamophobia and American foreign policy in the Middle East, there would have been no problems between Islam and the West?"

When I asked her, "Where was this interfaith dialogue group held?" she told me it was in Israel. Then I asked her "How many interfaith dialogue groups do you think exist in any majority-Muslim country?"

She answered, "I don't know but I know one in the West Bank."

"Who initiated it?" I asked.

She responded: "Israelis initiate them."

I then asked her, "Do you think there are interfaith dialogues between Sunnis and Shiites or between Egyptian Muslims and Coptic Christians?" She said she didn't know. I told her there are none because Islam prohibits it. Unfortunately, when the woman left, I could not tell if she was happy or disappointed with my answer.

The above dialogue is more or less repeated virtually every time I speak publicly—proving how the West is in need of the truth, regardless of how hard it is to hear.

Most of us would like to think that all religions share the same moral values, abiding by the Golden Rule and bringing out the best in their followers—making society work better and helping human-ity heal and seek the truth. We prefer to believe all men and women share the same goals and worship the same God, who loves all of humanity, even the sinners.

But sadly different religions don't share the same moral values, truths, and goals for their followers and for humanity. They don't even share the same God. This book is not about distinguishing good people from bad ones, but about comparing cultures, their moral values and purposes, what is advocated as right and wrong, good and evil in each, and what are the fruits that such cultures produce for their followers to reap.

A comparison of Islamic and Biblical values sheds light on how they are at odds with one another and reveals that the failure of Muslim assimilation in the West is not the fault of the West but the result of a concerted effort by the Muslim community and adherents of Islamic law.

Citizens of the West have been kept ignorant about the challenge of Islam to their values, culture, form of government, and way of life by Western politicians and media, who even underestimate the threat of terror. The misinformation forced on Western citizens by those who are covering for Islam—often out of multiculturalist embarrass-ment about criticizing other cultures, or simple fear of being called a racist—obstructs Western citizens' ability to do what is in their best interests.

No culture is void of goodness. My critique of Islam is not a critique of human beings, but of a toxic ideology I lived under and escaped from.

(Let me note here that I will often compare and contrast the Bible not just to the Koran, but to Islam. Unlike the Bible, the Koran is one of a trilogy of written sources for the religion it proclaims, including also the "hadith"—the various collections of the words and deeds of

Muhammad—and the "sira"—his biographies. Muslim theologians must rely on those other two sources to make sense of the Koran.)

MY TRANSFORMATION

Nothing helps us understand our culture better than looking at it from the outside in. It was in America that I first understood the big picture about Islam, the religion I was born in, and my culture of origin, Egypt. I lived under Islamic values the first thirty years of my life. It was only when I immigrated to the United States and began to live under Western values, which are ultimately derived from the Bible, that I could see those Islamic values for what they are.

The differences between moral and immoral, good and bad, honor and dishonor, and success and failure were totally different in America. I asked myself, Why is it that people in the West stand in line to wait for their turn while in the Muslim world people step on each other to get to be first? Why is it that in the West government leaders leave their office at the end of their term peacefully while in the Muslim world their term ends with either natural death or assassination? The list of questions I asked myself is long, and the answers are even longer. This book is dedicated to exploring those questions and answers.

In the West I found my peace and humanity. This is because of Biblical values that are the foundation of Western society. Among them are treating others as you would want to be treated, judging the sin but not the sinner, love, grace, peace, redemption, and healing.

Islamic society, on the other hand, looks up to the strongest fighters; respects power, those who enslave, bully, and shape others, and those with the most connections; and fears those who make the loudest noise, who will not hesitate to use terror and deception to achieve their goals.

A Black-and-White Matter

The world is hoping for Islam to reform. Many say that since Islam is an Abrahamic faith, if only violent jihad is taken out, Islam should be a great faith, able to co-exist beautifully with the non-Islamic world. In fact, that has been tried and failed miserably many times throughout history.

There are many reasons for that failure. But a central reason is that violent jihad is only the outward symptom of an ideology that is fundamentally hostile to the West and the values of the Bible.

But most nations and people around the world are building up their hopes with wishful thinking and denial of the truth about Islam. Islam has nothing to do with Abraham and Biblical values. In fact it awards the highest esteem to Muslims who kill the children of Abraham, the Jews.

After years of listening to Church sermons, reading the Bible, and interacting with Christians and Jews, I had adopted Biblical values, which, I had discovered, were contrary to all the values I grew up with under Islam. I started piling up a list of major foundational differences between the values of the Bible and of Islam. At first I had fourteen, but over time they reached almost sixty, and I am still regularly discovering additional differences.

My life is a miraculous transformation from the Koran to the Bible and from life under Islamic values to a life under Biblical values. The two different holy books have produced two diametrically different value systems and ultimately very different cultures.

Living under Biblical values saved my life. Today Biblically based societies are receiving millions of Muslim refugees who are mostly escaping Islamic society with its tyranny, chaos, destruction, and terror—though, as they're not properly vetted, some jihadis are certainly hiding among them.

What Led Me to America?

I was born a Muslim in Cairo, Egypt. Between the ages of four and eight I lived in the heart of the Arab-Israeli conflict in the Gaza Strip, where I lost my father to the jihad against Israel. Citizens in majority Muslim countries, Muslim and non-Muslim alike, must adapt their life to a state of permanent jihad, war, revolution, and counter-revolution, especially when the Muslims are financially and militarily strong.

After the trauma of life in Gaza, my family moved back to Cairo, Egypt, where, as I got older, I began to understand the harshness of life under Islamic law. In Egypt I lived through more war: the 1956, 1967, and 1973 Wars with Israel and many other skirmishes, political unrest, and fighting between Arab nations such as Egypt's war in Yemen. But the sudden loss of my father to jihad against Israel was by far the most traumatic event of my life. Out of that trauma I eventually learned to question how life could be so cheap in Islamic culture.

Asking questions and doubting is taboo under Islam. Islam failed to answer many important questions on my mind and the minds of many Muslims: *Why are the majority of Muslims poor, angry, envious, and unhappy? Why does distrust and fear control Islamic interpersonal relationships? Why are Islamic governments so proud to sacrifice the lives of men, women, and children for jihad? Why do distinguished Muslim leaders lie from the pulpit of mosques? Why are we, Muslims, not as tolerant and forgiving of one another as Christians and Westerners? Why don't we enjoy values of life, liberty, and the pursuit of happiness like the West? Why are we controlled and enslaved by other Muslims? Why do Muslims not appreciate the value of minding one's own business? And why are terror and violence the preferred solutions to so many of Islam's problems?*

It was only after I moved to America and became Christian that I figured out the answers.

Life Is Better under Biblical Values

Muslims are attracted to life in the West. This is obvious from the millions pouring into the West, while most Westerners would fear living in most parts of the Islamic world.

Very few immigrants to the U.S. attribute their attraction to America to the values of the Bible. Like most immigrants, I felt a natural attraction to American culture but did not fully understood why.

My journey to that understanding started when my flight landed on U.S. soil in late November 1978. Throughout the long flight from Cairo to Los Angeles, I had reflected on where I was and where I was heading. It felt like a scene from a movie about time travel. Flying to America felt like fast-forwarding ahead to the future. And yet the differences were not really a matter of time. Islamic culture will never catch up to Western culture because the differences between them are foundational. I didn't understand any of that yet. But one thing I was sure of, though; I had made the right decision.

On my passport was a visa to America, the land that Islamic preaching called "the Great Satan"—but where I found my salvation. The contradictions between Islamic propaganda about the West and the reality are huge. The role that propaganda plays in the minds even of Muslims who are eager to move to the West is astounding.

I looked at my passport before landing to make sure that all my documents were in order before I had to present them to U.S. customs authorities. I noticed that in my Egyptian-government-issued passport the word "Muslim" was written under my name. The Egyptian government was telling foreign governments that my religion was not a private matter and that it was assigned by the state. Even though I was about to land in America, I felt I was still in the grip of Islam.

Most of the immigrants I met in America in the late seventies and early eighties were Muslims or Coptic Christian Egyptians. Most of us were unaware of how deeply wounded we had been by life under Islam. But in fact even in the seventies and eighties the majority of Muslim immigrants to the West were escaping years of trauma. Life under sharia is traumatic in and of itself, and it took us many years to heal the wounds of shame, pain, terror, and war.

When I came to America I needed to talk, but none of the other Muslim immigrants wanted to open this sensitive and painful discussion over why we left and the hell we came from. Arab and Islamic pride, shame, and resistance to admitting sin all stood in the way of Muslim immigrants opening up to one another. Islamic cultural taboos prevented us from verbalizing the real reasons why we had all left our homeland. That delayed the process of healing and assimilation. A few never recovered or healed at all.

Opening Up in America

Old pain from the old country did not dissolve away quickly. Most first-generation Muslim immigrants live and die in America without fully ridding themselves of the impact of the indoctrination, pain, and trauma of life under Islam. I remember that in my first few years in America, when people asked me questions about how exciting Egyptian history was, I sometimes felt tears coming down my face uncontrollably. It took me almost ten years to fully open up about my past and confront the baggage I was carrying from life under Islamic values.

In my late thirties I started seeing a counselor for the first time in my life. In my early sessions I burst out crying to the counselor while telling him, "My father died." He said that he was so sorry to hear that and asked me when did it happen.

I said, "When I was eight." My whole body was shaking by then. Then he asked me if I ever talked about it before and my answer was "No." The counselor's question made me aware that I came from a culture where openly talking about one's true feelings, inadequacies, and vulnerabilities was taboo.

In Islamic culture, the wives and children of "martyrs" of jihad, like my mother, my siblings, and I, are not supposed to complain but rather to be proud of their hero jihadists.

The counselor was probably a bit staggered by my unusual story. I told him that I went to Gaza with my family as a toddler and left at age eight, that my father was head of the Egyptian military intelligence in Gaza and the Sinai, and that his job required him to continue the endless jihad against Israel. I told him he was assassinated in front of my little brother.

Life in the war zone of Gaza does not sound like the usual childhood, but we adapted to it. Children were not shielded from the bombing zones. Those who died died, and those who lived lived. No one around me questioned why.

As an adult in my late thirties, I once asked my mother why she didn't stay in safety in Cairo with us children while my father conducted the jihad against Israel from Gaza. Cairo was just a few miles to the west of Gaza by train. My mother seemed confused by my question, as though this possibility had never even occurred to her or to my father.

Arabs of Gaza, under the Egyptian administration back in the fifties, bombed and attacked Israel from near civilian homes, schools, and hospitals. I remember many nights sleeping under my bed out of fear from the constant bombing. But when my family woke up in the morning no one talked about the events of the night; we all just went about our business of living.

Now, looking back on my childhood, I see that the Islamic values of jihad and terror desensitized us to cruelty, terror, fear. Islamic values meant that a constant state of terror against Jews and non-Muslims was regarded as normal and honorable. Under Islam, terror was something to be tolerated and not talked about much. Not even in the media. What the Arab media talked about instead was how bad Jews and other non-Muslims are—to justify the terror.

The only time Muslims spoke about terror was when Israel shot back at Arabs. Suddenly terrorism was a horrible thing, because Arab lives mattered. But when terror was carried out by Muslims against Jews and Christians, especially against the state of Israel, it was not only tolerated, but celebrated as an Islamic holy right. After all, the prophet of Islam himself said, "I have been made victorious with terror" (Bukhari 4.52.220).[1]

My father, whom I adored, was assassinated, killed in his office by an explosive package sent by Israel, in the presence of my brother. My sisters and I were in a nearby cinema and heard the explosion.

Many of those who attended my father's funeral declared him a great "shahid," a brave martyr for jihad. Islamic society expected us to be proud of our sacrifice. As recently as 2015, my mother was on Egyptian national TV expressing her pride in my father's sacrifice as a shahid, and the sacrifices of our family for jihad.

Watching my mother on that show was difficult, especially as she no longer communicates with me because I became a Christian and support Israel. Islam's unforgiving nature, resentment, and the ruthless nature of Arab pride and shame have controlled much of my mother's life, unfortunately. She was a beautiful and intelligent woman, but she absorbed and lived by Islamic culture and Islam's moral values, and she was never happy. I spent most of my life trying to make her approve of me, to please her and make her happy, but nothing that I did worked.

I suppressed my family tragedy—outwardly expressing very little, even about my father's death, until I was in my late thirties in the office of a counselor in America, when finally I poured out my grief and started the mourning process.

It was at that point that I began to discover parallels between how Islam treats its despised enemies—Jews, the state of Israel—and how it treats its own people. Islamic culture sacrifices Muslim families for jihad. It even desecrates their bodies and makes a mockery of their grief. There are always extreme acts of mourning and wailing over the dead bodies when Muslims are killed in the jihad against Islam's enemies. Dead bodies are often paraded in the streets before media cameras. The purpose is to show the world how evil Israel is. And to achieve the goal of slandering Israel and justifying Islamic terror against Jews, Muslims have been caught producing videos of fake victims and fake funerals.[2]

The Arab-Israeli conflict is representative of the dysfunction of Islamic moral values. The heart of Islam is not in the well-being of anyone, either Muslims or non-Muslims. In Islam, everyone is exploited, except the few at the top of the pyramid scheme.

Discovering the Opposite Values

A recent story from Afghanistan illustrates what I am trying to relay about the opposite values of the Biblically based West and the Islamic Middle East. An Afghani rapist bragged to an American soldier about how he had chained a boy to a bed for seven days, and how, when the boy's mother tried to save her son, he beat her too. The young American Green Beret reacted by roughing up the bragging rapist. In doing that, he violated U.S. Army orders to ignore the rampant sexual abuse of young children, mostly boys, in Afghanistan and only to report the rape to local authorities. (Those orders are an example of how accommodation of Islam is undermining the Biblical values of the West.) The rapist was an Afghani police commander. The American Green Beret was discharged from the Army for disobeying orders.[3]

That story struck a chord with me because in the Muslim world it is not uncommon to be punished for doing the right thing, and standing up to oppression, tyranny, and the abuse of human beings. I could also relate to the Afghani mother and her son's disappointment with and distrust of their own culture and legal system. It took a young American soldier brought up on Biblical values to hopefully awaken the conscience of a nation.

Defending what one's gut says is right is often punished in Muslim culture. As a child and teenager I was punished for doing something similar to what the American soldier did in Afghanistan. I often witnessed brutal beatings and the abuse of maids, and I often defended the weak, standing between the maids and their brutal abusers. That got me in trouble and some of the anger and rage landed on me when I tried to stop the violence with my little body. I was blamed and told that it was none of my business; if I got hurt it was my fault for butting in to rescue the semi-slaves of society. There are many postings on YouTube showing the epidemic of physical abuse of housemaids and manual workers in Muslim countries, especially in Saudi Arabia and Arab Gulf nations.

It all goes back to moral values. Some actions that are commonplace and considered normal in Islamic culture would put people in jail in the U.S.

American jails are full of people who have done what Muslims in Islamic countries do in public and in the open and are never criticized for.

On the other hand, there are also many people in the Muslim world who are executed or jailed for "crimes" that are considered basic human rights in America. For example a Muslim girl who marries a Christian man is condemned to death if she refuses to leave the marriage, and the Islamic government also has the right to annul the marriage. When I wanted to marry a Christian man in Egypt, we had to wait for seven years until he and I were allowed to leave the country.

I have no childhood memories of being happy or being around happy people. Being happy and joyful was never a value in Islamic culture. Muhammad never said that he came to set us free, give us joy, or heal us from sin like Jesus did. On the contrary, happiness and good news were often concealed from people. If Muslims were happy, would they be able to hold onto the hatred and resentment that fuels the jihad against Islam's enemies?

Now thirty-seven years later, I am still transforming: from Muslim to Christian, from Egyptian to American, from an upbringing of pride and shame to forgiveness and joy, from a people pleaser to a God pleaser, from being judgmental to leaving judgment to God, from seeing what's wrong with others to seeing what's good in others, from oppressed to liberated, from chaos to harmony, and from anger to internal peace.

It is said that most Americans take their freedoms for granted because that is all they know from birth. That is especially true when it comes to linking American freedoms, democracy, and way of life to Biblical values. Not too many people notice that Biblical values are everywhere in America, even among those who call themselves secular, non-religious, or atheist. But I see Biblical values everywhere here. There is no other explanation for how different life in America is from life in the Islamic world. I see Biblical values in the joyful smile of a supermarket employee asking me, "Is there anything I can help you with?" I see them in the honesty of most Americans when I got my purse returned back to me after losing it in a public area. I see them in the sincerity and kindness of my elderly American neighbor telling me, "I will pray for you."

Below is a short list of just a few of the differences between Islamic values and Biblical values that I have personally experienced in my life. I will discuss each of these—and many others—in detail later in the book:

1. We Are All Sinners vs. They Are All Sinners
2. Life Is Sacred vs. Death Is Worship
3. Pleasing God vs. Pleasing Human Beings
4. Judge the Sin and Not the Sinner vs. Judge the Sinner, Not the Sin
5. Redemption from Sin vs. Immunity from Sin
6. Guided by the Holy Spirit vs. Manipulated by Human Terror
7. God the Redeemer vs. Allah the Humiliator
8. Healing of Spirit, Body, and Soul vs. No Healing Is Needed
9. Jesus Came to Save Us vs. We Have to Save Allah and Muhammad (and Muhammad's) Reputation
10. Jesus Died for Us vs. We Must Die for Allah
11. Confession of Sin vs. Concealment of Sin

12. At War with the Devil vs. at War with Flesh and Blood
13. The Truth Will Set You Free vs. Lying Is an Obligation
14. Trust vs. Distrust
15. Faith vs. Submission

It is unfortunate that many Americans take Biblical values for granted, assuming that kindness, honesty, and joy are the norm, with or without the Bible. Those of us who grew up in the parts of the world beyond the influence of the Bible know better. Biblical values are the product of the Bible, and they cannot be preserved separate from the Bible. I am writing this book because I want to tell America that many countries and religions around the world do not live by Biblical values. In fact the area of the world where Biblical values were birthed, the Middle East, no longer practices Biblical values.

Biblical values are a treasure that America must never lose. Many Americans today fear that Biblical values are eroding, and I share their fears. The following chapters will explore the differences between Biblical values and Islamic values that led me to choose the Bible.

2

THE SIN FACTOR

Sin is one of the most fundamental concepts in any religion. The ways Islam and the Bible explain sin are as different as night and day.

The holiest day of the year in Judaism is dedicated to cleansing oneself from sin—Yom Kippur, the day of atonement: "For on that day shall the priest make an atonement for you, to cleanse you, that ye may be clean from all your sins before the Lord" (Leviticus 16:30).[1]

Christianity teaches that "all have sinned, and come short of the glory of God" (Romans 3:23). It also teaches the concept of original sin—that the tendency to sin, inherited from Adam as a consequence of the Fall, is innate in human beings.

Unlike Judaism and Christianity, Islam does not recognize the concept of original sin. Islam has a very narrow interpretation of the sin of Adam and Eve. Islam's vision of humanity is not that "all have sinned, and come short of the glory of God."

Muhammad was perplexed by Jews and Christians' understanding of sin. He could not fathom how the fact that all of humanity has fallen short of God's standards does not mean that sin is acceptable. He did not relate to Allah as a loving God, a God who forgives sinners, rather than greeting them with a sword to chop off their heads at the doors of Heaven.

Muhammad regarded a prophet as the measure of perfection; he could not understand how Biblical prophets could admit flaws and imperfections. The Bible describes Jonah, Job, and Abraham himself as not always faithful servants of God—as sometimes even disobeying him. The fact that the Bible describes these men as human beings with flaws, moral dilemmas, and faults, was extremely confusing to Muhammad.

Muhammad understood sin not as the human condition but as a special curse afflicting Christians and Jews, who admitted their sins in their Bible. Muhammad was convinced that it was not he who must look within to recognize his own sin, repent, and change. Instead it was the Bible and its adherents that must change. If only Christians and Jews believed Muhammad's Koran and would totally submit to Allah, then they would not have to suffer anymore from their feelings of sin. But when Christians and Jews refused to follow Allah, Muhammad cursed them as still clinging to their disobedience and sinfulness. Muhammad could not understand the Bible, a holy book that allowed its followers to admit their sin.

Muhammad dedicated the majority of his preaching to condemning Christians and Jews who rejected the Koran and kept holding on to a Bible in which they admitted their disobedience and sin. To Muhammad, that was incomprehensible.

And so the majority of the Koran is devoted to the unbelieving kafir, rather than to the Muslims—according to Dr. Bill Warner, an authority on political Islam, 64 percent.[2] According to the Center for the Study of Political Islam, the amount of energy devoted to non-Muslims in the Koran and other Muslim texts is huge: "The majority (64%) of the Koran is devoted to the Kafir, and nearly all of the Sira (81%) deals with Mohammed's struggle with them. The Hadith (Traditions) devotes 37% of the text to Kafirs. Overall, the Trilogy, of the three, devotes 51% of its content to the Kafir."[3]

The Koran is totally obsessed with Jews and Christians, who are condemned as the symbols of sin and evil-living: "Say: O People of the Scripture!... and because most of you are evil-livers" (5:59)[4] "Don't take Jews and Christians as friends and protectors" (5:51). "Fight against such of those who have been given the Scriptures (the Jews and Christians)" (9:29). "Be merciful to believers [Muslims], and severe against unbelievers" (48:29). "Jews should long for death" (62:6). "People of the book [Jews and Christians] are perverted transgessors" (3:110). "[I]ndignity is put over them and they have drawn on themselves Allah's wrath" (3:112). Jews and Christians are "racing each other in sin and transgression" (5:62). "The path of those whom Thou hast favored [Muslims]; Not the (path) of those who earn Thine anger [Jews] nor of those who go astray [Christians]" (1:7). "Verily evil is their [the Jews'] handiwork" (5:63).

Even though Muslims don't observe a day of rest in the Koran, Allah punishes the Jews for having broken the Sabbath (a sin they admit in the Bible) by transforming them into apes: "And ye know of those of you who broke the Sabbath, how We said unto them: Be ye apes, despised and hated!" (2:65). The Koran also infamously describes Jews and Christians as pigs, unclean filth, treacherous, hypocritical, and enemies of Allah himself (Koran 7:166, 2:65, and 5:60).

Islam is the only religion on earth that dedicates the majority of its scriptures not to its own followers but to condemning whole groups of people outside the religion as cursed, doomed, and unforgiven sinners.

By being critical and unforgiving of Jews and Christians, Muhammad raised the bar for himself and Muslims almost to the level of perfection. Unlike the evil-livers, Muhammad and his followers had to appear as perfect role models and beyond reproach. Muhammad is thus described as "Al-Insan al-Kamil" meaning the perfect human being. In the same verse that describes Jews and Christians as perverted transgressors, Muslims are described as "the best of people for having the right conduct, forbid indecency and who believe in Allah" (3:110).

Neither the evil Jews and Christians nor the good Muslims are allowed freedom, grace, and forgiveness in the Koran. Muhammad's followers have no right to anything but perfect submission and blind obedience to Allah and Muhammad. Muhammad was not going to allow the acknowledgment of sin to be a virtue in his holy book. Islam is not about repentance. Nor is it about grace from a forgiving God. The death penalty awaits not only non-Muslims—the kafirs who reject Muhammad and the Koran—but also Muslims who do not fully submit, or who even imply any criticism or questioning of Muhammad and Allah.

Muhammad could not hide the fact that in his personal life he committed acts that were wrong and sinful not only by Biblical standards but also by Arabian Peninsula standards of the time. Muhammad cursed, he allowed lying and deception, he took eleven wives in addition to sexual slaves while limiting his fighting men to four wives. Muhammad also violated Arabia's traditions against ever killing those within one's own tribe when he ordered the killing of members of his Quraish tribe in Mecca who rejected him and of poets who wrote poetry ridiculing him.

So whenever Muhammad's behavior raised eyebrows even among his followers, Allah miraculously gave Muhammad his permission, with a new Koran verse of blessings on Muhammad's actions. When

Muhammad desired his adopted son's wife as his own, for example, Allah gave him his blessings in the Koran to cover him from any appearance of sin.

Whenever Muhammad changed his mind, Allah also changed his mind and allowed the abrogation of earlier contradictory Koran verses. Morality itself and definition of sin under Islamic law were determined by what Muhammad did and did not do. If Muhammad married a six-year-old girl at age fifty-two and consummated the marriage when the girl was nine then that was the moral female age of marriage under Islamic law. Even today, where sharia is the law, a girl can be married by her father's permission in a written contract at any age after her birth and the marriage can be legally consummated at the age of nine.

We Are All Sinners vs. *They* Are All Sinners

When I first became Christian I was amazed by the expression, "We are all sinners." It instinctively felt good to hear that; the saying had a ring of truth that comforted me and a depth of meaning that I had never heard from Islam. It was news to me that the God of the Bible forgave our sins without our having to do anything to earn forgiveness; it was called "grace," a concept hardly ever mentioned in Islam. The Biblical idea that God does not expect us to be perfect and does not hate us for our imperfections—that He hates sin but not the sinner—revolutionized my view of God and myself.

After I became Christian, the world was no longer split between non-Muslims (sinners) and Muslims (innocent non-sinners). The equality of all humans in the eyes of God—He knows we are all sinners—is a concept lacking in Islam. This is probably the crux of the huge divide between the two faiths, the essence of the difference between the two opposing value systems.

Realizing that all humans are loved by God even though they all fall short in not measuring up to God's standards was one of the most liberating experiences I felt as a new Christian. If only that concept—that God never hates people but only their sins—existed in Islam, then humanity could have been spared the suffering and killing of millions under the Islamic jihad that has gone on for fourteen hundred years and still counting.

The many obsessive attacks on Jews, Christians, and other non-Muslims in the Koran are staggering and hard to explain away. They simply don't fit in with the notion that Islam is a peaceful religion. By condemning others as evil sinners, Muhammad and his followers trapped themselves into the belief they must achieve perfection and nothing less. That perfectionism is a major source of both pride and shame in Islam.

Islam's response to the Christian concept of "We are all sinners" was and is a firm *No*. In Islam, it is *They are all sinners* (Christians, Jews, and all other non-Muslims, that is). Muslim preachers constantly preach that Muslims are innocent and non-Muslims are not innocent, *they* are the sinners.

Islamic law itself protects Muslims from being called sinful, "kafir," or "enemy of Allah." Islamic law states that non-Muslims are forbidden to point out the sins of Muslims or "show others the weakness of Muslims." These are considered enormous crimes under sharia law (*Reliance of the Traveller*).[5] But Islamic law does not give equal protection to non-Muslims from being called sinners, cursed as kafir, or being named as enemies of Allah. On the contrary, as we have seen, the Koran itself is a book devoted to cursing the kafirs.

Protection from being called a sinner, along with the right to call everyone else sinners, is a right and privilege accorded to those who convert to Islam. One hadith talks about three rights of any convert to Islam: "The Prophet said: Three things are the roots of faith: to refrain from (killing) a person who utters, 'There is no god but Allah' and not to declare him unbeliever whatever sin he commits, and not to excommunicate him from Islam for his any action" (Abu-Dawud).[6]

Islam's condemnation of non-Muslims as sinners, without admitting any sin on the part of Muslims, is the main cause of the dysfunctional and hostile relationship of Muslims to the rest of the world. But unfortunately Muslims refuse to admit that. Instead they claim that the West is "Islamophobic."

Jihad is built on the presumption that the sins of the others—non-Muslims—justifies conquering, subjugating, and converting them by force. Islamic logic does not see confession of sin by Jews and Christians as a virtue or as the starting point to redemption and an attempt to be better people. In Islam self-criticism, admitting sin, praying for forgiveness, and openly exposing one's vulnerabilities and imperfections in a search for the truth is worthy of punishment.

In my Islamic studies classes we were told that the Jewish people admitted their mistakes and sins in their Torah and that is why God cursed them. My culture of origin regarded the virtue of self-criticism as something to be ashamed of, something that could be used against Christians and Jews.

Judge the Sin Not the Sinners vs. Judge the Sinner, Not the Sin

The Bible says, "Judge not, that ye be not judged." Christians condemn sins, but not the sinner. Islam, on the other hand, encourages Muslims to judge sinners and punish them.

Punishing adulterers by stoning was a custom in the Middle East but that custom ended for Christians when Christ said, "He that is without sin among you, let him first cast a stone at her." Six hundred years after Christ, Muhammad brought back the stoning of adulterous women, commanded it, and participated in it himself.

One of the reasons Islam has to judge the sinner rather than the sin is that under Islam most sins are conditional. For example, murder and lying are sins in the Bible, but under Islam they are sometimes wrong and sometimes an obligation, depending on why a Muslim does the act. Muslims who commit murder under certain conditions are immune from being prosecuted, and the murder is not considered a sin under Islamic law. Islamic law specifically protects from prosecution both the killers of apostates and adulterers and also parents and grandparents who kill their offspring.

Muhammad, the prophet of Islam, never admitted personal sin or sin by Muslims. All his harsh criticism (as well as violence and terror) were directed at those who did not submit to his authority and rejected his message. Thus the Koran and the whole religious philosophy of Islam are based on condemning non-Muslims as sinful.

In Islam, whether or not you are condemned as a sinner depends more on who you are than what you have done. There are different rules for different classes of people, genders, and religions. Non-Muslims are punished harshly under Islamic law for criticizing Muhammad or mocking Muslims or pointing out the weaknesses of Islam (*Reliance* w52.1). But Muslims curse Jews and Christians and call them the most horrific names in their prayers and their holy book.

Confession of Sin vs. Concealment of Sin

The essence of Christianity is the healing forgiveness that God showers on us when we confess our sins. Under Islam, sin became something that exists primarily in the outside world, a world that is sinful and evil because it rejects Allah and Muhammad and thus must be conquered by Muslims. The sinful world of the "kafirs" should never be forgiven by Muslims, must be fought, must never be allowed to rule itself, and must be forced to submit to Islam. Muslims are told to never emulate it; they must constantly protect themselves from being lured by it. The job of the sinless Muslim believers is to change, correct, and harshly punish the sinful non-Muslim world through jihad. As we know from the horrific ISIS videos, Islam gives Muslims the responsibility and obligation to punish those who admit sin with the most barbaric and humiliating forms of punishments and torture such as beheading, flogging, and even crucifixion.

Islam's condemnation of others outside of Islam as sinful has brought Muslims and Islam itself a lot of criticism, which in turn just further stokes Muslims' anger and condemnation of non-Muslims.

And the same pattern asserts itself even within Islam. Pride and shame will not allow Muslims to confess that they themselves have sinned. But they are often eager to charge other Muslims with sinning. They especially accuse the weak and the vulnerable, such as women—who are often severely punished for sexual sins, and even for the least immodesty—or Muslims they disagree with—whom they often accuse of not being true Muslims. That's exactly what the Sunni and the Shia say about each other because of their theological differences.

Islam's doctrine of sin puts Muslims on the defensive in debates, which they often lose, as it is difficult to explain without offending non-Muslims and without admitting that some of Muhammad's behavior was appalling. To make Islam look better, Muslims are forced to conceal Muhammad's sins—and their own.

My life under a religion that punished sinners rather than condemning sin was full of cruelty and injustice. Only the powerful, the cruel, and the heartless could be happy in a culture where judging others was a sign of virtue.

That explains why most Muslims were obsessed with concealing their own sins while constantly pointing out the sins of others. It was only after I became a Christian that I started connecting the dots about the religion I was born in.

Since Islam was extremely critical, condemning, and unforgiving of the sin of others, Muslims and Muhammad have to appear sinless.

Confessing sin turns out to be a blessing for Christians and Jews that is lacking in Islam. No full healing and atonement can ever be achieved without it: "Confess your faults one to another, and pray one for another, that ye may be healed. The effectual fervent prayer of a righteous man availeth much" (James 5:16).

Instead of providing a road to healing by confessing their sins, the prophet of Islam commanded his followers to conceal them: "All of my community shall be pardoned, save those who commit sins openly.... a man who does something shameful at night... while in the morning he pulls away the cover with which Allah had concealed it for him" (*Reliance* r35.1, Bukhari 5721, Muslim 2990). Muhammad also said, "It is offensive for a person who has been afflicted with an act of disobedience or the like to inform another of it" (*Reliance* r35.2). What Muhammad tells Muslims again and again is that those who make their sin known will never be forgiven: "All of my Ummah will be excused, except for those who make their sins known" (Bukhari 6069).

Islam has a clear prohibition against exposing or admitting Muslims' sins. That prohibition just reinforces the shame and pride that hold sway over Arab culture. Muslims are not to admit sin, but to hide it even from one another. The Arabic word for concealment of sin is "satr" meaning cover, veil, and shelter. There is a famous Arabic saying, "Wa itha buleetum fastatiru," which means if you are cursed with a sin conceal it. Another common Arabic expression that I heard a lot growing up from the people around me was "Rabina yustur," meaning may Allah give us cover—from being publicly exposed.

To the Western mind, it is difficult to understand how a major world religion could command its followers to conceal their sins. Even though Jesus never tolerated sin, He still loved the sinner and forgave those who repented and sought forgiveness. In the Book of Ezekiel, both Christians and Jews read, "As I live, saith the Lord God, I have no pleasure in the death of the wicked; but that the wicked turn from his way and live." Islam, on the other hand, promotes hate against sinners when it says that Allah does not love unbelievers (sinners) (Koran 3:32 and 30:45), and will cast terror on them (8:12), and that Muslims should be severe against them (48:29), kill them (2:191), and not befriend them (5:51). So Muslims must conceal their sins. Appearances thus became everything in Islam.

But what about Muslims who find it difficult to conceal their sins, who would rather talk about them? As I know from personal experience living in an Islamic society, when I was honest and open about uncomfortable things, I was often called naïve or stupid for admitting to any wrongdoing.

Because of Islam's inability to confess sin, the state of Turkey still refuses to admit to the Armenian genocide, which happened a century ago. Sunni Muslim leaders as well as the Turkish government are denying that the killing of 1.5 million Armenians by the Turks ever happened.[7]

Another example of Muslims' never admitting sin or guilt is the fact that not one Muslim religious or political leader has apologized for 9/11 or for the worldwide epidemic of Islamic terrorism going on today. The only response the West gets from Muslims to the never-ending parade of thousands of Islamic terrorist attacks is that it has *nothing to do with Islam* and that it is the West that needs to be sensitive and do a better job of understanding what true Islam means.

Concealment of sin has been a curse on Islamic society. It conveys the wrong message: that people's approval is more important than the approval of God, who knows all our secrets, that how other humans perceive us is more important than how God sees us. For Muslims, it is only the appearance of innocence that matters.

This regime of concealing sins was torturous for me to live under, and I am sure many Muslims share my feelings. The majority of Muslims hear conflicting messages about sin. While they live in fear of exposure of their own sins, they are also commanded by Allah to harshly punish the sinners amongst them. Sharia law entrusts Muslims, who are commanded to conceal their own sin, to show little mercy toward sinners and condemn them on behalf of Allah himself. For example, Muslims are commanded to execute blasphemers of Muhammad, even if they repent. Muslims are thus left in a life of pretense that is void of truthfulness.

How can a just God do that? He can't. That is something Muslims would have to admit if they were willing to be honest with themselves and others. But such honesty is forbidden under Islamic law.

Here is a glaring example of what I am talking about from the real world of Islam. At one Islamic website that gives advice to Muslims a woman asked what to do after she caught her husband sexually assaulting their fourteen-year-old daughter. The answer by the religious expert started with a condemnation of what the husband had done to his daughter, calling it an abominable sin. But he very quickly advised the wife against leaving her husband: "What your husband did does not make you forbidden [sexually] for him and it does not invalidate the marriage. However, you should conceal his sin and not disclose it to people, but don't let him be in seclusion with your daughter, and Allah knows best."[8]

Redemption from Sin vs. Immunity from Sin

But concealment is not possible in all cases. Muhammad's marrying a child of six years old could not be concealed.

Muslims got tired of constantly defending Muhammad's actions and the actions of Islamic caliphs who followed him. Thus they came up with the doctrine of immunity from sin, to make Muhammad and others completely immune to judgment.

"Masoom" or "Isma," the Arabic word for infallible, implies immunity from condemnation and protection from accusations of having sinned. It is the concept of "incorruptible innocence" that covers Muhammad, all the prophets, and even imams and mosque leaders. The doctrine of immunity to sin varies slightly between Sunnis and Shiites but means essentially the same to both.

The same religion that condemns two-thirds of the world of being sinful kafirs who must be conquered by Muslims for not following Muhammad had to issue a decree ("fatwa") to protect Muhammad and other Muslim leaders from being called sinful: "The Muslims have unanimously agreed that the Prophets (alaihimus-salaam) along with the seal of the Prophets i.e., Prophet Muhammad (sallalalhu alaihi wa-sallam) are Masoom."[9]

I recently saw a Sunni Egyptian sheikh declare that the concept of "masoom" covers not only the prophet and caliphs but also all sheikhs in any mosque regardless of whatever sin they may commit. Egyptian Sunni Sheikh Musaad Anwar said on Al Rahmah TV that a Muslim in the hands of his sheikh should be like a dead body in the hands of a caretaker. Even if your sheikh commits adultery, don't say he committed adultery, but say, "It is my eyes [that are wrong to see] that committed the sin." The sheikh added, "Whoever objects to that must get expelled."[10]

According to Islam, Muhammad and other religious leaders are given immunity from sin regardless of what they do—and the blame is placed on the eyes of those who see the actual sin of those who are theoretically immune to it, Sins for which the ordinary Muslim could be beheaded are committed daily by Muslim leaders who act like they are above the law and even exempt in the eyes of Allah. Islamic society has legalized crimes for some but not others. Giving a few Muslims, such as sheikhs, the Prophet, and his companions the incredible privilege of being immune from sin regardless of what sins they commit has a devastating effect on Islamic society. It means that all human beings are not equal in the eyes of God and that the lucky few can literally get away with murder.

Naturally, Islam's demand of blind loyalty to Muhammad and other Muslim leaders has been abused. In fact the Islamic doctrine of "masoom" or "isma" has turned out to be a curse on Islamic culture. Perhaps that could explain why many Muslim ayatollahs, sheikhs, and even Arab political leaders not only abuse their power but flaunt their abuses as a divine right. In Islamic society the privileged feel entitled to practically do anything while the poor and ordinary Muslims are left with nothing but constant concealment of sin; some are flaunting their sin without a proper fear of punishment even from Allah himself while others are living in constant hiding, not from God, but from other human beings. Lawlessness, distrust, and chaos have thus permeated every aspect of Islamic society since the people at the top are immune from sin, with Allah's blessing.

A religion that encourages concealment of sin and gives special immunity to a few can never withstand the scrutiny that any ideology or religion must face. That is why historically, and still today, Islam has always responded very poorly to normal questioning and scrutiny. Muslims' typical response to questioning of Islam has always been to be offended, get angry, issue death fatwas, riot, and commit acts of terror. That has been the state of Islam for fourteen hundred years.

As for Muslims who nevertheless *are* guilty of sin—whether they are convicted by their own consciences, or if their misdeeds are simply too obvious—Muhammad and the Koran tell them that if they want their sins to be forgiven they must do jihad, holy war against non-Muslims. Killing kafirs is their only guarantee of forgiveness by

Allah, who will take the jihadi straight to heaven. More than one and a half billion Muslims around the world believe in this Islamic doctrine as the only way to be forgiven: every Muslim who conducts jihad is granted immunity from his or her prior life of sin. This is why when America kills Osama bin Laden thousands of bin Ladens rise up to follow in his footsteps, and when Al Qaeda is weakened ISIS quickly replaces it. Could this "forgiveness" be any more different from the way sinners are healed by God's mercy in Jesus' sacrifice on the Cross?

The Islamic doctrine of sin is unlike the Biblical doctrine of forgiveness of sin through grace. Islam points at non-Muslims as being sinners while giving Muslims immunity from sin, regardless of what they do, as long as they are able to conceal it or do jihad against non-Muslims to erase it. Islam is thus the only religion in the world mostly concerned with the sins of others.

3

HEALING, SALVATION, AND THE HOLY SPIRIT

The Bible tells us that we are made in the Image of God. Genesis 1:26 says, "Then God said, 'Let us make man in our image, after our likeness.'" Not only are we made in His image, but He also lavished His love on us as His children. The Bible promises to lift us up from our fears and guilt. It gives us an unmistakable and clear road to salvation, healing, forgiveness, and mercy. Nothing even comes close to this in Islam, which provides no road to salvation from human sin and suffering.

With my conversion from Islam to Christianity, my whole outlook on life, humanity, and myself was changed. I saw divine qualities, value, beauty, and dignity in every human being. I experienced healing and reconciliation with my Creator almost overnight. It was only through Biblical values that I was able to forgive those who hurt me personally in the past. I was able to heal and turn the worst thing that happened to me into the best thing that happened to me. That could never have happened without Jesus Christ.

After I became Christian, I was able to connect the dots as to why America is the envy of the world—why the life of every American citizen has value, while in the Muslim world a human being is valued only when he gives up his life for jihad.

Instead of promising healing to Muslims, Allah threatens those who turn down his offer to join Islam with increasing their disease: "In their hearts is a disease, and Allah increaseth their disease. A painful doom is theirs because they lie" (2:10). Allah is constantly focused on cursing non-Muslims rather than healing Muslims. In that same chapter two of the Koran, Allah calls non-Muslims hypocrites, liars, misguided, living in darkness, deaf, dumb, and blind. They are mocked by Allah, and will end up as fuel in Hell fire. This is all because they refuse to believe in Muhammad. In the days of Muhammad most of Arabia converted to his new religion out of fear and not out of conviction. That is why when Muhammad died they abandoned Islam and had to be brought back to it with the sword. It is obvious that many tribes around Muhammad, both Jews and Arabs, were stricken with fear. They were afraid to tell him no, and many of the brave souls who did were beheaded as example to the terrified others. In Koran 2:14 Allah wonders why the evil unbelieving kafirs are lying to Muslims about their faith in Islam: "And when they meet those who believe, they say, 'We believe'; but when they are alone with their evil ones, they say, 'Indeed, we are with you; we were only mockers.'" In other words, they were just kidding about believing Muhammad's revelations.

It was a terror-filled atmosphere. Obviously healing, salvation, and lifting up others were the last things on Muhammad's and Allah's minds.

Guided by the Holy Spirit vs. Manipulated by Human Terror

My pastor Jim Tolle talks about the relationships among body, soul, and spirit and about how God's Spirit is our guide. He guides us regarding sin, righteousness, and judgment. As a new Christian convert, being led by the Holy Spirit, I felt the internal guidance and gradually relied more and more on my instincts in a way that I had never experienced under Islam. When something felt wrong, I was led to a new and better way of thinking and behaving.

There is nothing equivalent to that in Islam. Islam uses human being against human being, an outside collective human pressure against the will of every individual. In any Islamic society fear of man—both of human judgment and of terrorist violence—is the driving force that controls the thoughts and behavior of individuals, to achieve submission. Islamic terror is nothing but man trying to control, manipulate, and destroy humanity in the name of Allah.

By making human beings into each other's judges, jury, and executioners, Islam has created social disaster, chaos, and turmoil in which literal survival belongs only to the fittest. And those who are most fit to survive and thrive in Islamic society are the strong, the relentless, and the cruel.

My life under Islam was a constant state of justifying myself to the people around me. The lower a Muslim is on the social ladder, the more the self-justification is required. Nothing pleases Islamic society, which takes away all freedom, joy, and spontaneity in life.

In contrast, life among people who are guided by the Holy Spirit is a miracle from God. This is the gift that the American church community has given me, saving me from slavery to man. The Spirit of God leads human beings to look at one another in a totally different way from the adversarial attitude they take toward each other under

Islam. When I became a Christian I discovered that in Jesus I am allowed to take responsibility for my thoughts and actions but under the guidance of a Spirit from God. My joy in Christ was nothing less than miraculous. This kind of freedom from the judgment of man was the most precious gift I experienced in America. The Holy Spirit guided me instead of Islamic terror.

God Lifts Up and Restores vs. Allah Shames and Humiliates

I had always wondered why Muslim society was plagued with hostile relationships, tit-for-tat score-keeping, distrust, and a tendency to put down others and to shame, blame, and humiliate especially the less fortunate. Why was Islamic culture so sensitive to issues of shame and pride, face-saving and public humiliation? I lived in such a society, but it wasn't until I left it that I could connect the dots about the judgmental nature of Arab culture. Those values moved from Arabia with Islam to became a predominant feature of all majority-Muslim countries. The daily humiliations in Arab culture flow directly from the Muslim God, who shames and humiliates both his enemies and his followers, while the God of the Bible lifts His creatures up—and tells us to do the same for each other.

After I became Christian these issues became more pressing. Biblical values encourage us to lift up, empower, and love one another and not to be judgmental. The contrast with the culture I had come from was striking.

The Bible is full of uplifting verses such as "And I, if I be lifted up from the earth, will draw all men to me" (John 12:32); "Humble your-selves in the sight of the Lord, and he shall lift you up" (James 4:10); "The LORD upholdeth all that fall, and raiseth up all those that be bowed down" (Psalms 145:14); "But thou, O LORD, art a shield for me; my glory, and the lifter up of mine head" (Psalm 3:3); and "Thou shalt increase my greatness, and comfort me on every side" (Psalms 71:21).

"Fear Not" vs. Fear as a Tool of Enforcement

"Fear not," the God of the Bible tells His people, "for thou shalt not be ashamed: neither be thou confounded; for thou shalt not be put to shame: for thou shalt forget the shame of thy youth, and shalt not remember the reproach of thy widowhood any more" (Isaiah 54:4). Allah never tells his followers not to be afraid. He wants everyone to be afraid of him. Fear is a tool of enforcement in Islam—to compel non-Muslims to submit, and to make Muslims comply with sharia. Fear of physical violence is used, but other kinds of fear as well.

A lot has been written about the violent verses in the Koran, but not much is said about the belittling, humiliating, and shaming expressions in Islam's holy book. The Koran is replete with words such as humiliate, disgrace, ignominy, and shame.

The word "shame" is repeated fifty-four times; "disgrace" sixty-one times; "humiliation" fifty-eight times; and "losers" forty-three times. The number of times they are repeated to describe those whom Allah does not love is staggering. When I discovered these numbers at a website that allowed me to search for any word in the Koran, my suspicions regarding the link between Islam and the shame-based Arab culture I grew up in were confirmed. Below are a few of the Koran verses that contain each of these words.[1]

Shame in the Koran:

"*Shame* is pitched over them" (3:112); "Thou coverest with *shame*, and never will wrong-doers find any helpers!" (3:192); "His will be a *shameful* doom" (4:14); "Allah will cover with *shame* those who reject Him" (9:2); "He will cover them with *shame*, and say ... are the Unbelievers covered with *shame* and misery" (16:27); "penalty of *shame*" (6:93 and 11:39).

Disgrace in the Koran:

- "surely Allah has prepared a *disgraceful* chastisement for the unbelievers" (4:102 and 4:151)
- "Fight them; Allah will punish them by your hands and will *disgrace* them and give you victory over them and satisfy the breasts of a believing people" (9:14)
- "the punishment of *disgrace* in worldly life" (10:98, 11:66, 11:93, 22:9, 22:57, 39:40, 42:45, and 48:6)
- "he will burn [in Hell] therein *disgraced* and rejected" (17:18, 25:69)
- "wilt sit in *disgrace* and destitution" (17:22)
- "drive them ... in *disgrace*, and they will be abased" (2:37)
- "*disgrace* in this world" (2:85)

There are also many verses regarding "chastisement, torment and punishment in *disgrace*" (41:16, 40:60, 33:59, 41:17, 2:90, 3:178, and 4:37).

Humiliation and Ignominy in the Koran:

- "*ignominy and humiliation* overshadowed them, and they earned the burden of God's condemnation" (2:61)

- "those who have earned evil will have a reward of like evil: **ignominy** will cover their (faces): no defender will they have from (the wrath of) Allah" (10:27)
- "his suffering doubled on Resurrection Day: for on that [day] he shall abide in *ignominy*" (25:69)
- "we will surely expel them therefrom in *humiliation*, and they will be *demeaned*" (27:37)
- *"Humiliation* and *disgrace* from Allah" (6:124)
- "you are of those *humiliated* and *disgraced*" (7:13)
- "that they might *humiliate* themselves (and repent to Allah)" (7:94)
- "obtain anger from their Lord and *humiliation* in the life of this world" (7:152)
- "Thus Allah made them taste *humiliation* in the life of the world, and verily the doom of the Hereafter will be greater if they did but know" (39:26)
- "will surely enter *Hell in humiliation!*" (40:60)
- "that We might give them a taste of a Penalty of *humiliation* in this life; but the Penalty of a Hereafter will be more *Humiliating* still: and they will find no help" (41:16)
- "so the thunderbolt of *humiliating* punishment seized them" (41:17)
- "to the Fire, humbled from *humiliation*" (42:45)
- "And he whom Allah *humiliates*—for him there is no bestower of honor" (22:18)

Allah condemns disbelievers to "a humiliating punishment" in numerous verses of the Koran (2:90, 3:17, 4:14, 4:37, 4:102,4:151, 22:57, 31:6, 33:57, 44:30, 45:9, 58:5, 58:16). And in several others he chastises those who hinder others from the path of Allah (from converting to Islam). Allah speaks of those who beg him for deliverance as having *"[h]umbled (subdued or humiliated)* themselves to their Lord" (11:23). The Koran commands Muslims to keep fighting non-Muslims "until they pay the Jizya (penalty tax) with *willing submission* and *feel themselves subdued (humiliated)*" (9:29).

The Koran also repeatedly calls Jew and Christians humiliating names such as apes and pigs (5:60), enemies of Allah and of Muslims (8:59), losers (3:5), najas (unclean) (9:28), and those who have earned Allah's wrath and went astray (1:7). Muslims believe the Koran is "the perfect book," which makes cursing, humiliating, and name-calling of others okay too. Whatever is in the Koran—whether it is violence, commandments to beat wives, and kill kafirs, humiliating words—is the norm for Muslims. Thus hostile relations, shaming, and degradation have become the norm in Islamic society.

On a recent religious program that aired on Egyptian television, Suad Saleh, a female Islamic cleric, discussed the doctrine of intentional humiliation and disgrace in Islam. She explained, "One of the purposes of raping captured enemy women and young girls was to humiliate and disgrace them and that is permissible under Islamic law."[2] There was no uproar in Egyptian society over this statement.

Healing of Spirit, Body, and Soul vs. No Healing Is Needed

Islam has no understanding that humanity is in need of healing. One of the stark differences between the Koran and the Bible is the number of words in the Bible dedicated to healing, encouragement, comfort, hope, peace, joy, love, atonement, and salvation.

Because in Islam there is no original sin in our relationship with God, consequently there is no need for healing, atonement, or salvation. If you asked a Muslim cleric how we can heal our relationship with God, the response would probably be, "Heal it from what?" That was the answer I got when, comparing the Koran to the messages of healing, hope, guidance, and salvation on almost every page of the Bible, I asked a Muslim friend if there were any healing messages in the Koran.

The word "heal" is mentioned only six times in the Koran.[3] And its implications there are totally different from what they are in the Bible. Take Koran 9:14, for example: "Fight them [non-Muslims]! Allah will torment them by your hands, humiliate them, empower you over them, and He will **heal** the hearts of the believers [Muslims], removing the rage from their hearts." While the beginning of the verse is violent, and typical of Allah's violent threats throughout the Koran, the end of it sounds like something you might read in the Bible.

But only until you know the historical context. According to *Al-Bidaya wa Al-Nihaya* ("The Beginning and the End"), Ibn Kathir's authoritative history of Islam, this verse is about the Battle of Badr, when a new convert by the name of Abdullah stepped on the abused body of Amr bin Hisham and placed his severed head in the hands of Muhammad. The dead man was the chief of a tribe in staunch opposition to Muhammad's message. Muhammad considered him a despised enemy and never called him by his real name but nicknamed him "abu Jahl" meaning "father of ignorance" in Arabic.

That was the kind of healing Muhammad felt—satisfaction and relief that his enemy was dead, and his body mutilated. This story still inspires jihadists today, who experience healing of their hearts when they kill non-Muslims, the people the Koran refers to as sinners.

There is another healing prescription for Muslims. According to several Islamic references and the sayings of Muhammad, his companions blessed themselves by drinking the Prophet's urine, sweat, and saliva. This prescription for health was confirmed in a recent book by the top Islamic leader in Egypt, Dr. Ali Gumaa: *Religion and Life—Modern Everyday Fatwas*. Gumaa quotes a hadith by

Muhammad: "Umm Ayman drank the urine of the Prophet, and the prophet told her: 'This stomach will not be dragged through the fire of Hell, because it contains something of our Lord the Messenger of Allah....'" This blessing can also "be done with the honorable saliva, sweat, hair, urine or blood of the Prophet."[4]

Muhammad also prescribed camels' urine for healing: "Some people of 'Ukl' or 'Uraina' tribe came to Medina and its climate did not suit them. So the Prophet ordered them to go to the herd of (Milch) camels and to drink their milk and urine (as a medicine)." But this story, too, like the verse about the Battle of Badr, has a horrific ending: "So they went as directed and after they became healthy, they killed the shepherd of the Prophet and drove away all the camels. The news reached the Prophet early in the morning and he sent (men) in their pursuit and they were captured and brought at noon. He then ordered to cut their hands and feet (and it was done), and their eyes were branded with heated pieces of iron, They were put in 'Al-Harr' and when they asked for water, no water was given to them" (Bukhari 1.4.234).

There are Islamic conferences today on the "wonders and secrets of healing from camel urine," whose participants argue that Muhammad was right and that "camel urine is the miracle of our time and is a gift from Muhammad to mankind." These are attended by Muslim scientists such as Fatin Khorshid of the King Fahd Medical Research Center, who sees the camel urine Muhammad prescribed as the ultimate solution to "all sorts of ailments" such as "cancer," "diarrhea," "sexual dysfunction," "liver disease," "skin ulcers," and so forth.[5]

Jesus Came to Save Us vs.
We Have to Save Allah and Muhammad

The Bible says that Jesus Christ came in the flesh to this Earth to save the lost and wipe away the sins of the whole world. While the

Bible calls Christians saved, the Koran describes Christians as "the lost" and those who went "astray," and it describes Jews as "those who earn Allah's anger" (1:7). All non-Muslims are considered the personal enemies of Allah and Muhammad, and they should be Muslims' enemies too. Thus the role of the devout Muslim with respect to Allah and his Prophet is the exact opposite of the Christian's relationship to Jesus Christ and His Father: the Muslim must save Allah from his human enemies on Earth. Thus the God who is supposed to be the all-powerful creator of all things actually needs his followers to devote their lives to converting or killing his enemies on Earth.

In Islam it is not humanity that needs to be saved, but Allah and Muhammad. Under Islam, pagans are given two choices, converting to Islam or death. Christians and Jews have one more option, to pay an extra humiliating penalty tax (jizya) for remaining Christian or Jewish but only under the condition that they live as second class citizens under an Islamic government and under Islamic law.

The most sacred duty that Muslim scriptures and laws have entrusted to the Muslim public is to protect and save Allah, Muhammad, and Islam itself from being slandered or insulted by anyone. Allah, the almighty, and Muhammad, his prophet, are very sensitive to any rejection and intimidated by criticism from most of Allah's creation, the non-Muslims who are condemned in almost every page of the Koran.

Thus the most sacred command by Allah to Muslims is to protect him and Muhammad from such rejection. The overwhelming and predominant message of the Koran is Allah's anger at non-Muslims, his cursing of them, and his instructions to Muslims to kill, subjugate, humiliate, and convert the human enemies of Allah for Allah's sake: "Fight against them so that Allah will punish them by your hands and disgrace them" (9:14). "Those who believe fight in the cause of

Allah" (4:76). "And let not those who disbelieve suppose that they can outstrip (Allah's Purpose). Lo! They [non-Muslims] cannot escape. Make ready for them all thou canst of (armed) force and of horses tethered, that thereby ye may dismay the enemy of Allah and your enemy" (8:59–60).

In his eagerness to entice his followers to fight, Muhammad promised salvation from Hell and admission to Heaven only to those who kill and get killed. The Koran promises Muslims that any Jew or Christian they kill will take their place in Hell. According to a hadith from Sahih Muslim, Muhammad said, "when it will be the day of resurrection, Allah will deliver to every Muslim a Jew or a Christian and say that is your rescue from Hell Fire" (Sahih Muslim book 37, number 6665).

In 2015 Abdullah al-Faisal, an Islamic sheikh in the UK, told his followers that killing is the only sure way for sinning Muslims to avoid Hell: "Some people are so sinful, after living in Dar ul-Harb (the West) for many years, the only way they can go to Paradise is for them to die on the battlefield fighting for Allah. When you go to the battlefield and you kill the kuffar (non-Muslims), they shall take your place in the hellfire."[6]

This means that a condemned Jew or Christian is the one who will rescue a Muslim in the afterlife, by taking his place in Hell. This might explain why Muslim jihadists are eager to kill others and get killed. It is the only way to salvation from Hell and admittance to Heaven.

The Laws of Islam were not designed to protect human beings from each other, but to protect Muslims and Allah from non-Muslim human beings who dare criticize Islam. Thus, under Islamic law, the severity of a crime depends on the degree to which it threatens Islam. The severest punishment under sharia is preserved for those who commit blasphemy against Muhammad and Allah; the punishment for that is execution even if they repent, meaning there is no forgiveness. In Pakistan blasphemers, Muslim or not, are burnt to death by other Muslims.

Many defenders of Islam blame the above Islamic teaching on ignorance or radicalism, but that teaching comes directly from the Koran: "Allah hath purchased from the believers their lives and their wealth for theirs [in return] is the Garden [paradise]: they shall fight in His cause, and shall slay and be slain. . ." (9:111). Muhammad also tells Muslims in several hadiths that the road to Paradise is through the sword: "Paradise lies under the shade of swords" (Bukhari 4.5.73).

When the lure of salvation from Hell was not enough for Muhammad's followers to sacrifice their lives for him, Muhammad became extravagant in his promises of fleshly pleasures in the Islamic Paradise, including even pleasures not allowed to Muslims on Earth. In the Islamic Paradise wine is going to be allowed to Muslims, who will also enjoy never-ending sexual pleasures with hundreds of beautiful women as white as pearls: "In the afterlife, Allah will give those in the Garden virgins of modest gaze whom neither man nor jinn have touched" (55:56). "Surely for the God fearing awaits a place of security, gardens and vineyards and maidens with swelling breasts, like of age, and a cup overflowing" (78:31–34). The Koran also promises Muslims who die in the jihad beautiful young boys: "And round about them will (serve) boys of everlasting youth. If you see them, you would think them scattered pearls" (76:19).

Unfortunately for Muslims, Allah gives conflicting messages in the Koran regarding their salvation from Hell and their admittance to Paradise. If Muslims read their holy book carefully, they must be disturbed when Allah seems to take back his promises of Paradise, telling Muslims that they will all go to Hell: "There will be no one of you who will not enter it (Hell). This was an inevitable decree of your Lord. Afterwards he may save some of the pious, God-fearing Muslims out of the burning fire" (19:71–72). According to this verse, Allah apparently changed his mind and is now promising a guarantee of Hell to all except for some pious ones who may be taken out of the burning fire after all are placed there.

But despite this reversal of Allah's promises, the common belief among Muslims everywhere today is still the same: to win Allah's approval, escape Hell, and enter Paradise, Muslims must kill and be killed while fighting the enemies of their God.

I have personally lived in the twisted world created by these beliefs about salvation. I was an eight-year-old child when my father was killed in the jihad against Israel. The president of Egypt at that time, Gamal Abdel Nasser, visited our home to pay his condolences since my father was one of his top military leaders. Nasser and his entourage asked my siblings and me: "Which one of you will avenge your father's blood by killing Jews?" At the funeral we were told that my father was now in Paradise. The Koran recitation during the funeral said, "Think not of those who are killed in the way of Allah as dead. Nay, they are alive with their Lord, and they are being provided for. They rejoice in what Allah has bestowed upon them from His bounty and rejoice for the sake of those who have not yet joined them, but are left behind (not yet martyred) that on them no fear shall come, nor shall they grieve. They rejoice in a grace and a bounty from Allah, and that Allah will not waste the reward of the believers" (3:169–71).

That very same verse was also quoted by Osama bin Laden in his "Letter to America" regarding the 9/11 attacks.

Jesus Died for Us vs. We Must Die for Allah

The Koran is replete with commandments to die for Allah and Muhammad's sake for the purpose of expanding Islam. Those who refuse to do so are called hypocrites; in Koran 4:66 they are ordered to "Lay down your lives or go forth from your dwellings."

That meant I was going to have no peace in my life and no reconciliation with Allah until I shed my blood or did some form of jihad.

Jesus, on the other hand, said, "I came that they may have life, and have it abundantly" (John 10:10). With Christ my burden is lifted, I have no enemies. No vengeance, no killing or dying for the sake of God is needed. Under Christianity I am allowed to live peacefully, lovingly, and fruitfully.

The Bible says that Jesus came into the world to die for us and to pay for the sins of all of humanity. He was crucified, died, and raised from the dead. He hung on the cross for our sins and the sins of the whole world.

This miraculous blessing from God, grace that human beings did not have to do anything to receive, is especially comforting to someone like myself, who grew up with the opposite value: that it is we who must die for our creator, Allah. With Christ I have been relieved from the burden of the commandment to Muslims to die in wreaking Allah's vengeance on this Earth.

Life Is Sacred vs. Death Is Worship

Six hundred years before Islam the Bible predicted the sharp difference between those who worship the real God and those who don't: "For whoso findeth me findeth life.... all they that hate me love death" (Proverbs 8:35–36).

The message of Islam is contrary to the Bible in regards to life and death. Islam glorifies death, and the highest reward is bestowed on those who die for the expansion of Islam which is what "to die for the sake of Allah" means. "Let those fight in the way of Allah who sell the life of this world for the other. Whoso fighteth in the way of Allah, be he slain or be he victorious, on him We shall bestow a vast reward" (Koran 4:74).

A common expression in Islamic preaching, political speeches, Arabic songs, and poetry is "We [Muslims] love death as you [Jews and Christians] love life." Another commonly expressed sentiment, repeated by Muslim groups such as Hamas, is "Killing Jews is worship that draws us close to Allah."

The Palestinian Media Watch often reports on parents holding not a funeral but instead a wedding to express (at least in public) their joy and celebration over the death of their suicide bomber children. While in the West such bombing is recognized as terrorism, the Muslim world celebrates terrorists for dying for the sake of Allah. Muslims are proud that theirs is a culture of death; the message again and again in Islam is worship of Allah through killing and getting killed as the only guarantee to Heaven.

Islam is all about death, whether it is for the purpose of reward or punishment. Suicide bombers and other dead "martyrs" are honored and become national heroes. And those who dishonor Islam or violate Islamic law are also condemned to death.

The sword is a symbol of jihad, conquering, taking the lives of Allah's enemies, and public beheadings that strike fear into citizens and make them submit. The flag of Saudi Arabia, the birthplace of Muhammad, proudly displays the sword as a symbol of jihad, killing and being killed for the sake of Allah. That is not a sign of a religion that regards life as sacred.

The last ten years of Muhammad's life were a constant state of fighting, battles, killing, beheadings, and glorification of death for the sake of Allah. Muhammad ordered the death of thousands during his lifetime and said, "If somebody (a Muslim) discards his religion, kill him" (Bukhari 52:260). Islamic solutions to those who violate Islam have often been "kill him/her/them."

If the ultimate worship of Allah is to die for him, killing and being killed, then the devout Muslim cannot respect the sanctity of life or be peaceful. To the contrary, he must reject love, life, liberty, and the pursuit of happiness. Muslim culture is thus extremely envious of, critical of, and threatened by cultures that promote joy and value life. Islam is a melancholy religion; the Koran is replete not only with humiliation and shame, but with doom, curses, killing, subjugation, and terror. Doom and gloom on Earth and making life not worth living for Islam's enemies have created a culture of death.

Even when they are not literally fighting wars, Muslims' lives are poisoned by the Islamic cult of death. For me, growing up in Egypt, life under Islam was a constant state of justifying oneself, not only to Allah, but to all the people around you. Nothing is ever enough for a Muslim to please Islamic society or Allah, and true joy and happiness is out of the question.

After becoming Christian I suddenly felt that I had permission from God to find joy in life. Living in a Biblically based culture, America, after having lived under the doom and gloom of a culture of death for thirty years was nothing less than miraculous for me. Christianity made me look at my life as a precious gift from God that I must make the best of. My psychological makeup was not easy to change, but I am grateful for the Holy Spirit directing me to finally put my tormented Islamic mind at rest and to allow myself to be transformed in the peaceful holy hands of God.

At War with the Devil vs. at War with Flesh and Blood

The Islamic doctrine that the way to be guaranteed Heaven is to die for Allah's sake refers to actual combative war, physical attacks on others, literally killing and being killed for Allah.

The Christian doctrine on "dying to self" has nothing to do with literal death.

While the Koran tells Muslims to fight other human beings and subdue them, the Bible tells us that we are fighting a spiritual battle between good and evil. Our hostility is directed at the Devil and not flesh-and-blood human beings: "For we wrestle not against flesh and blood, but against principalities, against powers, against the rulers of the darkness of this world, against spiritual wickedness in high places" (Ephesians 6:12). Jesus told us to love our enemies and not to judge the sinner.

Islam, on the other hand, does declare war against flesh and blood, namely the kafirs who reject Allah and Muhammad. In fact Islam externalizes and personifies evil and sin in the form of the other, the kafir. Islamic scripture speaks very little about a spiritual battle against the Devil. But it is full of commands to engage in literal fighting against flesh and blood infidels: "And slay them wherever ye find them.... Fighting is prescribed for you. . ." (Koran 2:191, 216).

In a nutshell, Islam makes it the primary goal of Muslims to be totally preoccupied with a constant war to make sure that those Allah considers to be wicked (non-Muslims), never prosper but in fact are killed by the hands of Muslims. That is very different from the role of Christians with respect to those considered to be sinners or wicked on Earth.

4

THE TRUTH WILL SET YOU FREE VS. LYING IS AN OBLIGATION

"[T]he Arab has no scruples about lying if by it he obtains his objective.... Arab society...is ruthless, stern and pitiless. It worships strength and has no compassion for weakness, the Arab is more interested in feelings than facts, in conveying an impression rather than giving a report."

—Sania Hamady[1]

Truth is a central theme of the Bible, where it is linked to human freedom: "And ye shall know the truth, and the truth shall make you free" (John 8:32). The Bible is very clear that we should search for the truth and abide by it. Jesus calls Himself "the way, the truth, and the life" (John 14:6) and promises to send the "the spirit of truth," (the Holy Spirit) Who "will guide you into all truth" (John 16:13). He calls Satan the father of lies (John 8:44). Christians and Jews are never commanded to compromise the truth for the purpose of achieving any goal. On the contrary: "But if ye have bitter envying and strife in your hearts, glory not, and lie not against the truth. This wisdom descendeth not from above, but is earthly, sensual, devilish" (James 3:14–15).

Unlike the Bible, the Koran and Islamic law promote a dualistic view on moral values, and particularly on truth-telling. Islamic law books start by saying that lying is "unlawful" (*Reliance* r8.0), but then they proceed to state the conditions under which lying becomes permissible, and even mandatory.

So in Islam, lying goes from being unlawful on one page to being an obligation on the next page—if it is for the benefit of Islam: "When it is possible to achieve an aim by lying but not by telling the truth, it is permissible to lie if attaining the goal is permissible, and lying is obligatory if the goal is obligatory" (*Reliance* r8.2). So if performing jihad, which is an obligation, requires lying, then a Muslim is obliged to lie. Islam allows lying under three conditions: in war with non-Muslims, in marital relations, "to smooth over differences" when a man is "talking with his wife or she with him," and in settling disagreements among Muslims (*Reliance*, r8.2). In one hadith, Muhammad claims that "inventing good information" is not really a lie if it's done to achieve a good purpose. In other words, the ends justify the means: "He who makes peace between the people by inventing good information or saying good things, is not a liar" (Bukhari 49:857).

Islamic law also obliges Muslims to slander, exaggerate, and mislead for the same reasons (*Reliance*, r2.16, r9.2, r10.3).

"Liars" are condemned in the Koran—when they are infidels who refuse to convert to Islam (Koran 9:107), or shirkers who refuse to go fight with Muhammad: "Had it been a near adventure and an easy journey they had followed thee, but the distance seemed too far for them. Yet will they swear by Allah (saying): 'If we had been able we would surely have set out with you.' They destroy their souls, and Allah knoweth that they verily are liars" (Koran 9:42). Thus in Islam lying could be a sin for some and a virtue for others; it all depends on how lying serves the goals of Islam.

Islamic doctrine is that deception is not only a valid tactic for Muslims—it is an attribute of Allah himself. Several times in the Koran, Allah describes himself as the greatest deceiver of all:

- "And they (the unbelievers) planned to deceive, and Allah planned to deceive (the unbelievers), and Allah is the best of deceivers" (3:54)
- "Are they then safe from Allah's deception? No one feels safe from Allah's deception except those that shall perish" (7:99)
- "And (remember) when the unbelievers plotted deception against you (O Muhammad), to imprison you, or kill you, or expel you. They plotted deception, but Allah also plotted deception; and Allah is the best of deceivers (8:30)

Muslim authorities have gone so far as to create several religious doctrines that justify lying as a tool to assist in Islam's own ascendancy:

- **"Taqiyya"**: dissimulation of the fact that you are a Muslim
- **"Kitman"**: lying by omission or partial truth
- **"Muruna"**: using stealth or flexibility to blend in with the enemies of Islam
- **"Tawriya"**: deliberate ambiguity, concealing, or creative lying

All of the above also allow Muslims to break their oaths—particularly if they violate only the intention of the oath, not its letter (*Reliance* o19.1–5). Such mincing of words and mixed messages regarding lying do not serve Muslim society—where appreciation of the truth is suppressed and distrust prevails—well.

It is permitted for a Muslim who lives in non-Muslim land to take an oath on the Koran and Allah and not be held accountable. While in the West that is called perjury, under Islamic law it is considered an honorable lie: "Allah will not call you to account for thoughtlessness in your oaths, but for the intention in your hearts" (Koran 2:225). That means if the intention is to benefit Islam, as in jihad, then taking a false oath on a Koran, the Islamic holy book, in a non-Muslim country would not be considered a sin in Islam.

While the Bible strictly forbids breaking one's oath (Numbers 30:1–2), Islam approves breaking one's oath when it is expedient to do so (Koran 2:225). If a Muslim discovers a better option after taking an oath, he is allowed to break his oath, take the better option, and make expiation (Koran 5:89; Bukhari 7.67.427; Muslim 15.4054). Islam provides that certain charitable acts can substitute for the performance of the oath (*Reliance* o20.0–4). Muhammad himself broke his oaths (at-Tahrim 66.2) and treaties (al-Anfal 8.58, al-Tawbah 9.3) with Banu Qaynuqa and the Quraysh, violating the treaty of Hudaybiyya by refusing to return Umm-Kulthum to Mecca (Bukhari 8.78.619 and 9.89.260). So according to Islamic sharia law, an oath is not binding.

These dubious Islamic doctrines, absolving Muslims from telling the truth and keeping even the most solemn kind of promises should be a clue to all Muslims that their religion is flawed. But somehow, Muslim apologists never give up on justifying Islamic teachings. As a matter of fact, they take advantage of the permission Islam gives them to lie to promote Islam. One example is their defense of the concept of jihad by defining it as an internal "struggle" in talking to Westerners—when they know that in their own books it is clearly defined as "war with non-Muslims to establish the religion"(*Reliance* o9.0).

Deception in defense of Islam and its goals is big business for Islamic organizations and lobbying groups in the West. It's an obligation under Islamic law, and it comes naturally to most Muslims. The reason I know this is that I was one of them and felt the exact same way. Lying in defense of Islam is something Muslims all over the world do. (Islamic governments regularly engage in it as well.)

Take, for example, new translations of the Koran from Arabic to English that intentionally mislead about what the original says, watering down its harsh, violent commandments. Koran 4:34 clearly orders men to beat ("wadribuhunnah" in Arabic) their disobedient wives. But a newly created website on the Koran called corpus.quran.com denies that the word "beat" is in the Koran at all.[2] Other translations, such as that of Muhammad Yusuf Ali, try to soften the Koran's message to beat women by adding the word (lightly) when the Koran clearly does not use the word "lightly."[3] Imams and other Muslim leaders claim that the commandment in the Koran for men to "beat" their wives really means they should "honor" their wives.[4] The deception is blatant.

"Awful doom," "fight for Allah," "shameful," "painful," "go to Hellfire," "terror," "slay disbelievers," "warfare ordained for you," "retaliation prescribed for you," and "Allah's curse" are some of the most common expressions in the Koran. In recent translations, however, these words are gone from the English.

Lying is practiced at the highest levels in Islamic society. While speaking in Germany, the top Sheikh of Al Azhar University denied that execution is the punishment for leaving Islam, but when he speaks in Arabic to Muslims he says the exact opposite, that apostates must be killed.[5]

Another example of Islamic lying for a greater goal is when the Arab media and Arab education establishment rewrite history about Israel and the West. Arab children, myself included, were taught that Jerusalem was originally an Arab and Islamic city. Still today, children in Gaza and West Bank Arab schools are taught that Yasser Arafat died as a result of being poisoned by Jews and that he was a martyr. And the Arab media refuses to expose such outrageous lies because those who expose Islamic lies are condemned as apostates.

Muslim leaders are often unaware of how ridiculous they appear when they lecture on Arabic TV on how beautiful it is for a Muslim to trick Jews into converting to Islam for Allah's sake. Cleric Mahmoud Al-Masri made this exact brag on Egyptian national TV.[6] The same preacher also taught children that it is necessary to lie to your wife, to Jews, and in time of war—though he explained they wouldn't understand the reasons, because they were children.[7]

The values of truth, honesty, and integrity are hardly mentioned in the Koran or preached by Islamic clerics. There are no Islamic legitimate examples of telling the truth for the truth's sake for clerics to teach from. Because Islamic doctrine is based on dual thinking and trickery, Muslims are not allowed to think for themselves. It is the job of the Muslim cleric to keep them ignorant, deceived, and confused. They lie to their own people, as well as to the kafirs.

Islamic education is focused on memorizing and not on analysis and interpretation. Competitions on memorizing the Koran are the most popular Islamic competitions. Muslims are allowed self-expression only if what they express redounds to the greater glory of Muhammad (the perfect man), the Koran (the perfect book), and sharia (the perfect set of laws). Muslims are in the habit of lying to promote Islam, but many of them are probably unaware of how explicitly their own law books command them to lie, slander, and deceive. Islam is in a constant race to keep its followers ignorant, confused, and unaware of the reality of their doctrine.

Likely it is hard on honorable Muslims who live in the West to lie for the benefit of Islam, or to look the other way when they see Islamic authorities saying things they know are not true. But it is the norm, the unspoken rule of life in Islam to just look the other way when you hear lies you don't like because there is no use in fighting them. Those who try to uncover lies in Muslim society end up getting badly hurt. Access to the internet has opened the eyes of some Muslims and given those who want to know the truth a free educational opportunity. Some are now learning about the contradictions and immorality of Islamic doctrine for the first time. But the majority of Muslims I know don't even want to know because uncovering Islamic lies could get them into terrible trouble, and end up cutting them off from their friends and family and entire life as they know it.

When I arrived in America, I learned more about my religion in just a few months than in a lifetime of education in the Muslim world. At first the process was intimidating. Muslims are often frustrated, not knowing what to say when asked what jihad is or what taqiyya is. No committed Muslim can venture to tell the truth about those Islamic doctrines, not even to him or herself. Those who leave Islam, such as myself, are the ones who simply could not continue with the lies. But many other Muslims continue to lie instinctively and without thinking, unaware that they have been indoctrinated into dishonesty by their own religion. Those are the hardest Muslims to convince of the truth.

It is hard for me to see Western nations treat Islam with equal respect, standing, and rights, allowing it to be practiced inside their countries on a footing equal to, if not better than, that of the Bible.

The number one enemy of Islam is the truth. And that has made the Bible itself the biggest threat to Islam. That is probably why there are two roads that Muslims who move to the West take; they either leave Islam altogether, like I did, often becoming Christians, or they go the other way and get radicalized, regardless of the truth.

Without living under Biblical truth, I personally could never have understood or discovered the sad truth about my former religion, Islam. I discovered for myself that life without the Bible leads away from the truth. That is probably the number one cultural shock every honest Muslim eventually has to confront.

"If lying is a foundation of a religion, then there is nothing one can build on." That statement by my pastor, Jim Tolle, opened my eyes as to why Islamic society is in a constant state of chaos and self-destruction. It's hard for me to shake my sadness over the misery inflicted on millions of Muslims, my family in Egypt included, who are unaware that the source of their misery is a God that tells them that lying, slander, and deception are holy.

My own personal experience with truth and lying was changed when I became Christian. When I wrote my first book on exposing and renouncing jihad I was already a Christian, and many Muslims regarded it as a betrayal of Islamic mores. I was called a "traitor" to Islam, a "liar," and a "Zionist." The taboo against being truthful to the West is so engrained in the Muslim mind that telling the truth is considered a sin in Islam. The Muslim community, both inside and outside the United States, ostracized me. I am unable to visit any Muslim country, including my birthplace Egypt, because of the death penalty for apostasy and blasphemy—in other words for becoming Christian and telling the truth.

It is hard for the West to understand that holy lying in Islam feels like a duty. That is how I felt when I was Muslim. The enormous power Allah's command to lie has empowered a whole culture into group think, pressuring millions of individuals into feeling that lying is normal. Thus one's conscience and one's gut feelings about what is good and evil become irrelevant.

I was not surprised to read an Intelligence Report at www.stratfor.com that confirmed my feelings about Islamic society. The report states that polygraph tests administered to Middle Easterners, Muslims in particular, could be seriously flawed. The explanation is both cultural and religious; it was discovered that lying did not cause stress on Muslims and Middle Easterners as it does to Western Christians. This allows Muslims to defeat polygraph tests.

In fact speaking the truth can cause stress to a Muslim. From personal experience in my early years as a Christian, I often caught myself feeling a bit guilty for speaking the truth in front of Muslims. I felt the urge to continue accepting the lies I was trained to overlook in the hope of getting approval from Muslims and the culture that I grew up in. It took me a while to fully wean myself from the destructive and powerful Islamic urge to lie for the sake of Allah and for the approval of Muslims.

There is one truth that Muslims are working day and night to hide, but that the West urgently needs to hear: the central goal of Islam is to make the whole world submit, to totally wipe out Biblical values and replace them with the twisted values of the Koran. They are willing to use any means to achieve that goal. In fact, Islam's endorsement of dishonesty and violence means that they can lie and inflict terror in pursuit of that goal while remaining guilt free and even passing a polygraph test. After 9/11, many Americans were sincerely asking "Why?" and "What did we do to provoke this?" These questions were the reason I started speaking out. I wanted to tell the American people that they had done nothing to provoke 9/11 or Islamic terrorism. That is how I started my journey to uncover the truth. I spoke out to warn America, and through that process of uncovering the truth I also started a process of personal healing and growth—ultimately out of a faith that feared the truth, and into a faith built on it.

Trust vs. Distrust

Trust develops in cultures where people are rewarded for speaking the truth, while distrust is the natural consequence in cultures that reward lying. But it's considered offensive and racist to point out this fact as it applies to Islam. Even though it is a well-documented fact that Islamic doctrine commands lying and deception, Muslims get extremely offended when such a doctrine is brought out of their own holy books and exposed in public to the infidels (kafirs).

A *Haaretz* article dated April 28, 2005, reported on a controversy over a lecture that had discussed lying in Arab cultures. Arabs complained that the lecture was racist because it raised the question. "So is it true that when an Arab opens his remarks with the expression 'Wal-lahi' [I swear by Allah], he is intending to lie?" (The translation in the brackets is mine.) The article reported some of what the lecturer had said: "Among Arabs, you will not find the phenomenon so typical of Judeo-Christian culture: doubts, a sense of guilt, the self-tormenting approach, 'Maybe we weren't entirely OK,' or 'Maybe we need to act or react differently.' These phenomena are totally unknown in Arab-Islamic society, toward outsiders. They have no doubts about their positions or the justice of their side. They have no sense of guilt that they may have erred. They have neither twinges of conscience nor any regrets that they may have done wrong to anyone else."[8]

In regard to the common Arabic expression "Wallahi," I am sure that most Muslims know that, yes, it is true that this expression is commonly used by Muslims who lie. And that should not be shocking in members of a religion whose God calls himself a deceiver and whose laws command them to lie, slander, and exaggerate.

The denial of this fact—for example, by the Muslim students who called the lecture racist—unfortunately is what prevents Islamic culture from transformation. The students were cutting off their nose to spite their face when they allowed their distrust to prevent them from benefiting from fact-based criticism, and even from taking a pause to consider the validity of what was said. All that they would have needed to do to check the accuracy of the lecture was to open their

Koran and sharia books and see for themselves the commandments to lie. But the lack of basic trust and comfort with the truth that is inculcated by a culture suffused with lies prevented them from doing that.

Trust is at the heart of religion. When one reads the Bible it becomes clear that building trust is one of its most vital principles. Trust is the glue that brings people and God together and the foundation upon which civilization is built. Bible-believing Americans who knew the importance of trust placed "In God We Trust" on U.S. currency. Having come from a culture where trust is considered an attribute of fools, it breaks my heart to see that some Americans actually want to remove that statement of trust in God from the dollar bill.

In the Bible, obedience is a product of trust: "The Lord is my rock, and my fortress, and my deliverer; my God, my strength, in whom I will trust; my buckler, and the horn of my salvation, and my high tower" (Psalms 18:2). "And such trust have we through Christ...." (II Corinthians 3:4).

In Islam, however, obedience is a product of fear. Islam forces submission through shaming, terror, and harsh and humiliating punishments rather than trust and persuasion. The obedience expected in Islam is similar to the submission of a slave to his master. This lack of trust in Muslim society places the individual in the wrong, in constant need of justifying himself. Islam has won many battles this way, but has lost the war for credibility and legitimacy.

The day Islam wedded itself to lying and slander was the day the trust factor flew out the window, to the detriment of the entire Islamic society. Yes, of course there are pockets of trust developed within certain families, clans, and sects by Muslims, whose humanity often wins out over their warped religion. But these are just rare pockets of trust—few and far between—in Islamic society. They do not fit the larger picture of Muslim society. Islamic law, by its very nature, challenges these loyalties and relationships of trust, which inevitably come into conflict with jihad and the best interests of Islam.

Islam's doctrine on lying also destroys any hope for building trust between different Muslim sects. And what Muhammad said in a hadith about divisions within Islam has led to further distrust: "'The Banu Isra'il split into about seventy-two sects. My community will split into seventy-three. All of them will be in the Fire except for one.' They asked, 'Who are they, Messenger of Allah?' He replied, 'Those who base themselves on what I and my Companions are doing today'" (At-Tirmidhi).[9]

So according to Muhammad all of the seventy-three sects of Islam will roast in hellfire except one, which he defines as the one that follows his own example. Given this hadith, no wonder all the Muslim sects point at each other in condemnation as apostates who will go to Hell.

The distrust is obvious even in Muhammad's own heart; the Prophet himself expressed fears and distrust of Allah's "schemes." Muhammad was uncertain whether Allah would save him: "I am not an innovation among the Messengers, and *I know not what shall be done with me* or with you. I only follow what is revealed to me; I am only a clear warner" [emphasis added] (Koran 46:8–9). "...some scholars have considered the words 'best of schemers' to be one of God's beautiful names. Thus one would pray, 'O Best of Schemers, scheme for me!' .... the Prophet used to pray, 'O God, scheme for me, and do not scheme against me!'" (Qurtubi, IV, pp. 98–99; cf. Zamakhshari, I, p. 366).

Muhammad's closest and most loyal companion, Abu Bakr, also expressed fear of Allah's deception in the following hadith: "Although he had such a faith, which was too great to suffice all the inhabitants of the earth, he was afraid that his heart might go astray. So, he used to utter, while weeping: 'Would that I have been a bitten tree!'

Whenever he was reminded of his position in Allah's sight, he would say: 'By Allah! *I would not rest assured and feel safe from the deception of Allah* ("la amanu limakr Allah"), even if I had one foot in paradise [emphasis added].'"[10]

As to non-Muslims, there is no hope for them at all to live in peace and equality under Islam. Non-Muslims have never had any reason whatsoever to trust Islam, which promises them Hell, doom, humiliation, subjugation, and discrimination. Allah even says in the Koran that he will purposefully lead them astray: "Whoever Allah guides is truly guided. But as for those He leads astray, you will not find any protectors for them apart from Him. We will gather them on the Day of Rising, flat on their faces, blind, dumb and deaf. Their shelter will be Hell. Whenever the Blaze dies down, We will increase it for them" (Koran 17:97).

As a Muslim, I often asked myself how an all-knowing God, the creator of the universe, could write a holy book that is so full of contradictions. A God that keeps changing his mind does not instill trust in his word.

The answer for inconsistencies in the Koran is the Islamic doctrine of abrogation—a principle unique to Islam among religions, and approved by Allah in the Koran itself:

- "When we cancel a message, or throw it into oblivion, we replace it with one better or one similar. Do you not know that God has power over all things?" (2:106)
- "When we replace a message with another, and God knows best what he reveals, they say: You have made it up. Yet, most of them do not know" (16:101)
- "God abrogates or confirms whatsoever he will, for he has with him the Book of the Books" (13:39)

- "If we pleased, we could take away what we have revealed to you. Then you will not find anyone to plead for it with us" (17:86)

I believe the contradictions in Islamic scriptures were not coincidental but have a purpose: to confuse the public, both Muslim and non-Muslim. Depending on what is needed in a conversation, Muslim sheikhs, who like magicians are experts in the art of deception, pull whatever verse is needed to fit their argument at the time, regardless of whether the verse has supposedly been "abrogated" or not.

For example Muslims like to tell the West that Islam is for religious freedom. In support of that lie, they quote a verse that has actually been "abrogated"—cancelled and reversed—but that is conveniently still on the books, in the Koran: "Let there be no compulsion in religion" (2:56). And yet public opinion in the Muslim world is overwhelmingly for the execution of apostates. According to an April 30, 2013, Pew Research survey, 86 percent of Egyptians are for executing apostates. How can that be?

The apologists for Islam who quote the "no compulsion in religion" verse know very well that Muslim public opinion has been shaped by other passages in the Koran—passages that demand the death penalty for apostasy, and that have not been "abrogated." The deception being practiced on the West is phenomenal. There are numerous Koran verses, hadiths, and sira, or actions of Muhammad, all saying that apostates must be executed. Islam's holy book orders Muslims to fight unbelievers until they relent and either convert to Islam or accept a state of humiliation under Islamic rule (4:89, 9; 11–12, 2:217, 9:73–74, 88:21, 5:54, 9:66, 9:29)—an obvious endorsement of "compulsion in religion." Muhammad himself decreed the death penalty for apostasy, in several hadiths: "If someone [a Muslim] changes his religion, kill him" (Bukhari 52:260); "strike off his head" (al-Muwatta of Imam Malik, 36.18.15);

"A man who embraces Islam, then reverts to Judaism is to be killed…" (Bukhari 89:271). According to every Islamic sect and all the different schools of interpretation of sharia law, apostates must be executed.

What level of trust can a religion have if it executes those who leave it? Very little. Muslims are told to rely—"tawakkul" in Arabic—on Allah. Some translate "tawakkul" as "trust,"[11] but that's not what the word really means. An accurate definition is *throwing one's body down (as in prostration) in servitude (to God) and attaching the heart to (his) Lordship.* Tawakkul has a fatalistic element of surrender to an inevitable predetermined future or destiny. It is simply blind obedience. The actual Arabic word for trust is "thiqah," which is not used in the Koran.[12]

One of the most common Arabic expressions is "inshallah," meaning "if Allah wills." The expression is often used in the context of making future plans, but Muslims also say it when they want to be vague and not respond to a request with a clear "Yes" or "No." This way a Muslim can give what appears to be a "Yes," and then, letting the request go unfulfilled, make the excuse that *I never promised with a positive yes, I only said "inshallah" and Allah did not allow me to do it.* This kind of word game adds to the distrust among Muslims.

There's a hadith that might explain why Muslims are obsessed with saying "inshallah" in almost every sentence. According to this saying by Muhammad, those who do not say "Allah willing" could conceive deformed babies: "Allah's messenger said, 'Once Sulayman Alayhissalaam said "(By Allah) tonight I will have sexual intercourse with one-hundred (or ninety-nine) women, of whom will give birth to a knight who will fight in Allah's cause." On that a companion of his said, "Say Allah willing," but he did not say Allah willing. Therefore only one of those women conceived and gave birth to a part of man. By him in whose hands Muhammad's life is, if he had said,

"Allah willing" (he would have begotten sons) all of whom would have been knights, striving in Allah's cause'" (Bukhari, Vol. 1, p. 395).

The Islamic doctrine of lying and deceit has been a curse on Muslims, leaving them with no choice but to feel constantly offended and angry at a world that does not trust them. They keep blaming the outside world for distrusting Islam and Muslims and accusing them of being "racists" who need to overcome their "Islamophobia"—when in reality what Muslims need to do to win the world's trust and respect is to reject the religious laws that oblige them to lie.

Belief vs. Submission

In the West, the word religion implies a set of beliefs that a human being voluntarily trusts and finds reliable. And belief requires a thought process leading to conviction. The Bible says "Come now, let us reason together" (Isaiah 1:18). Freedom of thought and conscience is a precondition for that process. Without freedom to think, reason, and believe, the very concept of religion makes no sense.

Muhammad started his religious movement with a promise that "there is no compulsion in religion," but when he could not win the hearts and minds of people with persuasion, he totally reversed his position—from no compulsion in religion to compulsion through terror. Muhammad even boasted that terror was one of Allah's gifts to him: "I have been made victorious through terror" (Bukhari 4:52.220). Then Allah confirmed Muhammad's change of heart: "Soon shall We cast terror into the hearts of the unbelievers (those who refused to believe in Islam)" (Koran 3:151). Allah changed his mind like Muhammad, and terror became Islam's tool for missionary work.

Reason and persuasion to belief became irrelevant to Islam, and blind obedience to both Allah and Muhammad became the theme of the Koran. Thus Allah himself says in the Koran, "The wandering

Arabs say: We believe. Say (unto them, O Muhammad): *Ye believe not, but rather say 'We submit,'* for the faith hath not yet entered into your hearts. Yet, if ye obey Allah and His messenger, He will not withhold from you aught of (the reward of) your deeds...." [emphasis added] (Koran 49:14) and "Whoever obeys the Messenger has obeyed Allah. . ." (Koran 4:79).

Muslims are also commanded to obey Muhammad. In the Prophet's own words: "Whoever obeys me has obeyed Allah. Whoever rebels against me has rebelled against Allah" (Bukhari 9:89:251). Allah and Muhammad agree that Muslims must not only obey Muhammad but also follow his example in every way. Allah says, "You have a good model in the Messenger of Allah for one who hopes for Allah and the Last Day" (Koran 33:21).

Islam promotes slavishly mimicking Muhammad in every way: his attire, beard, habits, and character; his love of jihad; his promotion of terror; and even his polygamy and ownership of sexual slaves. There are dozens of hadith on the topic of a Muslim's obligation to believe in, obey, and follow Muhammad and his Sunnah (way of life). Three examples follow: "Ash-Shafii said: 'Abdullah ibn 'Umar was seen making his she-camel turn round in a particular place and was asked why. He said, "I don't know. I once saw the Messenger of Allah doing it, so I do it."'"[13] Other hadiths show that Muslims kiss the black stone in Kaaba just because they were told to do so, not because it makes sense: "The Sunnah of the Messenger of Allah consists only in following it. When 'Umar looked back at the Black Stone, he said, 'You are a stone and can neither help nor harm. If I had not seen the Messenger of Allah kiss you, I would not have kissed you.' Then he kissed it" (Muslim 15:275). AbuSa'id said: I saw Wathilah ibn al-Asqa' in the mosque of Damascus. He spat at the mat and then rubbed it with his foot. He was asked: Why did you do so? He said:

Because I saw the Messenger of Allah doing so" (sunan Abi Dawud 484 w:94).

Thou Shalt Not Kill vs. Muslims Must Execute Apostates

The doctrine of Islam regarding apostasy is very simple: those who leave Islam are given three days to go back, and if they don't they must be executed.

Islam is the only "religion" in the world that makes it a moral and legal duty for its members to execute those who leave it.

Islamic law forces Christians and Jews into three choices 1) convert to Islam, 2) be killed, or 3) live as a dhimmi, with protection from being killed in exchange for living an oppressed life under Islamic law. The luxury of this third choice is not awarded by Islamic law to those born to a Muslim father, or to people Islam refers to as idol worshippers—to atheists, Hindus, or Buddhists.

Muhammad often called those who escaped Islam "hypocrites," even if they had been forced into it in the first place. Even if they had converted because of duress under the Islamic sword, Muhammad treated them as apostates if they went back on their forced conversions.

The proportion of the Islamic scriptures dedicated to commandments to terrorize human beings into accepting Islam, and then to terrorize them again if they try to escape from it, is astounding. That alone should disqualify Islam from being called a religion.

Looking back on my thirty-year life as a Muslim in Egypt, I don't remember ever being asked if I wanted to be Muslim. There is no baptism, bat mitzvah, or any kind of initiation ceremony to become a Muslim. In Muslim countries there is no offer of the Muslim message to those who are born into Islam. There is no attempt to persuade them to become Muslims. Born Muslims never freely accept Islam. So I was an unwilling participant; I never consented to being Muslim. All I knew was that the people around me followed Islam and told me I was a Muslim and that there was no other choice but to live under Islamic law.

In a speech to the United Nations in 2012, President Obama said, "The future must not belong to those who slander the prophet of Islam." When I heard that my heart sank. President Obama must have known that what he said was in line with the sharia law that forbids criticizing the Prophet and condemns such an action as blasphemy punishable by death.

Being a Muslim is a one-sided contract, a pledge of allegiance to Islam under penalty of death—and Muslims do not even have any choice about whether to make that pledge in the first place.

Besides being the only religion to enforce membership with the death penalty, Islam is also the only religion that uses the power of the State to claim newborns for itself. In the Muslim world, leaving Islam is not just a religious sin, but also a crime against the State.

In Egypt birth certificates of all newborns with Muslim fathers are stamped "Muslim" at birth by the government. All my Egyptian government issued–documents were stamped Muslim—my student ID, identification card, and any other government-issued documents such as passports. My original birth certificate, which I still have, was stamped Muslim at the time of my birth. Even now, it would be impossible for me today to persuade the Egyptian authorities to change any of those documents even though I am a practicing Christian today. If I visited Egypt today, I would still be legally bound to practice Islam only.

The same Islamic state that branded me Muslim since birth also made it legally impossible for me to marry a Coptic Christian man when I lived in Egypt. According to Islamic sharia law, Christian and Jewish men are not allowed to marry Muslim women—so we had to go through an eight-year ordeal before we could leave the country to get married in America.

Saudi Arabia and other Islamic countries have put pressure on Third World nations that are not majority Muslim to keep them from issuing marriage licenses to Muslim women and Jewish or Christian men. I was contacted by an Egyptian Muslim woman who was unable to get married to her Christian lover in his African country; she was refused a marriage license and finally had to go back to Cairo unmarried.

I am an American citizen and have lived in the U.S. for more than thirty-seven years, but Islam still does not want to leave me alone. I am now branded as an apostate under the laws of all Islamic countries.

Even though Egypt is described in the West as a moderate Muslim country, school books in Egypt today teach Muslim kids that killing apostates is a right for individual Muslims—and an obligation for Muslim governments. A recent program on Egyptian TV, discussing these school books and the right to kill apostates, revealed that cannibalism is also allowed in this situation. Schools in Egypt are teaching cannibalism, but the U.S. media and the Left in the West take no interest.[14] But anyone who pays attention cannot help learning that the death penalty for leaving Islam is very real.

No wonder double talk is necessary for Muslims who want to defend Islam's doctrine on apostates. They really approve of killing apostates, but they turn around and tell the West that Islam allows freedom of religion. Then when asked about the details, they say that a Muslim can be whatever he wants to be—in his mind. As long as the Muslim does not publicly declare he's a Christian then he cannot be accused of apostasy or subversion against the Islamic state.

Muslims who keep being Christian in their head are safe—obviously, because no one knows about it. The only problem is when a Muslim converts to Christianity and fails to conceal it. Here Islamic apologists are applying the same principle of concealment that, as we have already seen in chapter one, Islam encourages regarding sin. If you are not a Muslim in your mind, it's okay, because Islam does not care about persuasion, real faith, or what is in a person's heart, but only about his actions and being a loyal soldier for Islamic jihad. Only God knows how many people in Egypt who call themselves Muslim are really Muslim.

Thus Muslims who want to be Christians can go ahead as long as they keep it to themselves—as long as they never hold a Bible in front of family or in public, never befriend Christians or go to church, continue to carry government-issued ID stamped "Muslim," never marry a Christian, and continue behaving as Muslim—going to mosque, praying Islamic prayers and celebrating Islamic holidays, and being totally loyal to Islamic causes and laws and especially the Islamic state. Then they'll be safe and can practice Christianity in their mind. This twisted thinking allows Muslim apologists to feel justified in claiming there is freedom of religion in Islam—that it does abide by international human rights laws.

Freedom of religion is a Biblical value; it was never an Islamic value. Freedom of conscience has posed an existential threat to Islam from day one back in the seventh century. Islam is a violent rebellion against the Bible, a rebellion that has now lasted over fourteen hundred years. But Islam could not compete with the Bible when it began, and it still cannot compete with the Bible today. The reason freedom of religion is banned under Islam and by Islamic states is that Islam has no confidence it would survive in free competition with Christianity. Islam needs "compulsion in religion" to succeed. It is not adequate to compete with the Bible, and Muslims feel its inadequacy.

As we have already seen, one of the most respected leaders of Sunni Islam has said that the killing of apostates is essential for Islam to survive: "If they [Muslims] had abolished the punishment for apostasy, Islam would not exist today." What Yusuf al-Qaradawi said is the law of Islam in all schools of sharia law.[15]

The Organisation of Islamic Cooperation (OIC), which now has an envoy representing the United States, held a conference in Cairo that promulgated the sharia-based Cairo Declaration, in which words that are meant to sound like they affirm freedom of conscience actually confirm the death penalty for apostasy.

The Declaration's deceptive Article 10 says, "Islam is the religion of unspoiled nature. It is prohibited to exercise any form of compulsion on man or to exploit his poverty or ignorance in order to convert him to another religion, or to atheism." Notice that it's *not* prohibited to use compulsion to convert anybody *to* Islam. Even more ominously, articles 19 and 22 of the Declaration endorse the death penalty for apostasy and blaphemy—in a particularly devious way: "There shall be no crime or punishment *except as provided for in the Sharia*" (19d). Everyone shall have the right to express his opinion freely in such manner *as would not be contrary to the principles of the Sharia*" (22a). Everyone shall have the right to advocate what is right, and propagate what is good, and warn against what is wrong and evil *according to the norms of Islamic Sharia*" (22b). "Information is a vital necessity to society. It may not be exploited or misused in such a way as may violate sanctities and *the dignity of Prophets*, undermine moral and ethical values or disintegrate, corrupt or harm society or weaken its faith" (22c).[16] [Emphasis added throughout.]

The Declaration places sharia above international law on human rights, including freedom of conscience. And we know that sharia commands the death penalty for both apostasy out of Islam and criticism of Muhammad.

Even though Muslim groups in the U.S. say they are for freedom of religion, the truth is that they are not. In 2009 I joined a group of former Muslims in sending almost two hundred Freedom Pledge letters to Muslim groups in the U.S. asking them to sign in support of freedom of conscience and religion. Unfortunately, they refused. The pledge stated, "I renounce, repudiate and oppose any physical intimidation, or worldly and corporal punishment, of apostates who leave Islam, change their religion from Islam to another religion, or express unbelief in Islam, in whatever way that punishment may be determined or carried out by myself or any other Muslim including the family of the apostate, community, Mosque leaders, Shariah court or judge, and Muslim government or regime."

Only two moderate Muslim reformists responded to our pledge letter: Dr. Zuhdi Jasser of the American Islamic Forum for Democracy, and Dr. Ali Alyami of the Center for Democracy & Human Rights in Saudi Arabia.

Because of Islamic laws allowing the arrest, imprisonment, and execution of those who leave Islam, many former Muslims in the West, myself included, have decided not to visit any Muslim country. The danger of getting imprisoned, executed, or killed on the street for having left Islam is real in any Muslim country, including "moderate" Egypt and Turkey. The example of Pastor Saeed Abedini's arrest and imprisonment by the government of Iran, even with his U.S. passport, is a reminder to all of us American former Muslims never to visit our countries of origin.

The West is told that the majority of Muslims are moderate, but what does "moderate" really mean when, as we have seen, the overwhelming majority of Muslims in Egypt today support the death penalty for leaving Islam? Even though my family in Egypt is well educated and considered moderate, my mother and siblings in Egypt have severed all relations with me ever since I made it public that I am now a Christian.

Many in the West consider the execution of apostates under Islam to be an internal cultural matter among Muslims, something that does not affect the West. But the West should be concerned because killing apostates and honor killing is happening here as well. In 2009 there was the case of a seventeen-year-old girl, Rifka Bary, who escaped her home in Ohio after her Muslim father threatened to kill her when she became Christian. Instead of supporting the girl who ran for her life, the leftist media attacked her integrity and treated the story as just a family squabble. The majority of the mainstream media did not want to take the apostasy death sentence in Islam seriously.[17]

Few in the U.S. media seem to be interested in exposing this human tragedy. Instead, Western journalists are quick to condemn anyone who points out the truth about Islam as an "Islamophobe." To them I say this: My fear of Islam is not a phobia. I am afraid for good reason. But I will never submit to Islamic terrorism because I became Christian.

The lack of freedom of conscience in Islamic society is detrimental to peace and stability within a nation and between nations. The sharia law against apostasy brings the threat of violence to every level of society, from the president who must be a Muslim to the street sweeper who must obey Islam. To keep Muslims within Islam, Muslim governments must subjugate and dehumanize citizens, sacrificing peace and stability by the use of force.

Faith vs. Submission

The rejection of freedom of religion in Islamic morality is proof that Islam refuses to appeal to reason to persuade people to faith. Instead it relies on force to prevail and make others submit.

Whether a religion is based on freedom of conscience or not makes all the difference. If people have freedom, then religion relies on persuasion, which is the essence of what religion should be: "And ye shall know the truth, and the truth shall make you free" (John 8:32). A God who loves his creatures and sets them free will not encourage his followers to lie to trick others. He will not lead believers in him to live in a culture of manipulation, condemnation, enslavement, and jockeying for control and dominance between human beings. Thus the quality of life for all is greatly improved under religions that permit freedom of belief.

On the other hand, a religion that rejects freedom of conscience and demands total submission could never be from a loving God. A good God would never authorize human beings to judge and kill other human beings over religion—even to force people to believe in him.

5

FREEDOM IN THE BIBLE VS. FREEDOM IN ISLAM

As a former Muslim, I am in awe of the loving God of the Bible, Who desires for us not only to heal but to live an abundant life of freedom from bondage.

Nothing in the Koran comes close to Biblical verses such as these: "Now the Lord is that Spirit: and where the Spirit of the Lord is, there is liberty" (II Corinthians 3:17). "If the Son therefore shall make you free, ye shall be free indeed" (John 8:36). "For, brethren, ye have been called into liberty" (Galatians 5:13). "Stand fast therefore in the liberty wherewith Christ hath made us free, and be not entangled again with the yoke of bondage" (Galatians 5:1).

These references to freedom are uniquely Biblical and totally alien to Islam. In fact the Koran advocates the opposite. The word free or freedom, "hurriyya" in Arabic, is never mentioned in the Koran in the Biblical sense.

The Koran and other Islamic sources mean one thing by the words "free" and "freedom"—those terms simply describe men and women who are not owned by others as slaves, and the condition they live in. Islamic scriptures distinguish free men and women from slaves in the context of the widespread slavery in the Islamic world—something that is still regulated in Islamic law books today. Freedom of thought, religion, speech, and freedom from being subjected to cruel and unusual punishment are totally alien to Islamic culture. According to Ibn Arabi, the "Greatest Sufi Master," who died in 1240, the true freedom is "perfect slavery" to Allah. He refers to Allah as the "master" of his human "slaves."[1]

In the early twentieth century, however, as a result of Western influence, Islamic culture started to recognize the Biblical concept of freedom—but only to a limited extent, in a sense that does not explicitly contradict sharia law. That was a time when many Muslims were first exposed to Western education, literature, and the arts. At the end of the eighteenth century, the American Revolution and the French Revolution had spread the Biblical idea of freedom throughout Western culture. When, a little more than a hundred years later, many Muslims came into contact with the West, the pressure mounted on the Muslim world to import "freedom" in the larger sense, not just as a bare, literal description of the state of people who are not literally enslaved. That pressure also resulted in the curtailment of the literal institution of slavery throughout the Muslim world, where it had been accepted without question until that time.

Internal changes to Islamic values as a result of pressure from Muslims who demand it after being exposed to Western values are always threatening to Islam. Every time Muslims rebel against Islamic oppression, especially after being inspired by the West, Islam feels discredited and unsustainable. Even without exposure to Western culture, Islam is in a constant state of conflict and internal rebellion over sharia enforcement. And the mere existence of a successful Biblically based society that permits freedom and human dignity to its citizens is a huge challenge to Islamic sharia.

After America acted on its Biblical principles and endured civil war to abolish slavery, the pressure mounted on Arab countries that practiced slavery. The world now condemned slavery, and it seemed a sign of backwardness that there were still markets selling slaves and eunuchs in open markets in Islamic countries. Some Muslims began to wonder how Islam, which claims to be superior to the Bible, could still practice slavery when the people whom the Koran called sinners had abolished slavery.

Islamic pride in the birthplace of Muhammad, Saudi Arabia, was put to the test. In 1962 the Saudi government finally declared the end of the fourteen-hundred-year-old Islamic institution of slavery. That decision to make slavery illegal, meant to improve the reputation of the Muslim world, was ironically a slap to the credibility of Islamic sharia law. Riots immediately erupted in Mecca and Medina because Muslims considered slavery a religious right endorsed by the Koran, the example of Muhammad, and Islamic law.

Despite the riots, the laws against slavery stayed on the books. But in Islamic society there is always a way to work around the rules while maintaining appearances. Saudi Arabia and other Muslim countries may have abolished slavery officially, but the culture of slavery remains alive and well today in many parts of the Muslim world, where maids, drivers, household help, and anyone of a lower status—often immigrants from both Muslim and non-Muslim countries—have few rights and are often abused by their Muslim employers.

But maintaining de facto slavery while keeping up appearances is not good enough for some Muslims, who think that owning slaves is a right that Muslims should be able to practice out in the open.

Prominent Saudi religious leader Sheikh Saleh Al-Fawzan recently called for slavery to be re-instated as legal throughout the kingdom. According to the sheikh, who is a member of Saudi Arabia's Senior Council of Clerics: "Slavery is a part of Islam. Slavery is part of jihad, and jihad will remain as long as there is Islam."[2] And of course the world has watched in horror as ISIS actually did revive chattel slavery—including even public slave markets.

After the legal abolition of slavery and the trouble it caused to the status quo, Islamic leadership did their best to suppress any further challenges to Islam from the impact of Western values. A free competitive market of ideas threatened Islam to its core. The guardians of Islam felt that their system was on the brink of collapse. The influence of the West, the attractive Biblical culture that was the greatest threat to Islam, had to be stopped before sharia was further eroded. Islamic leaders felt that they had to mobilize all Islamic financial, intellectual, media, propaganda, and physical resources to block out the West. Western freedoms had to be portrayed as evil and corrupt. "Freedom" in the mind of Muslims had to be made to mean freedom from outside influences—essentially freedom from the freedoms the West stood for.

So Islamic intellectuals bombarded the Muslim public with negative messages, outright lies, and slander against the West; they denounced the little Satan (Israel) as well as the great Satan (the United States) in the strongest terms. "Istimaar" or "colonialism" was the concept that galvanized hatred and terror of the West throughout the Islamic world, unifying Muslims against the West and mobilizing a new jihad. Muslims were spoon-fed the notion that their freedom, wealth, resources, and oil had been stolen by the West. Under that theory, Muslims were brought together in unity despite the distrust and fear prevalent in Islamic society. The campaign for freedom in the Muslim world was very cleverly framed—Muslims' energy was channeled away from seeking freedom from Islamic oppression to seeking freedom from the Western Biblical values that formed an existential threat to Islam.

I grew up in the Muslim world in the '50s, '60s, and '70s hearing daily chants, songs, political slogans, and fiery speeches against the evil West. This campaign got more intense and worse by the day until it finally exploded in the face of the West on 9/11. It is still going on today, with smaller explosions of violence occurring every few days all around the world.

The only way for Islam to survive is by keeping sharia, which enables the absolute control that the religion has over the slaves of Allah—all ordinary Muslims. That's why the abolition of slavery was such a threat to Islamic society. It was an example of Western influence making illegal something that had always been legal under sharia, which still allows for it.

Muslims exposed to Biblical values had forced Arab media and political leaders to put into effect, if only in one discrete reform, the un-Islamic concept of "freedom." The only solution was for the Muslim leadership, terrified of what could happen to Islam if the trend continued, to constantly counter the influence of Western Biblical values with anti-Western propaganda before Islamic power was eroded further. Islamic law—with its divine endorsement of lying, slander, exaggeration, and terror against the kafirs in the best interests of Islam—was very helpful in the propaganda campaign.

In Islamic culture, demands for freedom rarely refer to human rights, much less to the rights of women and minorities as they are understood in the West. Even during the 2011 Arab Spring, in Tahrir Square in Egypt slogans on freedom never referred to freedom from the oppressive sharia law or for separation of mosque and state. Even the women were carrying signs against Mubarak but no signs demanding equality with men under the law. Not one member of the oppressed Coptic Christian minority carried a sign demanding to live free from Islamic law.

Demands for freedom in Muslim countries are always directed against a specific dictator, who is usually accused of collaborating with the evil "kafir" West. Islamic media does not differentiate between secular liberal Western values and Biblical values in its reporting. So if secularists in the West advocate gay marriage, Muslims do not see America as split over that issue and do not see that Biblical values disagree with gay marriage.[3] The Muslim world lumps liberal values with Biblical values because they are not familiar with a society that accommodates two opposite views. Thus the Islamic view of the great Satan is reinforced in the eyes of the unsuspecting Muslim public when Islamic propaganda claims that the Biblical West is corrupt. On an Arabic TV show aired by Christians in the U.S., a Muslim doctor caller said that Christians in the West are morally corrupt because of premarital sex. This doctor was under the impression that this Western phenomenon was sanctioned by the Bible. From the perspective of Muslims, anything that happens in Western society must be approved by the Bible.

Islam is currently in a fight for its survival against the Western and Biblical value of freedom; Muslims cannot understand that anything could happen in Western society without the approval of the Biblical religious authority—because in Islamic society nothing could happen without the approval of sharia. In that fight, Islam has no weapons that are based on truth, only the propaganda of lies, deception, getting offended, name-calling, and finger-pointing, all of which is coupled with the most powerful tool of Islam: terror.

The Islamic campaign of deception is impacting how the Koran itself is perceived in the West, with new English translations attempting to make the Koran's views on freedom similar to those of the Bible, when in fact it is the exact opposite.

For example in chapter 3, verse 97, of the Koran, Allah tells those who refuse to believe in Islam that: "Allah is independent (un-wanting) of the entire creation!" This is an accurate translation by Fridul Haque, in which Allah expresses his anger at those who reject Islam by telling them that he (Allah) does not need his whole creation. But a new translation at corpus.quran.com attempts to soften the image of Allah by translating the same verse as "Allah is "free" from any need of the universe.

The bottom line here is that the God of the Bible wants us to have freedom, while the God of Islam wants us to submit. Because unbelievers refuse to submit to Allah, Allah in this verse threatens to reject his whole creation, both believers and unbelievers.

Children of God vs. Enemies or Slaves of Allah

The Bible provides us with an amazing family to belong to. God sees us as His children whom He cares for tenderly: "Keep me as the apple of the eye; hide me under the shadow of thy wings" (Psalms 17:8).

In Islam, however, Allah sees the majority of his human creation—all the non-Muslims—as his enemies. The Koran says that Allah "does not love the unbelievers" (3:31, 30:45). And not even Allah's followers, the Muslims, are his children. He sees them not as children but as "O 'Ibadi," meaning "my slaves." Muslims are slaves who should worship Allah whether they like it or not: "And unto Allah falleth prostrate whosoever is in the heavens and the earth, willingly or unwillingly, as do their shadows in the morning and the evening hours" (Koran 13:15). Allah here says that everyone and everything—just like their shadows—bows to Allah twice a day whether they want to or not.

When I became Christian and learned that we are God's children, I wept. I finally had a father, after Islamic jihad had taken mine away from me at age eight. I was overwhelmed with comfort and love in a totally new relationship with a God who calls himself my father in the Bible. I was saved then.

Islam totally rejects the description of God as a father. It also sees the idea of God's Spirit within us as wrong and disrespectful. Islam recognizes the father-son relationship only in the purely biological sense; it has no concept of the fatherhood of God in the spiritual sense.

As a teenager I remember how embarrassed I was for a Christian friend of mine when a Muslim man reprimanded her for naming God as "the Father." Muslims in majority-Muslim countries feel entitled to correct Christians like this, lest young Muslims, including me back then, hear any good news about God that might contradict what the Koran says about Allah.

Islamic scriptures never refer to Allah as father. In fact the Koran insists that "Allah is a Father to no one" (5:18; 19:88–93; 21:26). Instead, the Koran describes Allah as a master (10:30) and human beings—including even Muhammad—as his slaves (2:23). Allah's approval even of Muhammad was dependent on his performance; Muslims who do not perform as Allah requires will suffer Allah's wrath and torture. Abdullah, meaning slave of Allah, is one of the most popular names for Muslims. And that is exactly how Muslims relate to Allah, as a far and distant God, angry, vengeful, and eager to punish. The Koran depicts a hostile relationship between Allah and his creation: "If you march not forth, He will punish you with a painful torment and will replace you by another people, and you cannot harm Him at all, and Allah is Able to do all things" (9:39). Again Allah here seems to be offended by his creation and threatens his followers with a painful punishment, and to replace them if they reject him.

The difference between how Christians and Muslims relate to God and how God relates to human beings in the Koran and the Bible is like night and day.

The Master-Slave Dialectic

A God who considers most of the human race his enemies and who desires the enslavement of his creatures unfortunately sets the tone for how Muslims relate to one another and to the world. The impact of Allah's master-slave relationship with his creation colors all Muslim social relationships and every interaction in Islamic society. Muslims relate to one another as cruel masters and servile slaves.

Thus to have enemies, to oppress, and to be oppressed has become normal, justified, and even God-like in Islam. One attribute of Islamic society that outsiders notice first is the ugly way citizens relate to one another. Oppression permeates every level of Islamic society; from the head of state to the street sweeper. Master-slave relationships characterize all social and political institutions from the military, the mosque, the political system, and corporations all the way down to the family unit.

It is not uncommon for Muslims to kiss the hands of religious and political leaders as proof of their submission and subservience. One incident in 2014 in Saudi Arabia sheds light on how the master-slave relationship dominates life in Islamic society. A Saudi woman by the name of Suad al-Shamari, co-founder of the Saudi Liberal Network, was held in a Jeddah prison on charges of insulting Islam. Her crime? Posting a photo on Twitter of a man kissing the hand of an Islamic cleric with this comment: "Notice the vanity and pride on his face when he finds a slave to kiss his hand."

People from such a background who come to live in America quickly notice the difference. People in the United States relate to each other as free citizens with human dignity. Most of us welcome the change, but there is often a side of the Islamic psyche that misses the power and unearned respect of the slave-master dynamic that Islam has created in all of us.

Transformation vs. Conformity

One of the most freeing verses in the Bible, one that helped me shed my bondage to Islam, is Romans 12:2: "And be not conformed to this world: but be ye transformed by the renewing of your mind, that ye may prove what is that good, and acceptable, and perfect, will of God."

That verse gave me permission to be transformed. The Bible tells Christians to be born again, to have purpose and meaning, to become like Christ. The very concepts of renewal, transformation, atonement, revival, and second chances are sadly alien to Islam.

Islam does not go much beyond Allah's demand for total conformity. Muslims demand a very high degree of conformity from each other, especially from family members.

While in the Bible Jesus says, "Behold, I make all things new" (Revelation 21:5), Islam resists any kind of novelty. Muhammad said, "For every newly begun matter is innovation, every innovation is misguidance, and every misguidance is in Hell" (*Reliance of the Traveller* w29.3 p. 914–915). Muslims today still reject change and shame and shun those who copy non-Muslim society. The Islamic ideal is to mimic and conform to the lifestyle of second-century Arabia, slavishly copying how Muhammad lived, dressed, and behaved.

The Islamic lifestyle is set in stone for the Muslim. Those who aspire to transform themselves and evolve beyond their roots, past the norms of their clan and birth conditions, are shamed and sometimes condemned as apostates. What Islam fears the most is for Muslims to be transformed so profoundly that they abandon the jihad against non-Muslims. Those who do are considered apostates under Islamic law and must be killed. An Urdu book on jihad quotes the eleventh-century jurist Al-Sarakhsi arguing that "One Who Rejects Jihad Is an Infidel."[4]

Hostility to nonconformity and change is common even among more moderate Muslim, like the ones in India. Remaining the same and protecting the status quo are Islamic values that go back to Arab pride and that have moved far beyond the Arab world into India and elsewhere. Transformation to follow one's conscience is prohibited to Muslims.

To the average Muslim the very word transform is foreign. *Why transform if the future is already pre-determined by Allah?* are the common words of wisdom spoken by Muslims. Muslims who look for new ways and solutions outside of the box of Islam are shunned, called names, and told *You forgot your roots and abandoned the culture that brought you up* or *Have you no respect for your origin?*

I have personally experienced this kind of Islamic shaming to enforce conformity. After 9/11 I called friends and family in Egypt because I wanted to be comforted after I saw many celebrating the carnage in the Middle East. I was hoping to hear some soul-searching from Egyptians, and a rejection of the hate education that we were all subjected to—which the 9/11 hijackers had acted on. But the response of one of my childhood friends to me was, "The flesh on your shoulders is from Arab generosity! How dare you accuse Arabs to be behind 9/11?" Even though I was already Christian then, the words still did hurt me. My friend's response to me was condemnation because I had dared to evolve, be transformed, and take the side of the enemies of Islam.

Even Islamic heads of State are not immune from harsh reactions, threats of removal from office, and even assassination—President Anwar Sadat of Egypt was killed for this very reason—if they veer from sharia and introduce novelty or innovation that is considered offensive to Islam. Islamic laws prohibit a Muslim head of State from being transformed, evolving, or accepting any novelty (*Reliance of the Traveller* o25.3 p. 640).

Islam is threatened by transformation. Conformity, uniformity, submission to group thinking, remaining the same, and protecting the status quo are what Islam expects of Muslims. These are all strong Islamic values.

Changing Yourself vs. Changing Others

The Bible teaches us to focus on changing ourselves instead of changing others: "how canst thou say to thy brother, Brother, let me pull out the mote that is in thine eye, when thou thyself beholdest not the beam that is in thine own eye? Thou hypocrite, cast out first the beam out of thine own eye, and then shalt thou see clearly to pull out the mote that is in thy brother's eye" (Luke 6:42).

Islam is all about changing, fixing, or at least impressing others rather than changing or fixing yourself. Holiness in Islam is measured by how committed a Muslim is to do jihad to bring others to Islam. When the word jihad is mentioned in the Koran, 97 percent of the time it refers to interacting with others in such a way as to force them to become Muslim. Because Muslims believe that non-Muslims are the sinners, it is the job of the Muslim to fix them. That is the main reason why Islam is in constant trouble with outsiders: the fact that the predominant message of Muslim scriptures is to use violence, force, intimidation, shaming, and humiliation to change others.

Changing others is the imperative of Islam, and it must be accomplished at virtually any cost, using the most violent means. The God of the Bible never tells us to do vengeance against His "enemies" on His behalf. On the contrary, the Bible admonishes Christians, "Dearly beloved, avenge not yourselves, but rather give place unto wrath: for it is written, Vengeance is mine; I will repay, saith the Lord" (Romans 12:19). But the Koran is full of commandments to Muslims to do just that. Allah entrusts Muslims with doing his bidding on Earth, commanding them to engage in retaliation, vengeance, fighting, and forced conversion for his sake—not to mention lying, slander, deceit, and exaggeration. All of that is for the purpose of changing others, so that they submit to Allah and conform to his commandments. That's the point of Muhammad's being "victorious through terror." It's the purpose for which the Koran tells Muslims to torture the enemies of Allah and smite off their heads. It's the reason Muslims demand that Christians and Jews convert, die, or pay the jizya. It's why Allah commanded Muslims to kill, torture, flog, behead, stone, and amputate the limbs of other Muslims who leave Islam, criticize Muhammad, or disobey sharia law.

As Muslims devote themselves to carrying out Allah's commands to change others, they remain oblivious to the need to change themselves. Even the most heinous crimes they commit are never their fault, but something they blame on their victims. *Look what you made me do!* is a frequently heard expression in Islamic society It is very common for Muslims to blame women for being raped. They say things like *She was not properly dressed, She wore perfume, She was not wearing Islamic clothes,* or *She allowed herself to be alone with me.*

Muhammad himself set the example of blaming others instead of taking responsibility. For example, when Jews refused to convert to Islam Muhammad beheaded six to nine hundred males of one Jewish tribe. Muhammad and the Koran justify the beheading, blaming it on the wicked Jews. The mere existence of non-Muslims (the kafirs) is offensive to Muslims. No wonder Muslims are constantly complaining about being offended by other religions, cultures, and people whose beliefs are different from theirs. Like Christianity, Islam is a religion that focuses on sins—but in the case of Muslims, it's the sins of others.

Fearing God vs. Fearing Man

While Christians and Jews try to please God, Muslims are focused on pleasing other human beings. The Bible tells us, "The fear of man bringeth a snare: but whoso putteth his trust in the Lord shall be safe" (Proverbs 29:25). Relations between citizens in the West are less formal and more at ease precisely because the God of the Bible tells us that He is in control; He does not abdicate His power to humans. He warns us against fear of man and depending on other people for approval and self-worth. Being in constant need of people's validation is not just a sign of insecurity. It is an indication that a person lacks fear of God.

When we are in Christ we are free from people-pleasing, fear of man, rejection, and tyranny. Biblical culture is accepting of those who express their weaknesses, sins, and vulnerability. A society shaped by the Christian Bible does not shame people, or subject them to social ostracism and humiliation.

But because the Islamic God delegated vengeance and punishment of sin to Muslims against others, both Muslims and non-Muslims, Islamic culture cannot help but be a man-fearing and people-pleasing culture. Muslims are forced to become people-pleasers to avoid other Muslims' wrath, shaming, and cruelty.

Arab culture is more concerned about public honor and appearances than the interior relationship with God. Being offended by the opinion of others can drive Muslims to horrific acts of violence, in which they feel completely justified.

Islamic culture has great respect for power, more than for integrity. Thus even bloodthirsty dictators like Saddam Hussein remain a hero to many Muslims no matter how many they murder and torture. Muslim culture pays the greatest honor to those who have power over other people. Because Muslim culture loves power, it ends up discouraging and punishing those who express their vulnerability or show any of their weaknesses. Those who do are often publicly shamed and humiliated.

This all goes back to how Muhammad arranged the social and legal structure of Islamic society so that Muslims are judge, jury, and executioner of one another.

"Khaf min rabbina" or "Fear God" is a common expression in Muslim society. Muslims express great pride in their devotion to Allah and Muhammad to the extent that whenever the name of Muhammad is mentioned it has to be followed with "Sallalahu 'alayhi wa sallam" or "May peace be upon him." Muslims always correct one another if they forget to say that. Muslim respect, devotion, and fear of Allah is exhibited daily in elaborate rituals, symbols, clothing, traditions, and the unified public Islamic prayers often held on street corners.

But behind this image of devotion to Allah one cannot but wonder whom Muslims are really trying to impress: Is it Allah, or is it one another? The truth as I personally felt it after living thirty years as a Muslim in a Muslim society is that Muslims are more terrified of one another than they are concerned about pleasing Allah. The life of a Muslim behind closed doors is totally different from his public life precisely because there is more fear of man than Allah.

During the month of Ramadan, government religious virtue police in countries like Pakistan and Saudi Arabia bring those who break the fast by eating or drinking water to a barbaric public flogging.

In less radical Muslim countries it is not the government that enforces fasting as much as it is the family, co-workers, and even strangers on the street—who will shame or in some extreme cases assault those who don't fast. The extreme social pressure to fast during Ramadan is felt everywhere. The poor Christians in Egypt have learned the hard way to never eat or drink in public during Ramadan.

Even U.S. troops stationed in Muslim countries are lectured on not eating in public during the month of Ramadan.[5]

Muslims feel justified in taking offense when others do not comply with Islamic sensibilities. Even in the West, Muslim taxi drivers reject customers carrying alcohol or dogs. Muslims seeking food from food banks are offended by the cans of pork 'n beans on the shelves. Muslim cashiers refuse to touch pork and alcohol products at the cash register.

And the pressure they bring to bear on their fellow Muslims is relentless. You don't have to go to areas controlled by ISIS, Al Qaeda, or the Muslim Brotherhood to see and feel the pressure that Muslims exert on one another to comply with sharia law. The reason for the extreme fear of the judgment of others is precisely that sharia law assigns the Muslim public the authority to enforce its severe and degrading punishments on those who do not fully comply or cooperate. Islamic law allows vigilante street justice, severe violence for non-compliance with Islamic morality.

When Allah seems to have abdicated prerogatives and made the average Muslim judge, jury, and executioner on his behalf, Muslims were given permission to do his vengeance right here on Earth; fear of God in Muslim society was transferred to fear of fellow man.

Muslims have developed elaborate traditions of maintaining appearances before others, traditions of appeasement and respect, especially to those with any degree of authority. There are many images of Saddam Hussein showing that even his military leaders would kiss his hand in public. Such elaborate appeasement rituals have developed over the centuries to allow Muslims to cope with the wrath and judgment of the people around them and live in relative privacy and peace.

It is not only political leaders who are honored in these rituals of respect for man. I remember as a child seeing my grandfather and grandmother's hands being kissed by the peasants who rented their agricultural land. Every quarter, they came to pay their rent, and as they entered the house my grandparents would pull their hands back, not wanting them to be kissed, even though that was the expected greeting to the landowner.

Such a culture of fear and appeasement of fellow man reflects the power of people over one another in the Islamic world. Islam has produced a culture of slaves and masters. Muslims do not live at ease with one another, except when they are brought together as a minority in the West. Then the dynamics change, and they start relating to one another as allies against the Bible-based culture of the West. As the Arab proverb says, "My brother and I against our cousin, and my cousin and I against the stranger."

6

THE BIBLICAL VALUES
THAT CHANGED ME

To see in a nutshell the difference between Bible values and Islam, a Westerner can simply watch any mosque service—or, better yet, a Muslim government–sponsored mosque service in the Middle East. The opposite is also true; a Muslim who wants to understand that difference should attend a worship service in a church or synagogue.

I learned a lot about the fundamental differences between Biblical values and Islamic values when I first attended church and synagogue. One thing stood out for me, and it probably would grab the attention of most Muslims if they allowed themselves to attend: cursing was simply not part of church and synagogue services. This surprised me because it was so different from what I was used to. The normal ending of a mosque service consists of prayers cursing those whom Islam calls the enemies of Allah.

Praising vs. Cursing

During the church service I could not help but hear in the back of my mind the angry voices of Islamic imams yelling words of incitement and hatred to their captive audience: impressionable and vulnerable young men. Below are excerpts from mosque preaching by different imams, aired on several Arab government TV stations:

- "O Allah vanquish the unjust Christians and the criminal Jews, the unjust traitors; strike them with your wrath; make their lives hostage to misery; drape them with endless despair, unrelenting pain and unremitting ailment; fill their lives with sorrow and pain and end their lives in humiliation and oppression; inflict your tortures and punishments upon the unjust Christians and criminal Jews. This is our supplication, Allah; grant us our request!" (from a Friday prayer service at the Grand Mosque in Mecca, Islam's holiest city)[1]

- "May Allah cut your tongue out! May he freeze the blood in your veins! May he inflict you with cancer and allow you no reprieve.... Allah, strike them with all sorts of disease, afflictions and pain! Allah, strike them with cancer! Allah, let your prophet overpower them! Allah destroy them! Allah destroy them! Allah destroy them! Allah destroy the criminals who challenge the noble prophet! [At this point, the preacher switched to very serenely addressing his Muslim viewers.] And peace upon you, and Allah's mercy and blessings." (popular Egyptian Sheikh Muhammad al-Zoghbi)[2]

- "Today, we realize why the [Jews] build walls. They do not do this to stop missiles, but to prevent the slitting of their throats.... My brother in the West Bank:

Stab!...Today, we have declared a curfew (in Israel)....
Stay at home, or go outside to your death. if you get
out of your homes you'll be killed.... Now, we are
imposing a curfew with daggers.... Oh Prophet of
Allah, incite the believers to fight.... Allah has brought
the Jews, His enemies and the enemies of humanity....
Form stabbing squads.... Attack them in groups, cut
them into body parts" (from an October 9, 2015, Friday sermon at the Al-Abrar Mosque in Rafah, Gaza,
by Sheikh Muhammad Sallah, who brandished a knife
as he was preaching).[3]

Growing up with this kind of religious message, I was amazed
that there was no cursing at all in Christian worship services. Eventually I learned that the Bible itself forbids Christians to curse their
enemies: "Bless them which persecute you; bless, and curse not"
(Romans 12:14; see also I Peter 3:9).

There should be no doubt about the direct link between the
widespread incitement to terrorize, stab, and kill coming from Islamic
places of worship and the phenomenon of worldwide Islamic terrorism and the rash of knife attacks on Jews in Israel. Some Muslim
defenders of Islam like to blame the phenomenon on misguided and
ignorant Muslim preachers, even though preaching like this is heard
in the most prestigious mosques in the Muslim world. I beg to disagree. These preachers and the governments that pay their salaries
did not invent cursing and preaching terror; the source of their vitriol
is the Koran itself, and the example of Muhammad, who dedicated
his dawn-time prayers to cursing his personal enemies. What a contrast to Jesus' teaching: "But I say unto you, Love your enemies, bless
them that curse you, do good to them that hate you, and pray for
them which despitefully use you, and persecute you" (Matthew 5:44).

Islam enthusiastically supports the cursing of non-Muslims by Muslims. And of course the opposite is forbidden by sharia law, on pain of death: if a non-Muslim is caught cursing Muslims, Muhammad, or Islam, or exposing the weakness of Muslims he is punished under the laws of blasphemy. Christians and Jews of the Middle East have lived with these laws for centuries. While hearing imams curse them day and night, they must tolerate it and never return the curse, or they will incur the Islamic penalty of death for blasphemy.

The dehumanization of non-Muslims in the Islamic world has been covered up—not only by Muslims but also by the international community. This injustice needs to be exposed for what it really is: a crime against humanity. This fact often hits me like a ton of bricks when I am at church listening to a sermon. As a new Christian, I often held back my tears when I looked around me and realized I was surrounded by the people Islam calls "enemies of Allah." The contrast between mosque and church services was as different as night and day.

It was only after I became Christian that I became fully aware of the depravity I had lived under. My heart was broken for the millions still living under Islamic slavery, robbed of their God-given freedom to discover the liberating truth of the Bible. The process of recovery from Islam took a while, but I am happy to say that I am now a new person in Christ. I wish the same healing for the Muslim people, whom I love and pray for.

It was the churches of America that helped in my transformation by messages of praise, love, fellowship, and peace. It was a blessing to leave behind the cursing culture of the mosque and become part of a culture of praise and blessing in the churches of America. Finally I was able to feel reconciled with God, with myself, and with the rest of humanity.

Looking back on the tragedy of cursing prayers in Islam, I am saddened to say that the majority of Muslims have no idea that the cursing, incitement to do violence, and profanity coming out of the mouths of Muslim preachers are in any way wrong or inappropriate. In fact during mosque services most of the worshippers respond to the cursing prayers at the end with a loud "Amen," considering them justified, normal, and even holy.

Personal Prayer vs. Exhibitionist Prayers

Prayers are commanded in both the Bible and the Koran, but Biblical prayers and Islamic prayers are totally different in multiple ways—in their purpose, in how and where they are performed, and in whether they are a private matter or mandated by the state.

Biblical prayers are usually discreet. In Christianity prayer is regarded as a personal matter between believers and God. Christians also pray together in fellowship within their families, at meals, at social gatherings, and at church services. The Biblical purposes of prayers are many, among which are to worship and be conscious of the presence of God; to draw closer to God; to give thanks, to confess and repent our sins; to ask for forgiveness and blessings; to ask God to change us from inside, empower us, and bring good results in the world around us; and above all to surrender ourselves into His hands.

The Bible tells Christians, "in every thing by prayer and supplication with thanksgiving let your requests be made known unto God. And the peace of God, which passeth all understanding, shall keep your hearts and minds through Christ Jesus" (Philippians 4:6–7). It also says, "Draw nigh to God and He will draw nigh to you" (James 4:8). Christians describe prayers as the way that the life of God in us is nourished and say that prayer is not a matter of changing things externally, but one of working miracles in a person's inner nature.

Christians pray in private in obedience to Jesus, Who said, "And when thou prayest, thou shalt not be as the hypocrites are: for they love to pray standing in the synagogues and in the corners of the streets, that they may be seen of men. Verily I say unto you, They have their reward. But thou, when thou prayest, enter into thy closet, and when thou hast shut thy door, pray to thy Father which is in secret; and thy Father which seeth in secret shall reward thee openly" (Matthew 6:5–6).

The Bible does not tell Christians and Jews to coerce, pressure, or shame others to pray. In Islam, however, prayers are not a private matter but socially enforced and in some cases made mandatory by the government. Islamic prayers are also ritualistic and synchronized; the words whispered are mandated. Men stand in a line shoulder to shoulder on prayer rugs and are led by an imam who initiates the prayers with a loud "Allahu akbar!," meaning "Allah is greater."

Christians do use some memorized prayers, especially the Lord's Prayer, which Jesus taught His disciples. But Christians typically pray in their own words, instead of repeating from rote memorization. As Jesus said, "But when ye pray, use not vain repetitions, as the heathen do: for they think that they shall be heard for their much speaking. Be not ye therefore like unto them: for your Father knoweth what things ye have need of, before ye ask him" (Matthew 6:7–8).

In Islamic theocracies such as Saudi Arabia, prayer is an institutionalized activity overseen by a special religious police force called the virtue police. In less radical Muslim countries like Egypt, prayer is enforced socially and often by the family.

Even in the West, Muslims come under social pressure to pray. A young Muslim man from Morocco confided in me on a visit to the United States that he had converted to Christianity but was unable to practice his new faith because of family pressure. They insisted on taking him to the mosque every Friday, and he was afraid they would discover his secret conversion. Today that young man is a good friend, a practicing Christian, and a loyal American citizen.

In 2001, just a few weeks before 9/11, my children, who were all born in the U.S., visited Egypt with me for the first time. My twenty- and eighteen-year-olds woke me up at 6:00 a.m. at my mother's home, in a nicer area of Cairo called Maadi, asking me if there was an emergency because of the loudspeakers blasting from every direction around the neighborhood. I laughed and told them that it was just the call for prayers from several area mosques surrounding us. It has been a custom since the invention of loudspeakers for mosques to use them for the call for prayers five times a day. My nephew once jokingly said that mosque sheikhs love to wake us "kafirs" all up to force us out of bed at 6:00 a.m.

The Islamic requirement to pray under societal pressure and the threat of punishment comes straight from Muhammad, who established many of the traditions still followed by Muslims today. For instance, the Prophet made it compulsory for all of his companions to gather at his mosque for prayers five times a day. Muhammad wanted to keep a close eye on them so none would abandon Islam or join forces with the people of Mecca against Muhammad.

A hadith describes how Muhammad went as far as punishing those who missed prayers with him by burning them inside their homes "The Prophet said, 'Burn all those who had not left their houses for the prayer, burning them alive inside their homes'" (Bukhari 1.11.626). Another hadith quotes the Prophet explaining this pattern of behavior: "I would order someone to collect firewood and another to lead prayer. Then I would burn the houses of men who did not present themselves at the compulsory prayer and prostration" (Bukhari 1.11.617).

The tradition of forced prayers established by Muhammad is still carried on today. In 2016 the Islamic State beheaded a fourteen-year-old boy in front of his parents for missing prayers.[4]

Islamic prayers are often performed in public streets and squares (reminiscent of Jesus' words about how "they love to pray standing... in the corners of the streets, that they may be seen of men," rather than indoors or in a private setting. Muslims often feel it is their right to stop traffic and close businesses to perform their mandatory religious duty and to remind everyone else of it.

Such prayers, causing traffic jams, blocking sidewalks, and accompanied with loudspeakers, have a strong element of exhibitionism. Islam is all about making an impression on others to express Islamic unity, power, obedience, submission, and solidarity. Some radicals even use street prayers as a way to intimidate non-Muslims and to convey an "us against them" show of force.

Christians in Egypt, who are not allowed to show any of their religious rituals and celebrations in public, usually avoid walking near mosques during the Friday prayers. This is because of fear of being targeted after an inciting sermon against the kafir Christians and Jews. Christians and Jews often hear Muslim preachers curse them on loudspeakers and TV sermons, and they must never object.

Mosques in the U.S. that I have personally attended encouraged prayers anywhere in public—on streets; in airports; inside airplanes, office buildings, and museums; and even at sporting events. Group Muslim public prayers do not happen by coincidence; they are planned. I personally heard Muslims planning to meet in a certain location to pray in public. The point is to impress on the American public how holy and devoted Islam is—and also to intimidate non-Muslims.

Islamic leadership in the West tell Muslims to demand Islamic prayer accommodations, such as special prayer rooms for Muslims and foot-level faucets (for the foot-washing that Islam requires before daily prayers) at their work places and on college campuses. Recently Muslims demanded a special prayer room at a Catholic university because crosses are offensive to Muslims.[5]

When I heard such demands by Muslims in the West, I knew immediately it was the same old game of intimidation and "I am offended" that was used against Christians and Jews in the Middle East. In the mind of Muslims, only they have the right not to be offended; everyone else must abide by their rules. Pushing the envelope and testing the patience of non-Muslims is a way of life in the Muslim world, something that the West does not yet understand.

When I worked at the Middle East News Agency, in Cairo, there were no prayer rooms for employees and no foot-level faucets either. The Cairo airport never had any prayer rooms or special faucets at the time. Muslims simply want to push the envelope with intimidation to see how far the West will go out of its way to accommodate demands that are extreme even by a moderate Muslim country.

Some Muslims want to demand a holy life style, like that at Mecca, be provided to them at taxpayer expense in the West. I often don't know whether to laugh or cry when I see Islamic exhibitionist intimidation playing out in public. I once saw several Muslim mothers in the Burbank, California, airport blocking a corridor to pray while their kids ran wild. It was not easy for me to get around them with my luggage while their children were bumping into me. I knew exactly what their purpose was, and it was not communion with God. It was a show of power and intimidation to tell America, *We are here, we are Muslims.*

In 2014, a Muslim family filed a $5 million lawsuit against the owners of the Empire State Building, claiming they had been booted out of the building's observation deck because they were praying together there.[6]

On a recent flight to the Philippines a Muslim man stood by the door of the airplane and shouted "Allahu akbar!," calling out that it was time for prayers and causing a scare among passengers.

There is a popular video on YouTube of an attractive Muslim woman with lots of makeup praying on different street corners in New York City. She engaged in these very public prayers and had them videotaped by her friends to make some kind of statement—to impress passersby, to look holier than thou, or to claim she is a victim and accuse ignorant Americans of being Islamophobes.[7]

I wonder what would happen to a Jew or Christian if he did the same thing, pray on public street corners in Islamic countries? I would like to suggest to this Muslim woman trying to teach Americans a lesson on respecting freedom of faith not to throw rocks when you live in a glass house.

A message of one-sided rights for Muslims only is promoted by Islamic leadership in America, who cannot help but follow the model of the tyrannical Islamic sharia of the Middle East. Such leaders call themselves moderate, but they have never publicly protested the mistreatment and mass murder of Christians in the Middle East, the practice of not allowing Christians to pray or hold a Bible in public, and the burning of churches that are not allowed to be rebuilt.

Prayers for All vs. Prayers Only for Muslims

While Christians and Jews pray for everyone, Muslims are prohibited from praying for non-Muslims. In the Koran Allah clearly tells Muhammad not to pray for dead disbelievers nor attend their funerals: "never offer prayer for any one of them who dies and do not stand by his grave; surely they disbelieve in Allah and His Messenger and they shall die in transgression" (9:84). "It is not for the Prophet, and those who believe, to pray for the forgiveness of idolaters even though they may be near of kin after it hath become clear that they are people of hell-fire" (9:113).

The Koran also says that it is pointless to pray for forgiveness for non-Muslims. Such prayers will not be accepted by Allah: "Ask forgiveness for them, (O Muhammad), or do not ask forgiveness for them. If you should ask forgiveness for them seventy times never will Allah forgive them. That is because they disbelieved in Allah and His Messenger, and Allah does not guide the defiantly disobedient people" (9:80). Allah's unforgiving attitude makes him very different from the God of the Bible, Who, as we have seen, does not want the wicked to die, but to "return from his ways, and live" (Ezekiel 18:23). The Koranic principle that asking forgiveness for non-Muslims even "seventy times" is useless is an ironic contrast with Jesus' command to forgive sinners "seventy times seven" (Matthew 18:21).

After a recent Islamic terrorist attack in Brussels, a Belgian Muslim Iman said that to pray for the non-Muslim victims of terror at the hands of Muslim terrorist is against Islamic law.[8]

One of the most touching experiences I felt after I moved to America was when my American neighbor told me that she was going to pray for me. The words, "I will pray for you," were amazing to hear and unheard of in Muslim society even among Muslims.

In that sense Islamic prayers fundamentally differ from Christian or Jewish prayers in every way.

Vengeance Is the Lord's vs. Vengeance Is Prescribed For Muslims

The overwhelming message of the Bible is love, peace, forgiveness, wisdom, and that vengeance is to be left to God. What I personally feel after reading the Bible is freedom from the urge to be vengeful of someone who hurt me. Proverbs 20:22 says, "Say not thou, I will recompense evil; *but* wait on the Lord, and he shall save thee." Romans 12:19 reads, "Dearly beloved, avenge not yourselves, but rather give place unto wrath: for it is written, Vengeance is mine; I will repay, saith the Lord."

Even though the Old Testament does have the law of retaliation—
"An eye for an eye" (Exodus 21: 24, Leviticus 24:20, and Deuteronomy 19:21, as quoted in Matthew 5:38), the majority of rabbis do not
interpret the law literally. The Old Testament also includes many
messages of forgiveness, telling the people of Israel to leave vengeance
to God: "To me belongeth vengeance" (Deuteronomy 32:35). "Thou
shalt not avenge, nor bear any grudge against the children of thy
people, but thou shalt love thy neighbor as thyself: I am the LORD"
(Leviticus 19:18).

The Koran adopted the law of retaliation ("qasas" in Arabic),
taking it literally: "O you who have believed, retaliation (*qasas*) is
prescribed for you for those murdered—the free for the free, the slave
for the slave, and the female for the female.... He who transgresseth
after this will have a painful doom" (2:178). The last sentence in this
verse tells Muslims that if you don't follow the law of qasas, or retaliation, a painful doom will be awaiting you. And so they do follow
it. Just sixteen years ago an Egyptian man had an eye surgically
removed in a Saudi hospital as punishment for an acid attack he had
carried out against another Egyptian.[9]

The God of the Bible never commands Christians or Jews to do
vengeance on His behalf or for His own sake. As we have already seen
in the last chapter, Allah does.

Arab scholar Dr. Sania Hamady, one of the greatest authorities
on Arab psychology, has said, "There are three fundamentals of Arab
society... shame, honor and revenge."[10]

The reason vengeance is a fundamental feature of Arab society is
that Allah himself promoted values of vengeance and not values of
forgiveness in the Koran: "Lo! Those who disbelieve and deal in
wrong, Allah will never forgive them, neither will he guide them unto
a road" (4:168). "Indeed, the vengeance of your Lord is severe"
(85:12). "Surely (the ones) who have disbelieved in the signs of Allah

will have a strict torment, and Allah is Ever-Mighty, Owner of vengeance" (3:4).

Vengeance is rooted and enshrined as a value in the Koran. Muhammad obliged Muslims to perform cruel, disproportionate, and irreversible punishments against others; punishments that amount to extreme vengeance, cruelty, and anger. It has always been the law in Islam, from in the seventh century up until today, to literally cut the hands off thieves, stone adulterers, behead apostates, and blasphemers and throw gays off of buildings. Muslims who were repulsed by carrying out such punishments were told by Muhammad that vengeance was good and healthy for them: "And there is life for you in retaliation, O men of understanding, that ye may ward off (evil)" (Koran 2:179).

In the Koran Allah says, "And who is more unjust than he who is reminded of the signs of his Lord, thereafter veers away from them? Surely We will be the Avengers against [Literally: avenge (Ourselves)] the criminals" (32:22). The Arabic word for revenge in this verse is "muntaquimun," which literally means vengeance. But some Muslim translators try to soften the message of the Koran by falsely translating muntaquimun as retribution or requite: "And who doth greater wrong than he who is reminded of the revelations of his Lord, then turneth from them. Lo! We shall requite the guilty." The people who are called "guilty" and "criminals" in the Koran are simply people who were offered the Koran but turned it down; in other words the Koran here is encouraging vengeance against non-Muslims whose only act of criminality is to dare reject Islam.

Promoters and defenders of Islam in the West are constantly warning against the danger that Americans may judge or retaliate against all Muslims because of the actions of a few Muslim terrorists. And yet Muslims are taught by their own religion to take vengeance against non-Muslims for the crime of rejecting Muhammad's Koran.

They seem to be unaware of the contradictions in their position: they demand forgiveness from the world for terrorism, which they claim is perpetrated by just a few bad apples, while at the same time they must obey Allah's commandment to do vengeance and jihad against those who reject the Koran.

Muhammad's dedication of his entire religion to vengeance against those who rejected it has caused the world a lot of bloodshed. Islam is literally all about vengeance.

There is a fundamental difference in worldview between Christianity and Islam. Christianity accepts the fact that we live in an imperfect world where perfect justice is unattainable and consequently the wicked can often prosper in our world. The God of the New Testament is patient, letting good and evil men "both grow together" until "the end of this world" (Matthew 13:30, 40). Jesus says that His Father "maketh his sun to rise on the evil and on the good, and sendeth rain on the just and on the unjust" alike (Matthew 5:45). Islam, on the other hand, is obsessed with molding this world into perfection by forcing human beings into perfect submission. Muslims believe that perfect peace can and will come on Earth when Islam wins over all nations and takes control of world government under the Islamic Ummah. Consequently, in pursuit of a worldwide Islamic State, Muslims allow themselves to use any means for the destruction of everything un-Islamic.

Six hundred years after Christ taught humanity forgiveness, love, and salvation, Muhammad turned back the clock to bloody vengeance.

Forgiveness and Mercy vs. Reveling in Unforgiveness

Muslims call Allah "the merciful," but for the most part the Koran is about unforgiveness and reveling in torturing and humiliation. One must read a credible translation of the Koran to understand the extent of Allah's anger and vindictiveness.

Allah seems to revel in torturing those who turn their backs on Islam, "yoked together in chains, wearing shirts of tar, their faces enveloped in the Fire." (49–50). They will "stare in terror" (21:97). and be "made to drink pus"—"he gulps at it but can hardly swallow it down. Death comes at him from every side but he does not die. And beyond him is relentless punishment" (14:17). "[T]he sinner's desire will be: Would that he could redeem himself from the Penalty of that Day by (sacrificing) his children, and his wife and his brother, and his kindred who sheltered him, and all that are in the earth, so that it might save him. By no means! Verily, it will be the Fire of Hell! Taking away (burning completely) the head skin! It invites he who turned his back [on truth] and went away [from obedience]" (Koran 70:11–17).

While Jesus also warns about hellfire in the New Testament, His descriptions are not anything like as graphic as Muhammad's. The Prophet and his God seem to take an unhealthy delight in the punishments they are promising.

Allah is also comfortable with extreme humiliation and public disgrace in this life. He describes the shame of those he wants to punish: "And those who earn ill-deeds, (for them) requital of each ill-deed by the like thereof; and ignominy overtaketh them—they have no protector from Allah—as if their faces had been covered with a cloak of darkest night...." (Koran 10:27).

The Koran mentions Allah's humiliation and painful torment of his enemies *420 times*.[11] But the joy of vindictiveness does not end there. Allah appears to be giving a lesson on torture: "Like boiling oil, it will boil in the bellies, Like the boiling of scalding water. Seize him and drag him into the midst of Blazing Fire. Then pour over his head the torment of boiling water" (Koran 44:45–48).

Biblical Angels vs. Islam's Warring and Vindictive Angels and Jinn

In the Bible, angels are spiritual beings created by God to serve Him. Some angels remained obedient to God, while others disobeyed Him and fell from Heaven. These bad, fallen angels are called demons or devils, and they stand in active opposition to the work and plan of God. Christians are warned to be on guard against the deception of the bad angels (demons), especially of Satan, the chief fallen angel: "Put on the whole armour of God, that ye may be able to stand against the wiles of the devil" (Ephesians 6:11).

The Bible teaches that angels guard those who make the Lord their refuges (Psalms 91:11). They protect us from physical harm and give strength to overcome difficulties. Angels also proclaim God's Truth and do battle with Satan and his demons.

The good angels in Islam, however, are totally different from the good angels in the Bible. Muhammad claimed to have communicated with angels, including Gabriel, who he said had relayed the Koran to him. Muhammad told his reluctant fighters that angels under the leadership of Gabriel accompanied Muhammad to battle and helped him persuade people to convert to Islam.

Muhammad told stories of how Gabriel mounted a horse called Haizum, and fought alongside Muhammad in his battle dreams. The angel Gabriel even amassed an army force of three thousand angels to fight with Muhammad against his enemies in the battle of Badr.

Muhammad's angels also help Allah at the doors of Hell. The Koran describes angels standing at the door of Hell: "when the angels take the souls of the Unbelievers (at death), (how) they smite their faces and their backs, (saying): 'Taste the penalty of the blazing Fire'" (8:50).

Jinn are supposed to be supernatural creatures that Arabs in the culture that preexisted Islam believed in. They were retained by Islam; in fact, an entire chapter of the Koran, called "Al-Jinn," is dedicated to them (chapter 72). When I was a Muslim I never personally believed in jinn, but I heard many stories of how people had to protect themselves from jinn and of people who used jinn to empower themselves against others. Belief in jinn has caused social and cultural trauma in the Muslim world, victimized many people, and caused mental problems for some Muslims. This superstitious side of Islam is often denied by Muslims. But it should be hard to deny because it is in the Koran.

American TV shows on Arabian "jeanies" are not total fabrications after all.

Upholding Human Rights vs. Sacrificing Human Rights

Many people in the West paint all religions with the same brush. Some assume that Islam is as peace-loving and respectful of human rights as Christianity, while others see all religions as anti–human rights. But the truth is that Biblical values and the Ten Commandments have been proven to be in harmony with human or natural rights—in fact they are the ultimate source of those rights, expressed in the U.S. Constitution and Bill of Rights, for example—and that the same cannot be said of Islam and its laws.

The list of Islam's violations of the basic human rights and freedoms of both Muslims and non-Muslims is very long. Here is a brief list of some Islamic laws and doctrines that violate human rights:

1. No freedom of religion.
2. No freedom of speech.
3. All men are not created equal.
4. Lying and slander are an obligation.
5. Cruel and unusual punishments are in store for those who disobey Islamic law.
6. Killers of apostates, adulterers, and parents who kill their offspring are protected from prosecution.

7. The right of non-Muslim countries to protect themselves against Islamic jihad is denied under the laws of sharia.

8. A Muslim head of State can come to power through force, without the consent of the people.

9. The Muslim public has the right to remove a Muslim head of State from office at any time if he is no longer a Muslim or refuses to rule by sharia.

10. The age limit for marriage for girls is nine.

11. A husband has the right to beat his wife.

12. A husband can divorce his wife, but she cannot divorce him.

13. The Testimony of a woman in court is half the value of a man's.

14. To prove rape a woman must have four male witnesses.

15. Slavery is legal under Islamic law and is still unofficially practiced in many Islamic countries—and officially in the Islamic State.

16. Islam guarantees Paradise only to those who kill and are killed in jihad against the enemies of Allah (non-Muslims).

Islamic law also allows jihadists, those who are fighting for the expansion of Islam, to rape, enslave, and take possession of the property of non-Muslims. There are "fatwas" (Islamic rulings based on sharia) that allow girls to give themselves to the mujahideen in Syria. Even homosexuality, which is prohibited in Islam, is allowed for suicide bombers. In 2010 a fatwa was issued in an Arabic news video permitting sodomy to a suicide bomber to "widen" his anus in order to accommodate the explosives. That video, which I have personally watched, has recently been removed from the internet after Islamic leaders felt the public backlash.[12]

Islam is simply not compatible with human rights, life, liberty, and the pursuit of happiness. It demands that human rights and basic decency be sacrificed to empower Islam's totalitarian ambitions over people, territory, and governments.

That might explain why almost all Muslim countries are in constant political instability, coups d'état, and revolutions, with Islamists wanting to take control of government by force. Unless those who are loyal to Islam have total control over the government, they cannot impose sharia, and thus they feel impotent. As Alexis de Tocqueville said, "A man's admiration for absolute government is proportionate to the contempt he feels for those around him." Islam demands and even romanticizes absolute government of the entire human race under sharia law. And its proponents have absolute contempt for their fellow man, and for his rights.

Islam has contempt for human rights because they conflict with Islamic goals of totalitarian control. That is just another major example of the differences between the Bible and Islam. The Bible is a bulwark protecting us from the tyranny of man on man and government on citizen, but Islam came to reinstate the enslavement of man to man and individuals to their rulers.

Work Ethic vs. Wealth through Conquest

The Bible is filled with verses on the ethics of hard work and relying on one's own labor: "For thou shalt eat the labour of thine hands; happy shalt thou be, and it shall be well with thee" (Psalms 128:2). "Commit thy works unto the LORD, and thy thoughts shall be established" (Proverbs 16:3). "He becometh poor that dealeth with a slack hand: but the hand of the diligent maketh rich" (Proverbs 10:4).

The Bible commends those who work hard: "He becometh poor that dealeth with a slack hand: but the hand of the diligent maketh rich" (Proverbs 10:4). "The hand of the diligent shall bear rule: but the slothful shall be under tribute" (Proverbs 12:24). All hard work brings a profit, but mere talk leads only to poverty. Both Old and New Testaments make it clear that hard work should benefit the worker: "The husbandman that laboureth must be first partaker of the fruits" (Proverbs 14:23). "For even when we were with you, this we commanded you, that if any would not work, neither should he eat" (II Thessalonians 3:10). "The husbandman that laboureth must be first partaker of the fruits" (II Timothy 2:6).

The work ethic found in the Bible has blessed the West for centuries with a prosperous civilization. Today, despite the petro dollars, many majority-Muslim countries are among the poorest nations in the world. Besides being poor, the Muslim world also contains the most war-torn, unstable, and chaotic places to live. Muslim refugees are pouring into the Biblical West without realizing that their own religion has not promoted the political, social, economic, and spiritual environment for prosperity and stability.

Even though the Koran, like the Bible, warns Muslims not to get attached to material wealth, Islamic values about acquiring wealth are totally different from those of the Bible. The Prophet of Islam, Muhammad, bragged that he acquired wealth through terror: "I have been made victorious with terror (cast in the hearts of the enemy), and while I was asleep, the keys of the treasures of the world were brought to me and put in my hand...." (Bukhari 4:52:220).

Islamic values on this, as on every other subject, are rooted in the example and life of Muhammad. And Muhammad accumulated his wealth through offensive wars and battles against tribes that refused to convert to Islam.

Muhammad rewarded Muslim fighters who died with Paradise and those who survived with wealth: "Allah guarantees that He will admit the 'mujahid' in His cause into Paradise if he is killed, otherwise

He will return him to his home safety with rewards and war booty" (Bukhari 4:52:46).

The last ten years in Muhammad's life were nothing but a series of battles and attacks on others to expand his power and acquire wealth—goods, land, homes, and slaves—from his enemies. Under Islamic law these are the lawful spoils of war.

The example of Muhammad and his Muslim fighters is in stark contrast to that of the Mecca merchants and to the Jews who lived in Medina, the same town as Muhammad.

Three major Jewish tribes resided in Medina before the arrival of Muhammad. It was not hard for the outside world to notice how different Muhammad and Jewish tribes were when it came to earning their living. The Jews became prosperous through hard work: tool-making, agriculture, and trade. Before Muhammad, Medina attracted some poorer Arab tribes who were able to benefit from the prosperous Jewish economy. It was these poor Arab tribes who invited Muhammad to move in after they converted to Islam.

Muhammad utilized the poor Arabs of Medina to build wealth through war instead of following the example of the Jews that those Arabs originally worked for. Muhammad destroyed, burnt, enslaved, and beheaded his way to wealth, all taken from his victims, whom he called "kafirs." The "spoils of war" were a big motivation for his fighters, and a whole chapter in the Koran is dedicated to their legitimacy. Muhammad made sure to announce a law saying that he and Allah were to take one fifth of the booty (8:41), and he warned his fighters against stealing any of it (*Reliance* w52.1).

The contrast between the style of life of Muhammad and his fighters and the Jewish tribes probably alarmed the Jews—with good reason. Muhammad, who called himself an Abrahamic prophet, envied the Jews' power, wealth, property, and women. Muhammad's solution was to expel two of the Jewish tribes, seize their property, and give four-fifths of it to his fighters as a reward. The six to nine hundred men of the third Jewish tribe were all beheaded. After the slaughter, Muhammad had his first pick of the women, who were divided amongst the Muslims as sexual slaves. The Jewish children, women, land, homes, cattle, and goods were Allah's gift to Muhammad and his fighters.

It may be that the mere existence of Jews and their hard-working way of life made Muhammad look and feel illegitimate. In any case, he wanted their possessions. The Jews had to be gotten rid of. And not just the Jews of Medina. Muhammad entrusted Muslims till the end of time with the mission of killing Jews wherever they find them. After Muhammad died, his followers continued to hunt down and kill Jews until finally, one hundred years later, they built a mosque right on top of the ruins of Solomon's Temple, thinking they had erased Jewish history from existence.

Conquest became the most honorable model for acquiring wealth in Islam. When Iraq invaded Kuwait in 1990, all the wealth in Kuwait that could be removed was taken by the Iraqi soldiers. That was sharia-approved behavior.

This has always been the model for Muslims to build wealth. Islam became an ever-expanding machine of conquest that could not stop—or else it would run out of money—sucking up the wealth of many great civilizations including Persia, Syria, Turkey, Iraq, Coptic Christian Egypt, and the Biblical lands in and around Jerusalem. And it explains why manual labor and those who work in both farming and trade are looked down upon in Muslim culture and often despised and treated as slaves.

Today, as Muslims are escaping their vast, poverty-stricken Islamic territories in fifty-four Islamic nations for the greener lands of Europe and America, Westerners seem to think they are rescuing refugees. But this is just the latest version of a story that has been repeating itself for fourteen hundred years.

Muslim clerics today are still advocating jihad for the acquisition of wealth. Prominent Egyptian sheikh Abu-Ishaq al-Huwayni gave a recorded lecture on how Muslims' financial difficulties are due to the fact that they have abandoned jihad. The solution, he told the Muslims attending his lecture, is to go back to jihadist raids a few times a year. The purpose of the jihad Huwayni was recommending would be to bring back wealth and slaves—prisoners of war including women and children—who could be sold in the market to bring in extra income when times are tough for Muslims. His lecture explained the economic benefits of the sharia code: after Muslims do an offensive invasion of a non-Muslim nation, the properties and persons of infidels are to be seized as "ghanima" or "spoils of war."[13]

But at least one Muslim leader has noticed that the lack of a work ethic is hurting the Islamic world and tried to come up with an argument for recommending one from Islamic sources. "[W]e (the Muslim World) don't work and if we work, we don't do it professionally. We do not produce... and we import everything from the needle to missiles," said Sheikh Yusuf al-Qaradawi. He admitted that he could not find one Koran verse or hadith about a proper work ethic. But he did say that "Muhammad ordered us to excel in everything 'if you kill, do it properly, and if you slaughter, do it properly...' How come the Zionist gang has managed to be superior to us? They have become superior through knowledge and technology and work ethics."[14]

The lack of a work ethic in the Islamic world helps explain why Muslims' eyes are always focused on the outside, non-Muslim world, the greener pastures, for more and more to conquer and expand into. Capturing wealth from others rather than creating wealth is an Islamic value, established as an honorable and holy legal right of

Muslims. As Muhammad said, "Booty has been made legal for me" (Bukhari 53:351).

The Islamic model of acquiring wealth that was promoted by Muhammad is unsustainable. It only keeps digging Muslim nations into more war, terror, bloodshed, and poverty.

Muslim leaders today can no longer openly use piracy on Western ships or engage in government-against-government jihad because it is against international law. In addition, Muslim nations are weaker militarily compared to the West, at least at the present. Muslim ambassadors today can no longer afford to be as honest as their counterparts two hundred years ago. During the Barbary wars the Tripoly envoy, Sidi Haji Abdul Rahman Adja, told Thomas Jefferson and John Adams that Muslims' rights to piracy against American ships was "written in their Koran."

Muslim governments today have no choice but to delegate the job of holy jihad to paramilitary groups, called jihadis in the Muslim world, but terrorists in the West. Many such groups are created, coddled, and financed by Muslim governments and ironically many threaten the Muslim governments that created them. Under Islamic law jihad should be the job of every Muslim head of State, but today the power of the West and of international institutions founded by the West has forced many Muslim governments into a love-hate relationship with jihad and jihadist groups.

Unlike the Tripoli ambassador, Muslim leaders today insist that neither they nor Islam have anything to do with terrorism, and many Western leaders repeat this lesson.

Islamic governments and groups who are really engaged in jihad, as they are required to do under Islamic sharia law, must convince the world that they have a different cause, one that is just and noble. Daily Islamic attacks, terror, and aggression must be explained as in aid of liberation from occupation and imperialism, righting past injustices, or addressing land and border disputes. Muslims must appear to the world to be the victims in order to justify jihad. Many people around the world have fallen for claims that Muslims are victims rather than aggressors. Today Europe and America are rescuing Muslim refugees rather than rescuing the people being targeted by the jihad: Coptic Christians, Yazidis, or Kurds.

Islam's long history of wealth creation through terror and conquering continues today, but the West today is still in denial and refuses to learn from history.

More than Conquerors vs. to Conquer Is to Prevail

Conquering has a totally different meaning in the Bible from in the Koran. Romans 8:36–37 says, "As it is written, For thy sake we are killed all the day long; we are accounted as sheep for the slaughter. Nay, in all these things we are more than conquerors through him that loved us."

Those Bible verses appear to speak directly to me about my life of suffering under Islamic oppression and terror. With Christ's love I have become more than a conqueror, and that with Jesus, I have been saved from a horrific life of conquering—a very different kind from the conquering that the Bible promises Christians—for which my father lost his life.

Values of conquering are all over the Koran and unfortunately ingrained in the psyche of most Muslims as the highest honor.

I once saw an Egyptian tourist in a U.S. airport wearing a provocative tee shirt that Americans hardly noticed; they did not even understood its meaning. The shirt said "To conquer is to prevail." That pretty much sums up the purpose of Islam and its goals in America and around the world. Islamic values are often paraded before the eyes of the West, but few ever notice. After a few moments of internal outrage and sadness over the obvious challenge to the West by Muslims, my mind took me to Romans 8:37: "We are more than conquerors through Him who loved us."

Unlike the Bible, Islam measures its success as a religion by its ability to violently conquer. The aim of Islam is to control governments and people and suck the wealth of a nation dry. Islamic preaching is all about triumph—prevailing over all nations and religions. There are many video clips of Muslim preachers stating in no uncertain words that they want to turn the White House into the Muslim House and conquer Buckingham Palace, Rome, and so forth, to turn them into Muslim capitals. This is how Islam measures religious success.

Muhammad is quoted as saying: "Verily Allah has shown me the eastern and western part of the earth, and I saw the authority of my Ummah (nation) dominate ALL that I saw" (Muslim, 2889). As the prominent twentieth-century Islamic scholar Abul A'la Maududi said, "The purpose of the Holy Prophet's appointment as a Prophet was not merely to preach this Religion, but to make it prevail over all others."[15]

7

THE FRUITS OF THE SPIRIT VS. THE FRUITS OF ISLAM

The Holy Spirit has done miracles in my life and is still doing them. Under His guidance, I am evolving from a morally confused woman under Islamic enslavement into the kind of woman God intended me to be. Becoming a Christian totally changed the direction of where I was heading under Islam. The transformation that took place within me exceeded my expectations. Jesus has snatched me out of a slow and painful death.

The Bible tells us that when Christ ascended, He sent the Holy Spirit in His place to be present within us to guide us. Where the Spirit is, there is freedom, wisdom, insight, guidance, healing, transformation, and growth in Him. The Christian life bears "fruits of the Spirit," just as a healthy tree bears nutritious fruit.

Jesus says, "Ye shall know them by their fruits" (Matthew 7:16)—we can identify false prophets by their fruits. Fruit here is a metaphor referring to the external manifestation of a person's faith through his or her work, words, and behavior.

Islam does not recognize that human beings are made in the image of God, nor the existence of a Holy Spirit whose guidance brings blessings to our lives, allowing us to bear good fruit. Islam has a very different understanding of life—dividing the world into Muslims and non-Muslims, with Muslims having authority from Allah over non-Muslims. Under Islam, Muslims are Allah's vice regents on Earth, which means that they can act on Allah's behalf, especially in regards to enforcing Allah's laws and punishments on kafirs and other sinners.

The Bible says, "But the fruit of the Spirit is love, joy, peace, long-suffering, gentleness, goodness, faith, meekness, temperance...." (Galatians 5:22–23). Under Islam, these positive attributes are not valued.

Instead, the Koran is all about cruelty and harsh treatment of non-Muslims, who were the majority on this Earth back when Muhammad was alive and still are today. The Koran teaches that the kafir is worth less than a Muslim and unworthy of good treatment. Far from treating non-Muslims with love, gentleness, and the other fruits of the Spirit, Muslims are authorized to kill them.

We have already looked at the hadith in which the Prophet of Islam says, "Three things are the roots of faith: to refrain from (killing) a person who utters, 'There is no god but Allah' and not to declare him unbeliever whatever sin he commits, and not to excommunicate him from Islam for his any action" (abu-Dawud 2532 15:56). This basically says that to be a good Muslim you should stop killing non-Muslims you are about to kill if they declare Allah is their God, and that, whatever converts do after becoming Muslim, they are immune from sin and cannot be excommunicated for any action, good or evil. So killing and mistreating people outside of Islam is OK until they say "I believe in Allah."[1]

Islam is very serious about depriving non-Muslims of love, joy, peace, patience, kindness, goodness, faithfulness, and gentleness. And

Islam most certainly does not teach self-control to Muslims, but rather gives them not only permission but encouragement to take out their anger and resentment on the infidel kafirs.

Love

The Bible says that God loves us unconditionally and also commands us to love God with all our hearts, souls, and might. The miraculous identity of God with love is summed up in I John 4:8 "He that loveth not knoweth not God; for God is love."

The blessings of God's love, and our love for Him, bear fruits in the Christian life. Love is extended to all our relationships: "A new commandment I give unto you, That ye love one another; as I have loved you, that ye also love one another" (John 13:34).

While love is at the center of the Bible, the word "love" is hardly mentioned in the Koran, which never refers to Allah as loving to all of humanity. Allah's love for some humans is conditional. It is limited to Muslims, to those who do good, and to those who love Allah and the prophet Muhammad. But above all, Allah loves those who fight in His cause; "Truly Allah loves those who fight in his Cause in battle array, as if they were solid cemented structure" (Koran 61:4).

Allah never commanded Muslims to love all of humanity, nor even to love one another. One of Allah's ninety-nine names is "wadud," meaning "friendly," but the Koran never refers to Allah as "mahibba," meaning "loving."

I have translated an Arabic internet clip posted by Egyptian fans of the late president of Egypt, Anwar Sadat. The clip shows Sadat speaking before the Egyptian Parliament about what he had learned from reading a German book during his incarceration, when he was a young military officer back in the mid-1940s. This is what he said: "During the incarceration I studied the German language and what intrigued me the most in studying that language were the examples that expressed the most important moral value in the life of humans. I still remember what the German book said: 'To love and be loved is the greatest blessing in our existence.'"[2]

According to his fans, this is one of the "Greatest Quotes by Sadat." This quotation by Sadat made such an impression on them because the topic of love as a blessing to humanity is alien to the Islamic mind. The only kind of love discussed in Islamic culture is romantic love, or else love between a mother and child. The larger concepts of love for all of humanity, and of God's love for us and ours for Him, are simply lacking in Islamic culture.

Even romantic love between a man and a woman is not celebrated but rather discouraged and even prohibited in Islamic culture. Some Islamic countries, including Saudi Arabia, ban any celebration of Valentine's Day; it is illegal to sell red roses on February 14. The Koran talks about the sexual reward of virgins to men in Paradise, but it never speaks of the sacredness of loving relationships between men and women. Hadiths brag about Muhammad's sexual prowess as equal to that of forty men—"He [the Prophet] once said of himself that he had been given the power of forty men in sex" (Ibn Sa'd, Kitab Tabaqat Al-Kubra p. 139)—and claim that he used to have sex with all his eleven wives in one night—"'The Prophet used to visit all his wives in a round, during the day and night and they were eleven in number.' I asked Anas, 'Had the Prophet the strength for it?' Anas replied, 'We used to say that the Prophet was given the strength of thirty (men)'" (Bukhari 1:5:268).

God Loves Us Unconditionally vs. Allah Hates Non-Muslims

The Bible revolutionized my life when I read about the joy of loving people. Unlike the Koran, the Bible describes what love looks like: Love "suffereth long, and is kind… envieth not… vaunteth not itself, is not puffed up... Doth not behave itself unseemly, seeketh not [its] own, is not easily provoked, thinketh no evil; Rejoiceth not in iniquity, but rejoiceth in the truth; Beareth all things, believeth all things, hopeth all things, endureth all things" (I Corinthians 13:4–8).

Messages like that cannot be found in the Koran, in Muhammad's example, or in Islamic teaching. That is why Muslims are starving for messages of love.

On the other hand, the Koran has plenty of verses about those whom Allah does not love—especially the kafirs (see for example Koran 3:31–33 and 30:45).

When the word love is mentioned in the Koran, it is often conditional or even in a negative context. Neither Allah nor Muhammad tells Muslims to love people of other religions. The messages to Muslims to love one another are not unconditional, but are usually commanding loyalty to one another against the kafirs. Even the love of Muslims for their prophet Muhammad is conditional upon hating Jews. Prominent Muslim theologian Muhammad al-Maghili declared in his writings that "Love of the Prophet, requires hatred of the Jews."[3]

Love Your Enemies vs. Terrorize Your Enemies

Allah's excessive hatred of non-Muslims is the most prominent feature of the Koran. As we have seen, the majority of the Koran is devoted to the kafirs, rather than to the Muslims—according to Dr. Bill Warner, an authority on political Islam, 64 percent.[4] According to the Center for the Study of Islam, the amount of energy devoted to non-Muslims in the Koran and other Muslim texts is huge: "The majority (64%) of the Koran is devoted to the Kafir, and nearly all of the Sira (81%) deals with Mohammed's struggle with them. The Hadith (Traditions) devotes 37% of the text to Kafirs. Overall, the Trilogy, of the three, devotes 51% of its content to the Kafir."[5]

Not only does the Koran say that Allah does not love the kafirs; it commands Muslims not to befriend them, in fact to kill and terrorize them. The word kill appears in the Koran 102 times; terrorize 32 time; slaughter, 39 times; slay, 46 times; and humiliate, 58 times. Not all of the passages in which those words appear are direct commandments to terrorize and kill the kafir, but many are, such as "strike terror into the hearts of non-believers" (8:12).

The Muslim Brotherhood emblem is made up of two swords above the first word ("Make ready") of a verse from the Koran, which translates, "Against them make ready your strength to the utmost of your power, including steeds of war, to strike terror into (the hearts of) the enemies of Allah and your enemies, and others besides, whom ye may not know" (8:60).

The Koran is replete with verses threatening killing, cursing, torment, torture, and Hellfire to the enemies of Allah, the non-Muslims. A small sampling: "And kill them wherever you find them" (2:191, 4:89, and elsewhere). "Then take them and kill them wherever ye find them. Against such We have given you clear warrant" (4:91). "As to those who reject faith [Islam], I will punish them with terrible agony in this world and in the Hereafter, nor will they have anyone to help" (3:56). "I will cast terror into the hearts of those who disbelieve" (8:12). "Fight against them so that Allah will punish them by your hands and disgrace them" (9:14) "O Prophet! strive hard against the unbelievers and the hypocrites and be unyielding to them; and their abode is hell, and evil is the destination" (9:73).

I grew up hearing Islamic imams openly preaching offensive and not defensive war against the kafirs "even if they do not fight you." This very same kind of preaching is still going on today.[6]

Because Islam's main goal is to conquer and expand, the command to "Love your enemies" is perceived as a weakness that Muslims should take advantage of, not as an expression of restraint that should be appreciated. Any accommodation, yielding, concession, or compromise is considered a weakness to be exploited by Muslims. The very concepts of love and mercy are considered weaknesses. Iran's Ayatollah Khomeini said, "Show no mercy! Stamp out all those who oppose Islam."[7]

Joy vs. Anger, Shame, and Misery

One of the pleasant surprises I found in the Bible—a surprise because of my Islamic background—was God's wish for us to experience joy in Him and also in our lives. I had never remembered hearing that joy could be godly, growing up in Islam.

To confirm my memory, I checked the Koran, and it confirmed what I thought. There was no mention of "joy," or of "delight," or "rejoice." I also found nothing similar in meaning to Biblical expressions such as "my heart is glad" (Psalms 16:9), "cheerful giver" (II Corinthians 9:7), or "songs of deliverance" (Psalms 32:7).

The closest thing I found in the Koran was the description of the Paradise that is promised to those lucky Muslims who die fighting Allah's enemies on Earth as "Gardens of Pleasure." But pleasure is not joy. The Islamic Paradise promises not spiritual joy but sexual pleasures with virgins, young beautiful light-skinned boys who serve you, and fruits and rivers of wine (forbidden on Earth). There is no joy—only sensual pleasure—in the Islamic Heaven. And as far as life on this Earth is concerned, Muslims are not even supposed to enjoy it.

In fact Islam teaches Muslims to despise life on Earth and shames those who want to flee from jihad for the sake of Allah in order to live: "Let those fight in the way of Allah who sell the life of this world for the other" (Koran 4:74). "The comfort of the life of the world is but little in the Hereafter"(9:38). All the fun Allah promises to the good Muslim is after he dies.

The Koran encourages Muslims to embrace pain and suffering to achieve the worthy goal... of causing pain to others: "And be not weak hearted in pursuit of the enemy; if you suffer pain, then surely they (too) suffer pain as you suffer pain...." (4:104).

So it should come as no surprise that there is a shortage of joy in Muslim society. Instead of seeking joy and contentment, it is more common for Muslims to seek opportunities to get offended by others. One of the most noticeable features of the Arab street is one face after another expressing anger, discontent, envy, and the victim mentality.

A lack of joy, to put it mildly, is also very noticeable in Islamic preaching. Muslim imams—loud, cursing, condoning and inciting violence—seem always to be angry. The fact is, if they follow the values of their scriptures, Muslim clerics have no choice but to teach discontent, anger, finger-pointing, shame, and the demonization of others.

Under Islamic law, laughing is actually considered offensive and is regulated. (*Reliance of the Traveller* r32.7 and r19.2).

Iran's Ayatollah Khomeini said, "There are no jokes in Islam. There is no humor in Islam. There is no fun in Islam."[8]

Islamic societies often prohibit singing and dancing. As a six-year-old child I remember being beaten by my father because he saw me belly dance with my siblings at home. People in the entertainment industry, such as singers, dancers, actors, and artists, are often looked upon as unacceptable and even un-Islamic.

Entertainment that brings men and women who are not blood relatives together is also forbidden in traditional Islamic society.

A culture that is geared toward ridding the world of the enemies of Allah fears embracing joy. It is more comfortable with anger and resentment. It treats the ordinary pleasures of this life as an unnecessary and even shameful distraction from its bloody mission.

As Jesus says in the Bible, "The thief cometh not, but for to steal, and to kill, and to destroy: I am come that they might have life, and that they might have it more abundantly" (John 10:10).

Another feature of Islamic society that I was surprised not to find in the West is shame about any public expression of happiness or joy and the downplaying, even the concealment, of good news. Of course Muslims celebrate weddings and other festivities, but the Islamic religion puts a taboo on being happy in life.

Melancholic themes of abandonment, rejection, disappointment, victimhood, and even anger fill most Arabic songs about romantic love, while other songs are about jihad, pride, and destroying the enemies of Allah. It was not until I played a song by the late Arab diva Oum Kalthoum to an American neighbor that suddenly it dawned on me how sad the song sounded.

Arabic movies often include scenes of domestic violence.

Arabic TV also carries children's programs with violent themes, even showing children telling other children that to die as a shahid, martyr, is a beautiful thing, better than living in peace.[9]

Peace

The Koran puts peace in a negative light: "So do not weaken and call for peace while you are superior" (47:35). Allah is telling Muslims that to call for peace is a sign of weakness and that as long as Muslims are powerful or superior they should not pursue peace. Another translation of the same verse says: "Be not weary and fainthearted, crying for peace, when you should be uppermost." Peace is not an option for Muslims when they are strong. This verse is sarcastic about those who want peace, describing them as weaklings, wimps, and fainthearted. In Arab culture such a description—particularly when applied to young men—is extremely shameful, making peace-seeking itself a shameful act.

Under Islamic doctrine, Muslims should never accept peace if they are winning. They can only accept it, temporarily, when they are weak or if they need a breathing space to regroup and then come back to win. Temporary peace is allowed under Islam as a period of "Hudna" or truce that should never exceed ten years. If you notice, most of the peace treaties Palestinians sign never exceed ten years. Also the recent Iran nuclear deal was limited to ten years. In any case, Muslims also allow themselves to breach their agreements with infidels as soon as they feel ready, regardless of what they signed. It is common for Arabs after signing ceasefire agreements to go ahead and strike Israel almost immediately, before the ink on the agreement dries. All of that is okay under Islamic values and law.

In the history of Islam there were some periods of relative peace and even prosperity, but that was not because of Islamic values. In fact Islam allowed periods of peace only after Muslims had conquered non-Muslim countries, seized control of their governments, and forced sharia on their citizens. The borders between Muslim and non-Muslim countries were never peaceful by choice, only when Islam was weak—and even during periods of Muslim weakness, those borders were constantly plagued by tension and bloody confrontations. Then, as soon as Islam became more powerful, the Muslims' need to have the upper hand reasserted itself.

Even during periods of weakness, you can still see Islam's bias against peace with non-Muslims. Some Muslims today argue that the Islamic greeting "Salamu Aleikum" which wishes peace on others, is proof that Islam values peace, but that is not true. In a hadith by Sahih Muslim (14/144), Muhammad said, "When the People of the Book (Jews and Christians) say 'salaam' to you (greet you by saying *al-salaamu alaykum*), say '*Wa 'alaykum*' (and unto you)'"—in other words, the Prophet told Muslims to take the word "salam," or peace out of the greeting when addressing non-Muslims. According to this hadith, even a greeting that wishes peace is restricted to Muslims only.

It was the Jews who first used the expression "shalom aleichem," which is Hebrew for "peace be upon you," many centuries before Islam came on the scene. Muhammad obviously failed to fully understand or appreciate it—just as he did with most of what he borrowed and copied from Biblical customs and traditions. It is obvious from the above hadith that the Jews of Medina greeted Muslims with "shalom aleichem" in just the same way as they greeted one another. But Muhammad did not want to reciprocate the peaceful greeting. That says a lot about the tension and animosity Muhammad created between Muslims and the Jews and Christians of Arabia from the very inception of Islam.

Covenant of Peace vs. Covenant of Permanent War

In Isaiah 54:10 God assures us of His covenant of peace: "For the mountains shall depart, and the hills be removed; but my kindness shall not depart from thee, neither shall the covenant of my peace be removed, saith the Lord that hath mercy on thee." Peace is also a key value in the the New Testament: "Now the Lord of peace himself give you peace always by all means" (II Thessalonians 3:16). "These things I have spoken unto you, that in me ye might have peace" (John 16:33). "And the peace of God, which passeth all understanding, shall keep your hearts and minds through Christ Jesus" (Philippians 4:7). "Let him eschew evil, and do good; let him seek peace, and ensue it" (I Peter 3:11). In other words, don't just desire peace, actively pursue it. And, in stark contrast to Muhammad's message against peacemaking by Muslims, "Blessed are the peacemakers: for they shall be called the children of God" (Matthew 5:9).

This kind of peace does not exist in the Koran and is never taught as a value in Islam. I never heard anything in Islam even close to the Bible's endorsement of peace of the heart, mind, and soul; its urging to actively pursue peace with God, oneself, and humanity. When I became Christian, it took me a while to fully understand the concept of peace as something that God wants us all to live under.

In contrast, the Koran advocates a covenant of war. That is the doctrine of jihad. As Hasan Al Banna, founder of the Muslim Brotherhood, said, "All Muslims Must Make Jihad. Jihad is an obligation, from Allah on every Muslim and cannot be ignored nor evaded."

As we have seen, the only kind of "peace" Islam endorses is a cease-fire in which there is—temporarily—no physical violence. In fact, Islam divides the entire world between "the House of Islam," meaning the land where Muslims (and conquered non-Muslims) live in submission to an Islamic government that rules by sharia, and "the House of War," meaning the part of the world where non-Muslims live under their own governments and non-Muslim laws, against which Islamic war must be directed until they submit.

"Warfare is ordained for you," the Koran tells Muslims (2:216). Allah promises hellfire to those who are happy to stay home rather than commit their wealth and lives to the fight (Koran 9:81). He says to those who stayed behind, "So let them laugh a little and weep much" (9:82) and tells them that Muhammad will not pray over any of them when they die because when they did not go with Muhammad to fight they were defiantly disobedient to Allah (9:84). Allah's threats to those who refuse to fight along with his Messenger, Muhammad, extend to his assurance that they will never enjoy their wealth and their children (9:85–86). As for the good Muslims who fight alongside Muhammad, "Allah will bestow a vast reward" on them (4:74). The contrast between the punishment of hellfire and the reward of physical pleasures in the Islamic paradise is relentless in the Koran.

When I was a student of Islam all I learned was a perverted view of peace: that those who seek peace with non-Muslims in Europe, America, and Israel are committing treason against Islam and Muslims. Muslim religious authorities, intellectuals, and political leaders who dare advocate peace with taboo nations do not survive. The assassination of Anwar Sadat is a prominent example.

I grew up in the Gaza Strip where as a child I leaned that "killing Jews is worship that brings us closer to Allah." The terror group Hamas still advocates the same thing in Gaza and the West Bank today. I often wonder what my life would have been today if I had remained in the Middle East. It is not a pleasant thought. Looking back on my childhood often makes me deeply sad because I lived in a culture that was hostile to peace: "Fighting is what pleases the prophet" is a hadith by 'Ali, the son-in-law of the Prophet Muhammad and Islam's fourth "Rightly Guided" caliph.[10]

According to the Center for the Study of Political Islam, which I highly recommend as a source of information and statistics on Islam, when Islamic scriptures are compared with the Bible, both Old and New Testaments, the difference between the Bible and Islam is very clear—particularly when it comes to violence. This chart is a good response to those who claim that all religions are equally violent:

Words Devoted to Political Violence

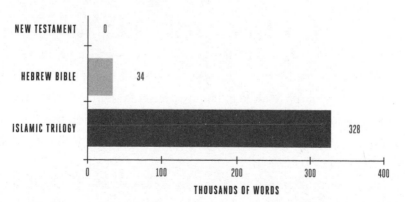

A comparison of political violence in the passages of the Hebrew Old Testament, Christian New Testament, and the Islamic Koran, sira, and hadith.[11]

It is thus not a coincidence—or something that can be explained by their ignorance—that Islamic preachers are consumed with promoting violence, hatred, and anger. Those who equate criticizing Islamic violence and terror with speaking ill of or even threatening all Muslims are using fear tactics that remind me of the culture of fear that silences truth seekers in the Muslim world.

To them I say that even up to today, the Al Azhar Islamic University in Cairo has not issued a religious ruling (fatwa) stating that the actions of ISIS are un-Islamic. Saudi sheikh Adel Al Kilbany has even said, "ISIS didn't come [up] with anything new, this is all in the core of our books, the seeds are in Salafi Islamic thought."[12]

Many brave and well-intentioned Muslim activists today are protesting the lack of peace values in Islamic education. But their task is hopeless, given the 164 verses in the Koran dealing strictly with jihad and violence against non-Muslims. How can Islamic education teach peace when every time Muslims turn a page in the Koran they find at least one verse teaching animosity, hatred, or violence?

The "Religion of Peace" Deception

The slogan "Islam is a religion of peace" was specifically created for Western consumption—I never heard that expression in all my decades living in the Middle East—and it has convinced many. I never heard that expression in the Middle East. The deception over "peaceful Islam" has reached alarming levels even when it came to translation of the Koran.

As we have seen, people who don't speak Arabic need to be very careful about which translation of the Koran they are reading. When it comes to the word "peace," the mistranslation is flagrant.

According to the Islamic website legacy.quran.com the word peace is mentioned in the Koran fifty times. Most of the mentions of peace are in the context of a greeting and a blessing to the prophets and to

Muslims, or about reconciliation between spouses or between Muslims, for example, "And if a woman fears cruelty or desertion on her husband's part, there is no sin on them both if they make terms between themselves; and making peace is better" (4:128).

The word peace in Arabic is "salam," while the word "aslihu" means to reconcile, but some translations of the Koran confuse the two. For example in Koran 2:224 the English translation used by legacy.quran.com reads "If two parties among the believers [Muslims] fall into mutual fighting, make peace between them." The Arabic word used here was "aslihu" meaning reconcile them. Note, too, that the call for reconciliation here is between Muslims—and that the recommendation for reconciliation even between Muslims is conditional, as is clear from the continuation of the verse: "then if one transgresses against the other, fight the one who has transgressed until he returns to the commands of Allah." So even amongst Muslims the recommendation is yet again to fight those who transgress the commands of Allah.

Patience and Gentleness

Patience is considered a virtue in Islam and is often mentioned in the Koran, which praises "those who persevere in patience, and put their trust on their Allah" (16.42). On the surface, Islamic society appears to value patience. But if you carefully examine patience in Islam, you will see that it's very different from the kind of patience or "longsuffering" that is a fruit of the Spirit in the Bible. The patience preached in the Koran is limited to the patience and tolerance of the Islamic system and its heavy-handed laws that are required of the subjects of the Muslim state.

For the inhabitants of Muslim countries, submission to Islamic sharia law and Muslim culture is not an option, it's a necessity. Impatience with the Islamic political leadership, and especially with the Islamic laws that control every aspect of life, is considered rebellion and severely punished with the harsh penalties of sharia. That may explain why Muslims in general exhibit enormous patience and tolerance of the unjust Islamic system, with its many abuses.

But while Islamic scriptures and preaching encourage Muslims to bear the yoke of sharia law patiently, Muslims are told to be harsh with non-Muslims: "let them find harshness in you" (Koran 9:123). This harshness often means being impatient, intolerant, and unreasonably demanding when living in Western culture. Muslims are not shy about expressing their sense of entitlement rather than expressing gratitude for all the goods they enjoy in the West. Anti-Semitic, anti-Christian, and pro-sharia Muslim groups in the West are rarely criticized by the Muslim public.

Muslim citizens in the West, by and large, are doing exactly what the Koran preaches, which is treating each other gently while treating the majority non-Muslim citizens of the West harshly—with criticism, imperious demands, violence, and sporadic acts of terror. And after every act of terror, instead of apologizing for or protesting against Islamic terrorism, Muslim groups immediately go into victim mode and demand that we never judge them by the actions of the terrorists, who are rarely reported by their Muslim friends and relatives.

Historically Muhammad himself was patient with his followers, especially those who fought on his side, but he was totally the opposite with non-Muslims. Usually his first resort in settling differences with those who disagreed with him was the sword. The Prophet's immediate response to poets of Arabia who mocked or criticized him in their poetry was beheading—in one case he demanded the beheading of a female poet; she was breast-feeding her baby when she was killed on Muhammad's orders.

Muhammad was impatient and easily offended by anyone who disagreed with him. He exhibited no tolerance for criticism or any kind of challenge. In fact the Koran and hadiths are predominantly about punishment, violence, and terror against those who rejected Muhammad and his Allah. Islamic scriptures describe in detail

Muhammad's many intemperate and violent actions, supremely unfitting to a man who called himself the final prophet of God.

Because Muslims are told that Muhammad was the perfect man, rightly or wrongly those who follow Muhammad's example in impatience and intolerance toward the outside world are thought of as the most devout

Strangely, Allah himself warns Muhammad in the Koran to be patient with those whose hearts he himself has sealed against Islam: "Thus doth Allah seal the hearts of those who know not" (30:59). "So have patience (O Muhammad)! Allah's promise is the very truth, and let not those who have no certainty make thee impatient" (30:60). But this is one command that Muhammad does not seem to have taken to heart. Neither at the time of Muhammad nor in today's Islamic culture do Muslims have any patience with outsiders, but rather demand infinite patience from them.

One Islamic site says that "Kindness"—which is the name for the same fruit of the Spirit as "gentleness" in some Bible translations—"is very highly regarded in Islam," but it provides only one Koran verse (plus a few hadiths) that purportedly encourage kindness: "Invite to the way of your Lord with wisdom and beautiful preaching; and argue with them in ways that are best and most gracious; for your Lord knows best who have strayed from His Path, and who are truly guided" (16:125). This is not a verse encouraging disinterested kindness; it is telling preachers of Islam to preach with beauty and wisdom for an ulterior motive—so they can gain followers. Neither "kindness" nor "gentleness" is found in the English, or in the Arabic original that sits right on top of it at the website.[13]

Goodness, Faithfulness, and Meekness

Islamic scriptures do not celebrate the values of goodness, faithfulness, meekness, and temperance. When I checked the word "goodness" in the Koran on legacy.quran.com, it said there were four mentions. This was the first of the four mentions of goodness, defending the Prophet: "And among them are those who abuse the Prophet and say, 'He is an ear.' Say, '[It is] an ear of goodness for you that believes in Allah and believes the believers and [is] a mercy to those who believe among you.' And those who abuse the Messenger of Allah—for them is a painful punishment" (9:61). This is hardly the "goodness" that the Bible is talking about.

When I checked for the word "faithfulness" there were zero mentions. So I tried "faithful" just to be sure and found two mentions. One is in a verse threatening Muhammad's wives: "Perhaps his Lord, if he divorced you [all], would substitute for him wives better than you—submitting [to Allah], believing, devoutly obedient, repentant, worshipping..." (66:5). This is not the faithfulness of the Bible; it is just about Muhammad getting more devout and obedient wives.

I finally checked "gentleness"—another way of translating the Biblical fruit of the spirit "meekness"—and found two mentions of "gentle." This was the first on the list: "you dealt with them gently. And had you been severe..." which at first sounded great to me—apparently Allah was asking Muhammad to deal gently with someone. But it turned out to be another contrast with the Bible, where gentleness is a fruit of the Spirit to be practiced by all Christians in a disinterested way. In this Koran verse, Muhammad is asked by Allah to be lenient (gentle) with his followers (not with non-Muslims) because of the practical effectiveness of that course of conduct: "[O Muhammad], you were lenient with them. And if you had been rude [in speech] and harsh in heart, they would have disbanded from about you. So pardon them and ask forgiveness for them and consult them in the matter" (3:159). The Koran verse has nothing to do with telling all Muslims to be meek or gentle in character.

In fact the Koran does command Muslims to be "humble," but only "towards believers," and "stern towards disbelievers" (5:54). "Fight those of the disbelievers who are near to you, and let them find harshness in you," it commands (9:123). "Strive against the disbelievers... be harsh with them. Their ultimate abode is hell" (9:73). "Do not take the Jews and the Christians for friends; they are friends of each other; and whoever amongst you takes them for a friend, then surely he is one of them" (5:51).

Meekness or gentleness in the Koran is restricted to what happens between Muslims. The opposite—harshness, un-forgiveness, and physical violence—is what a devout Muslim should do to non-Muslims.

Feeling sorry for or grieving with non-Muslims is against the Koran: "So do not grieve over the disbelieving people" (5:68). In fact, as we saw on 9/11, Muslims are happy to celebrate the grief of non-Muslims. Taking delight in non-Muslims' suffering is not considered distasteful, inappropriate, or a sin in Islam; it is in perfect harmony with the Koran and hadiths.

Even a simple greeting to a non-Muslim is discouraged in Islam. In one hadith by Muslim (book 026, number 5389), "Abu Huraira reported Allah's Messenger as saying: Do not greet the Jews and the Christians before they greet you and when you meet any one of them on the roads force him to go to the narrowest part of it."

Muslim preachers are all over the internet prohibiting Muslims from wishing Christians a Merry Christmas and telling them it is equal to committing blasphemy or apostasy and worse than murder.[14]

A Muslim shopkeeper was recently murdered in Glasgow in the UK, for wishing his customers a Happy Easter. He was declared an apostate—which under sharia law was an encouragement to kill him, and someone did just that.[15] The Islamic teaching against gentleness to non-Muslims is a life-and-death matter.

The lack of the fruits of the Spirit in Islam goes a long way to explaining why life in Muslim communities in Europe is often void of expression of love, peace, joy, and a sense of humor. Instead, what is common in such communities is a quick bad temper, anger, and offense-taking.

Self-Control vs. Controlling Others

One of the most striking differences between the Bible and the Koran is the contrast between self-control (one way of translating the fruit of the Spirit "temperance") and controlling others.

Self-control is a crucial Biblical value. With the help of God's grace, Christians build their inner strength to monitor their actions, become more aware of what their thoughts and motivations really are, and take more responsibility for their lives. This is truly a fruit of the Spirit, and a blessing that successful societies cannot do without. Self-control is the only way people can overcome self-absorption, selfishness, and anti-social impulses.

Christians and Jews see that their role in the world requires changing themselves. Their focus is on *How, with God's help, can I make myself better and this world a better place*. The Bible teaches Jews and Christians to be in control of their thinking, impulses, emotions, and behavior. For Christians, the purpose is to eventually be transformed and born again into becoming more Christ-like. The Bible is full of verses on self-control. "A man without self-control is like a city broken into and left without walls" (Proverbs 25:28). " ... [M]ake every effort to supplement your faith with virtue, and virtue with knowledge, and knowledge with self-control, and self-control with steadfastness, and steadfastness with godliness, and godliness with brotherly affection, and brotherly affection with love" (II Peter 1:5–7).

Muslims, on the other hand, see their role in the world as fixing and changing others: *I can make others better for Allah's sake.* Islamic law places the enforcement of religious laws such as performing prayers and fasting in the hands of Muslims, authorizing them to punish other Muslims who do not comply.

Islam is consumed with controlling others. It produces bullies who often have unreasonable expectations of others, such as obedience, compliance, admiration, approval, and special treatment of themselves. Islam has a very strict code of conduct, in which Muslims are extremely accountable to one another. And that accountability is all about external appearances—it works to impose conformity to sharia by social pressure and violence. Allah rarely talks to Muslims about their inner selves and their consciences. He does not urge them to cultivate self-restraint and self-control in order to be at peace with the world. Instead, the Koran is a book about action, telling Muslims what they must do and not do. Muslims are focused on what they want to accomplish and whether it benefits Islam or not. And, as we have seen, the moral rules for their behavior are different depending on whom they are dealing with. Thus their sense of their need for self-control is conditional and flexible, while their need to coerce their neighbors into obedience to sharia is absolute.

And jihad is the ultimate tool for controlling others. Muslims are often told never to hesitate or be discouraged by guilt in killing Allah's enemies, the non-Muslims: "Fighting is prescribed for you, and ye dislike it. But it is possible that ye dislike a thing which is good for you, and that ye love a thing which is bad for you" (2:216). "Fight (kill) them (non-Muslims), and God will punish, (torment) them by your hands, cover them with shame" (9:14). The message from Allah is for Muslims to use the most violent means to compel non-Muslims to submit, without hesitation or remorse.

This kind of teaching in the Koran and hadiths explains why jihadists lack empathy, guilt, or second thoughts about the barbarities they commit against their victims. Instead of the normal human feelings of empathy, Muslim society encourages them and their families to celebrate and express pride in such acts of terrorism. There were celebrations after 9/11 in every Muslim capital around the world, often publicly but also in private.

There is a huge difference in how Muslims and Christians interact with other people. Muslims rarely second guess themselves or reflect that it may be their fault when something goes wrong in their interpersonal relationships. They seem always sure of others' fallibility, and of their own right to correct them. Thus their first impulse is to be offended, which gives them an excuse to blame and even violently attack other people.

This happens between Muslims, whose friendships are volatile; they often get offended and sever relationships. And there is a huge amount of abuse in families in the Muslim world.

And it also happens in Muslims' relationships with non-Muslims. When Muslims move to the West they are not shy about expressing how they are offended by Western culture, customs, music, dancing, pork, dogs, wine, women, and so forth. The first time in my life I heard the expression "I hope I did not offend you," it was from a Christian.

The Koran itself is all about reacting to others; Allah and Muhammad were both consumed with anger toward others, especially those who refused to convert to Islam and totally submit to them without questioning. That is why the Koran is all about the kafirs. Even if they reject Islam in good faith, non-Muslims must be conquered, prevailed upon, judged, punished and terrorized—until Muslims have absolute control over them. It is not a coincidence that Muhammad often bragged about being victorious through terror; the ultimate act of controlling others.

It was truly a relief and a blessing over my life when I moved to the West and was freed from the persistent and judgmental eyes of the Muslims around me. Native-born Americans have no idea what a blessing life in this country is for immigrants from around the world who are escaping Islam. They also have no idea how dangerous it is to bring radical Muslims and jihadists into the country.

As we have seen, not one Islamic political or religious leader has apologized for 9/11. An apology from them would be appropriate because while mainstream Muslim leaders were not directly involved in what happened on 9/11, there is no doubt that Islamic culture, preaching, and education provided the fertile soil for terrorism to flourish all over the globe. It is a shame that Muslim apologists refuse to take responsibility for their role in fostering terrorism, denying any link between terrorism and Islam. As a product of the education in hate and jihad that millions of Muslims around the world receive, I can speak from experience: it took me decades to rid myself of it.

Not all Muslim individuals are bad apples, of course, but there is no doubt that the West is taking a huge risk by opening the door to the bad fruits of Islam that have been poisoning Islamic society for centuries. It should be no surprise when strife results when people believe that God is giving them his authority to hurt other human beings. And because of their value for peace, Christians and Jews are often regarded by Muslims as sitting ducks who deserve nothing better than violence.

The difference between the two cultures is astounding. Because Christians and Jews are oriented toward changing themselves, when they encounter a problem their first reaction is *What can I do to fix it?* When I met Jews for the first time in my life, in the United States, I was very impressed when I heard them say that one of their priorities in life was to "leave this world a better place." This phrase reflected a sense of personal responsibility that is totally lacking in Islam.

When I was not yet a Christian, I could already see that Jews and Christians must feel very special in the eyes of their God because they believed His wisdom, love, inspiration, care, and guidance were focused on helping humanity. And He was building their character and inner strength so that they could contribute to that project. Their God was so different from Allah, who used his followers as human bombs to hurt others.

When I was a Muslim I never felt that God loved me or cared for my internal life. There was no sense that Allah was blessing his followers with goodness and compassion—much less a peaceful life. All that he cared about was sacrificing us and our families for the permanent war called "jihad for the sake of Allah." The permanent war that took my father's life when I was eight years old.

To me as a young Muslim woman, Allah often felt like an abusive parent rather than a God who loves humanity. Instead of blessing Muslims' lives, Allah tests them to find out if they are ready to sacrifice their lives for him. The God of the Koran says that he tests Muslims' devotion by seeing if they are afraid to go to war. Those who fail the test will suffer a painful doom: "O ye who believe! Allah will surely test you, in the matter of the game, which ye take with your hands and your spears, that Allah may know him who feareth Him in secret. Whoso transgresseth after this, for him there is a painful doom" (Koran 5:94).

Unfortunately millions of Muslims and thousands of their leaders worldwide are inspired rather than repulsed by this message. And they have created a whole civilization ready to "kill and be killed" for Allah.

After being exposed to the Bible and starting to doubt Islam, I thought of a few questions to ask the almighty Allah: How come you are so angry at the majority of your creation that you are willing to sacrifice your own devoted followers to satisfy your urge for vengeance? If you want Muslims to kill and get killed to prove their loyalty to you, then what is the purpose of life on Earth? As God couldn't you have destroyed us all instead of sending a prophet with a book to order us to kill each other? Is your hatred of the kafirs stronger than your love of Muslims? Do you realize how Islam has turned this world into an ugly and hateful place? Do you know that focusing on punishing and killing others—the way you do in the Koran—is a formula for disaster, where no one is a winner?

I heard nothing back from Allah. And eventually I escaped life under Islam—with the help of a different holy book that I began to read in America, where it has shaped the entire society in accordance with the loving commandments of a very different God. I am grateful that I now worship my Lord and savior Jesus Christ.

Fruits of the Bible vs. Fruits of Islam

The chief fruit of Islam is terror. And terror stands in the way of Muslims' ability to recognize the importance of the Biblical fruits of the Spirit. Terror manifests itself in every aspect of Islamic society, keeping Muslims from recognizing hate, war, harshness, lawlessness, and control of others for the evils they are.

In Islam, no virtue is equivalent to Jihad: "A man came to Allah's Apostle and said 'Instruct me as to such a deed as equals Jihad (in reward).' He replied, 'I do not find such a deed'" (Bukhari, v1 p:391). All sin—lying, deception, terror, torture, war, and killing—is excused for the jihadist. The Koran calls the jihadist the most superior Muslim: "Allah has preferred in grades those who strive hard and fight with their wealth and lives above those who sit (at home). Unto each, Allah has promised good (Paradise), but Allah has preferred those who strive hard and fight above those who sit (at home) by a huge reward" (4:95). The best deed a Muslim can do—apart from being a Muslim in the first place—is jihad: "The prophet was asked 'which is the best deed?' He said 'To believe in Allah and His Apostle.' He was then asked, 'Which is the next (in goodness)?' He said, 'to participate in jihad in Allah's cause'" (Bukhari Vol 2, Book 26, p. 594).

Thus it makes sense that the Nation of Islam in the U.S. named its security force "Fruit of Islam." A Nation of Islam website urges men to enroll in the FOI and describes members as "brave fighter[s] for Allah" engaged in "a unique war for the very heart and soul of a people." Unfortunately, the jihad is not just a war for hearts and minds. It is also a very literal, physical, violent battle to conquer those of us who belong to Biblically based Western civilization—which some Western converts to Islam have joined, on the other side.

8

THE SEVEN DEADLY SINS

The seven deadly sins—pride, envy, lust, anger, laziness, greed, and gluttony—are fatal to our spiritual progress. These are not obvious external sins, transgressions like murder, rape, robbery, and so forth. But if we indulge them, eventually they can lead us to crimes like these, against society—and to self-destruction.

The Bible delves into the disorders of the soul and character that, if neglected, can gradually pile up to block our ability to see right from wrong, eventually separating us from God, stealing our joy, damaging our psyche, and hurting the people around us. The Bible says the wages of sin is death. The God of the Bible loves us and does not want anyone to die from sin.

God the Redeemer vs. Allah the Humiliator

Unlike the God of the Bible, Allah is full of anger, vindictiveness, and pride. Muslims have given their God ninety-nine names, derived from the Koran's descriptions of Allah. Some of them are: Al-Mutakabbir and Al-Mutaali, meaning the Prideful and Above Others; Al-Muntaqim, meaning the Avenger; Ad-Darr, the One Who Harms, or the Afflicter; Al-Mumit, the One Who Causes Death; Al-Muzill, the Disgracer or He Who Causes Humiliation; Al-Khafid, the Abaser or the Downgrader. That's all in addition to the fact that Allah, several times in the Koran, calls himself the greatest deceiver.

Obviously, what is considered a sin in the Koran is different from what is considered a sin in the Bible.

At the essence of Christians' understanding of the seven deadly sins is our faith in the great love of Jesus for us. Jesus demonstrates to us, through His own character, that one can live life without having to resort to negative and harmful behavior and attitudes. Jesus became a flesh-and-blood example to us to guide and save us from indulging in what would only bring us terrible harm and death.

After I became Christian I realized that the difference between Jesus and His Father, on the one hand, and Allah, on the other, was astounding. Jesus died to save us from a painful death caused by sin, while Allah rewards Muslims with forgiveness of all sin if they die for him; perhaps that is the crux of the difference.

The Wages of Sin Is Death vs. Forgiving Sin with Death

Jesus wants to save us from death by sin, and He wants our lives on Earth to be holy and wholesome. But Allah wants us to die in order for our sins to be forgiven.

The relationship between sin and death in the Koran is the reverse of the relationship between them in the Bible—because the Koran connects intentional death (of jihadists) with forgiveness of sin. The death of a Muslim martyr is the highest virtue, his sins will be all forgiven, and he is guaranteed paradise: "And if you are slain, or die, in the way of Allah (meaning for Allah's sake) forgiveness (of sin) and mercy from Allah are far better than all they could amass" (Koran 3:157).

To the Muslim, sin on Earth thus has one solution, to die while killing the enemies of Allah. And who has not committed sin? No one. So the motivation in Islam to die killing Allah's enemies is extremely seductive, tempting and powerful.

Unlike the God of the Bible, Allah never says that sin leads to spiritual or physical death—in a negative way. He makes the connection between death and sin a positive one: death in jihad gains the Muslim the reward of forgiveness of sins for himself and all his family members This is how the Koran solves the problem of sin.

As a result, Muslims view sin in a completely different way from how Christians see it. The more guilt a Muslim builds up from sin, the more motivated he will be to turn to the only way out—death by jihad.

This should explain why Muslims often brag, "We love death and they love life." In Islam, sin and death are connected in a convoluted way, so that terrorists are free to commit all the sins that they can imagine before blowing themselves up with as many non-Muslims as possible. The 9/11 terrorists went to Las Vegas for a few days before their act of terror and committed all kinds of sins forbidden to the ordinary Muslim.

In Islam, most sins are permitted if they are in aid of jihad. In that context, Islamic law allows lying, rape, and many other forbidden acts. This principle is taken to truly appalling extremes: "Saudi cleric Nasser al-'Umar issued a fatwa permitting mujahidin [jihadis] in Syria to have sex-jihad with their sisters [muharamhum] if no one else is available." As Raymond Ibrahim points out, "The rationale and justification of these fatwas is based on the Islamic maxim, 'necessity makes the prohibited permissible,' not unlike the more familiar adage, 'the ends justify the means.'"[1]

The jihadists of ISIS, Al Qaeda, and the other Islamist groups who commit unspeakable atrocities are told by preachers—quoting Allah—that all will be forgiven at the doors of Paradise, when they are greeted by eagerly waiting virgins in the sky.

And over and above Islam's explicit forgiveness of the most horrifying sins is its recommendation of Muhammad—a man guilty of truly heinous crimes—as the perfect example for all Muslims. Verses in the Koran do warn Muslims against vices here and there, but the character and actions of Muhammad conflict with those warnings. And, as we have seen, the God that Muhammad preached is nothing like the God of the Bible. The examples of Allah and his Prophet enshrine lust, hate, pride, envy, anger, and greed as positive values.

Pride Is a Sin vs. God Himself Is Prideful

Islam sends mixed messages about pride. A few hadiths do warn Muslims against pride, but this warning is contradicted by the character of Allah, one of whose ninety-nine names is "Al Mutakabbir," meaning "the Prideful."

The hadiths that warn Muslims against pride do so not on the grounds that it is bad for them, but because pride is exclusively a characteristic of Allah. Allah says he will torture any one who claims the mantle of pride from him: "Pride is My cloak and greatness My robe, and whoever competes with Me I shall throw him into Hell" (Sunan Ibn Majah Vol 5, 37,4174). This hadith is confirmed by another hadith "Pride and Glory are My garments, whoever claims them, I torture him" (Muslim 1:618).

The influential imam Ghazali defined "al-Mutakabbir" as "He is the One Who sees everything and everyone as insignificant besides Himself, Who sees greatness and pride justified only for Him; so, He looks upon others as kings look at slaves.... *Istikbar* is to think of yourself as being great, instilling the attitude of pride.... Such a quality is not fit except purely for Allah.... Quoting the Lord of greatness, the Almighty God, the Messenger of Allah has said, 'Pride is My cloak; Greatness is My shirt; whoever disputes with Me regarding either one of them, I shall surely hurl him into the fire.'"[2]

Muhammad talked the talk against pride, but he did not walk the walk. He preached against pride, just as the Jews and Christians of his time did. But in his character and his actions, the Prophet utterly failed to exhibit humility like Christ's. It is obvious from the Islamic scriptures that Muhammad felt he was above other people; in fact he literally humiliated, tortured, and even beheaded those who challenged his self-regard. Muhammad's life was all about destroying anything and anyone who stood in the way of his voracious pride—the exact opposite of the character of Jesus.

Muslims were thus left with no examples for humility. All they have is the warning that those who will take Allah's pride will be tortured, as if pride were a prize only Allah and Muhammad are worthy of. Such sad and conflicting messages are all over Islamic scriptures.

Islam has failed to provide its followers with a comprehensive and well-integrated value system or with examples of true holiness and godliness. The behavior and character of Muhammad certainly do not qualify.

Even as a young girl the contradictions in the character of Muhammad made me uncomfortable. I can see now that Muslims—particularly the so-called moderate Muslims—were importing Biblical values to Islam. Insofar as Muslims I knew growing up saw

Muhammad as an example of humility, they were—consciously or unconsciously—borrowing their picture of him from the character of a very different religious figure: Jesus Christ. The moderates' picture of Muhammad has no warrant in the Islamic doctrine or the Muslim scriptures. Those moderate Muslims never checked their claims against the Islamic scriptures but just operated on the assumption that Islam is basically the same as the other Abrahamic religions. The fact is, there are moderate Muslims, but there are no moderate Islamic scriptures to support what they claim.

Humility vs. Pride

While Islam claims to advocate humility, it strongly encourages the supremacy of Muslims vis à vis all others. Muslims are commanded, not only to assault, terrorize, and kill the kafirs, but also to discriminate against them and treat them with contempt, shunning, and humiliation. For example, Muslims are urged not to greet Jews and Christians when they are passing, but rather to assault and push them: "The Prophet said, 'Do not give the People of the Book the greeting first. Force them to the narrowest part of the road'" (Muslim 2167 and Bukhari Book 25, Number 5389).

How can there be any logic or integrity in a religious ideology that claims to value humility and yet at the same time preaches assaulting others on the road instead of greeting them?

People talk about "Arab pride" for a reason; pride is certainly a leading feature of the Arabs' culture. But it is a cultural reality that was reinforced by Muhammad and enshrined in Islamic scriptures. The supremacist nature of Islam is both a reflection and an extension of the culture that birthed Islam, that of the Arabian Peninsula. Islamic culture values pride and sees it as a positive thing. In the Arab world pride is associated with success and power. Muslim society has a very condescending and abusive attitude toward the underprivileged, the weak, and the poor. Muslims are eager and proud to say that they don't need others. I often heard my grandmother pray for the preservation of her "karama," her pride—not to need anyone in her old age.

Humility, being nice, and uplifting others without expecting anything in return are rare behaviors in Muslim society; when they do occur, they are often mistaken for weakness. In the Muslim world, people who appear poor or unimportant—those with no pride, so to speak—are mistreated.

The Koran and hadith collections are predominantly books about rejecting the other—other religions, cultures, and ways of life. Islamic supremacy is taught on every page of the Koran, where Muslims are commanded never to stop until Islam dominates and destroys all other religions. Slogans such as "Islam Will Dominate" are displayed with pride by Muslim protestors all over the West.[3]

Muslims are more interested in impacting and impressing the outside world than in finding peace and improving themselves from within. What is that but pride?

The pride that plays such a large role in Islamic culture has its roots in the pre-Islamic culture of the Arabian Peninsula. In fact, as we shall see in chapter fourteen, that Arab pride is a key reason that Islam was created in the first place.

Even non-Arab Muslims, such as the Pakistanis, often complain about Arab pride. A Pakistani Muslim once wrote, "I myself come from a Pakistani background and I always question my family members and friends on why they take so much pride in Arabs' culture rather than our own. In the West, we are allowed to own businesses, gain citizenship, and marry their women, yet if you tried to do this in any Arab country, especially Saudi Arabia, they will simply deport you…. So much for the universal Muslim 'brotherhood' in Islam."[4]

A culture based on pride is hard to live in. It was never easy for me personally to adapt to a culture that treated the prideful as special and deserving of respect, while showing contempt for those with humility. I grew up surrounded by people who responded to me with respect only when I acted prideful, something which was totally against my nature and happiness. Society was harsh on those who did not wear a prideful mask at all times. Even families were hard on people who appeared to be vulnerable in any way. My own mother was in the habit of asking me, "Have you no pride?" when I expressed my need for her love and affection. That took a toll on me; it was years before those wounds healed.

It was not easy for me to recover from the Islamic culture of respecting the powerful, the arrogant, and the proud and holding the weak and the humble in contempt. For Muslims, pride stands in the way of getting close to God (Allah "the Prideful"), and it stands in the way of forming true friendships, so that many Muslims have been forced into a life of isolation, shunning people and being constantly on their guard. That is especially true of Muslim women, who must also live in physical isolation behind the Islamic burqa—the garment that protects their husbands' pride.

The Bible says, "Pride goeth before destruction, and an haughty spirit before a fall" (Proverbs 16:18). It is pride that is bringing Islam's fall from grace today. As we shall see in chapter fourteen, Arab pride veiled the eyes of Arabia to the Bible. And Islam has entangled Muslims in a never-ending cycle of Arab pride, in a supposed greatness that never truly was and never will be as long as pride continues to reign supreme in the hearts of Muslims.

Islamic culture does not distinguish between pride and honor. To the contrary, the culture gives more honor to the proud; those who express pride are responded to with admiration and even regarded as being virtuous. Those who are lucky enough to have a superior place in Muslim society treat others with contempt; they act as though they don't need others, they don't need to be nice to or smile at those who are below them socially.

Pride and supremacy were attributes of the Arabian Peninsula culture long before Islam, but unfortunately Muhammad, instead of identifying and correcting this aspect of his culture, reinforced it. In fact he enshrined Arabian supremacy and pride as a right Muslims have in the Islamic legal system—and made it a holy virtue instead of sin. Then unfortunately, after the discovery of oil, petro-dollars came along and gave another shot in the arm to Arab pride.

Envy
Envy Is a Sin vs. Envy Is a Curse

Pride often leads to envy. An inflated view of yourself tends to lead you to compare yourself with others and desire what they have, whether their traits or their situation. Thus it should be no surprise that the Islamic culture of pride is deeply immersed in envy as well.

The Bible warns us against envy: "A sound heart is the life of the flesh: but envy the rottenness of the bones" (Proverbs 14:30). "Wherefore laying aside all malice, and all guile, and hypocrisies, and envies, and all evil speakings, as newborn babes, desire the sincere milk of the word, that ye may grow thereby" (I Peter 2:1–2).

Envy, which can grow like cancer (rotting the bones) will ruin our relationship with God and hinder our happiness, internal peace, and spiritual maturity. It can also hurt others who are the objects of our envy, if we act upon our feelings.

But it is clear that the Bible focuses on envy as a sin that is deadly *to the one who envies.* The Koran, on the other hand, never mentions envy as a sin that is self-destructive. Instead, in the Koran, envy is regarded as the powerful source of a vicious curse—"the evil eye"—that can be intentionally placed on one person by another.

The Koran contains only three mentions of the word envy, and none of them are on envy as a sin to be avoided by Muslims. Instead they are about seeking protection against those who envy: "I seek refuge in the Lord of daybreak; From the evil of that which He created; And from the evil of darkness when it settles; And from the evil of malignant witchcraft, And from the evil of the envier when he envies" (Koran 113:1–5).

The Koran describes those who stayed behind during jihad but who later came to collect the spoils of war as being envious of the jihadists: "Those who were left behind will say, when ye set forth to capture booty: Let us go with you.... Ye shall not go with us.... Then they will say: Ye are envious of us" (48:15).

The third mention of envy, in Koran 2:109, is about Jews and Christians who are portrayed as envious of Muslims: "Many of the People of the Scripture wish they could turn you back to disbelief after you have believed, out of envy from themselves...."

Not one mention in Islamic scriptures is about envy as a sin or character defect. Instead of warning Muslims against this deadly sin and teaching them how to eradicate it from their lives, Islamic culture has created elaborate protective customs, activities, objects, and spells against those who envy, or have "the evil eye." It is sad for me now to remember how many people I knew who were accused of envy or having an evil eye who were broken-hearted when they were told that by others, sometimes by close relatives.

Arab markets are stacked with jewelry and decorative figures for the purpose of repelling the evil eye of envy—for example, the "Hand of Fatima" and blue beads with eyes ornaments to place at one's doorstop for protection from envy.

In addition to the jewelry, Muslim society has also developed barriers of doubt, suspicion, and distrust between people to guard against the curses of the envious. All Muslims know from the Koran that Allah wants to protect us from other people who have an evil eye. And some Muslims go as far as resorting to witchcraft and placing spells on others suspected of envy.

In times of good news—a wedding, the birth of a baby, graduating with honors, a promotion—Muslims are careful about whom to tell the good news to, and whom to hide it from.

The words of the most popular Egyptian wedding song are focused on protecting the bride and groom from the evil eye of the envious, who are probably among the guests. "may the eye of the envier be poked with a rod, haleluya, the groom is beautiful and his bride is well chosen. And tonight we have annoyed and provoked our enemies…" This rather horrifying song is played at most Egyptian weddings.

I remember being told as a child, by both my mother and grandmother, not to tell good news to others because of the evil eye. I once heard my mother say that one of the reasons my father was killed was because of the evil eye—because he had reached a high position in his career and was popular. All the adults in my family agreed with her interpretation. They said the curse of envy is in the Koran. Which is true.

I personally knew many people in Egypt who stopped communicating with others, including even friends, after a supposed evil eye incident. For example, one time a woman told a new mother I knew that her baby was beautiful, and the next day the baby got sick. The new mother then ended her relationship with her neighbor because of what she perceived as an evil eye attack on her baby.

The pain, suffering, and destruction to friendships that are caused by the concept of envy in Islam are serious tragedies. No good God would have given envy the power to drive people apart, creating terrible divisions between friends and even in families. My life in the Muslim world was not a happy one, with everyone having to walk on eggshells so as not to offend anyone with even a hint of the evil eye.

The way envy is understood in Islam, as the source of curses that can do terrible damage, is truly destructive to human relations. Muslims are not taught that we are all sinners, that we are all prone to the sin of envy, and that we have to do our best to avoid feelings of envy of others when they surface because envy is a sin that interferes with our emotional growth and happiness. They are not taught that God knows we all struggle with envy, that He loves us anyway, but that He does not love the sin. Those Biblical ideas on envy are totally alien to the Muslim mind. Instead, Muslims are taught that envy is a force that gives the envious a terrible power over those whose good fortune they envy.

Lust
Lust Is a Sin vs. Allah Seduces Jihadists with Lust

Lust is an intense craving for the pleasures of the body, especially regarding sex. Lust is considered by Christians to be one of the deadly sins that enslaves and damages us, others we interact with, and our relationship with God.

Both the Bible and the Koran contain standards and prohibitions regulating sexual ethics and behavior. On the surface, Islam appears to be the most restrictive religion when it comes to sex outside of marriage. Among all the religions of the world, Islam has the most severe punishments for those who commit sexual violations such as adultery: flogging, execution, and honor killing by the sinner's relatives. Islamic society also has almost total gender segregation, and most women are covered from head to toe. Sex in the Muslim world appears to happen only between husband and wife.

But we should never judge a book by its cover. On sexual morality, as about virtually everything in Islam, there are many contradictions. While making an ostentatious display of sexual purity, Muslim culture is in fact obsessed with sex, sexual rituals, virginity, concubines, sex slavery, and Muhammad's sexual prowess. We have seen that the Koran rewards jihadists with sexual slaves and promises each of them seventy-two perpetual virgins in Paradise. There are many gratuitous and graphic hadiths regarding the personal sexual behavior of Muhammad and his eleven wives.

Restrictions on sex in Islam mostly fall on women; in regards to men, such restrictions are very superficial. A Muslim man, married or unmarried, who understands all the games and loopholes that sharia allows to men will have no problem having sex as often as he wishes with any number of women; the only real restrictions will be the limits of his financial resources and physical stamina.

Muslim men have the right to up to four wives, in addition to any number of temporary contractual marriages (pleasure marriages) in exchange for money. This kind of marriage can last for one night or a few hours and does not require a divorce when the contract—which can be merely an oral one—expires. A Kuwaiti man recently posted a wedding photo with his four brides in one wedding, putting Hugh Hefner's playboy lifestyle to shame.[5]

Muslim men are also allowed any number of sexual slaves and concubines under Islamic law. These are traditionally captured in war, taken for sex against their will. This is what is called rape in the West. Many Muslim men take that right as permission to rape non-Muslim women in virtually any circumstances, something that explains the epidemic levels of rape of Coptic Christian women in Egypt, and of European women by Muslim migrants.

Thus the term adultery means totally different things in Islam and Christianity. With all the sexual opportunities that Islam allows for men, it is hard to catch a Muslim man committing adultery. In the Muslim marriage contract, loyalty is expected only from the woman.

Islam also uses lust in all forms, especially sexual lust, as a lure to recruit jihadists. The Islamic Paradise in the Koran is all about promises of sexual pleasures beyond the imagination. Every Muslim man who dies in jihad is promised a non-ending supply of virgins. And to those who prefer little boys—well, they too can have what they want: boys described in the Koran as glittering like jewels.

Muhammad also rewarded the lust of his fighters who survived the battle. The Prophet encouraged them not to be reluctant to rape the captured women in front of their husbands: "They met their enemy and fought with them. They defeated them and took them captives. Some of the Companions of the Apostle of Allah were reluctant to have intercourse with the female captives in the presence of their husbands who were unbelievers. So Allah, the Exalted, sent down the Qur'anic verse" (Koran 4:24). "And all married women (are forbidden) unto you save those (captives) whom your right hands possess" (Abu Dawud 2150; Muslim 3433).

Muhammad had several chances to reverse his sanctioning of rape of captured non-Muslim women even in front of their families, but he continued with his encouragement of the practice and then afterward he permitted his men to sell the women as slaves:

"Then the apostle sent Sa-d b. Zayd al-Ansari, brother of Abdu'l-Ashal with some of the captive women of Banu Qurayza to Najd and he sold them for horses and weapons" (Ibn Ishaq 693).[6]

Muhammad offered and allowed all kinds of carnal pleasures to his men to inspire them to fight, conquer, and expand his control. It is no wonder that he was willing to offer them the bribe of sexual pleasure; after all, he even forgave them for not praying or fasting, as long as they were fighting. This is still happening before our very eyes today, not only when it comes to ISIS, but in many other jihadist groups such as Boko Haram, whose jihadists keep kidnapping and raping hundreds of underage Christian school girls.

While lust is used and abused to seduce jihadists for Islam's expansion, Muslim women are living without any kind of freedom. In Islamic society a woman can't have a boyfriend even in a Platonic way. She can't even be seen walking with a man who is not a blood relative. She can't choose the man she wants to marry, or even at what age she must be married. The disparity between men's and women's sexual lives under Islam is obscene and offensive.

Islam is a religion obsessed with pleasures of the flesh, offering sex and even rape as a lure to men while honor-killing young girls for rumors of sexual impropriety or even falling in love. Judged by Biblical values, this is an abomination. As the Epistle of James says, "Let no man say when he is tempted, I am tempted of God: for God cannot be tempted with evil, neither tempteth he any man." But the God of Islam uses the temptation and lure of sex to get his followers to obey.

Anger
Anger as a Sin vs. Anger as a Tool to Gain Power

Expressing anger is not regarded as appropriate or civilized behavior in the West. It is interpreted as a sign of weakness, self-indulgence, and lack of self-control. In the West, losing one's temper is the fastest way to lose friends and respect.

But that is not the case in Islamic culture, where anger and taking offense are often seen as signs of power, strength, and means. Those who do not respond with anger to even the slightest degree of rude behavior are considered weak.

Discussions on Arab TV often end up with fighting, slapping, and throwing tables and chairs—something that explains why guests on Arab TV are often seated far from one another. As a young girl in Egypt I remember an older high-ranking military man we called "uncle." He was a nice man until we went with him to a restaurant.

The poor waiters had to suffer from his fits of anger throughout the meal. The culture never told him his behavior with waiters was wrong or shameful. No one around the table acted like it was a big deal, but his behavior left me feeling uncomfortable and sorry for the poor waiters.

Muhammad himself had no tolerance for anyone who came into conflict with him; he reacted to any challenge throughout his life with angry physical violence. Also Allah described himself as an angry God in the Koran.

Pressure from the example of the West has driven Islamic culture to adopt some Biblical values, insinuating that they are also Islamic values—when it fact they are never mentioned in the Koran, but only in the Bible. When I lived in Egypt, I heard the expression not to go to sleep angry, and I presumed that was a wonderful Islamic value. But when I checked the Koran versus the Bible I found out that this is a value that exists only in the Bible: "let not the sun go down upon your wrath" (Ephesians 4:26); "[f]or the wrath of man worketh not the righteousness of God" (James 1:20).

What you find in the Koran, in contrast, are many warnings and threats about the horrific consequences to making Allah angry and suffering his wrath: "Already have defilement and anger fallen upon you from your Lord" (7:71); "anger from their Lord and humiliation in the life of this world" (7:152); Jews are mentioned as "those who have evoked [Allah's] anger" (1:7); and here is a reference to those who are the targets of the "anger of Allah and whose refuge is Hell? And wretched is the destination" (3:162).

Allah uses angry, graphic, and cruel words against people in the Koran, placing curses, doom, and torment on people he hates and sending them to a despicable, sorry, and miserable destiny.

Allah and Muhammad themselves are, in fact, the perfect examples of anger and cruel retaliation. Naturally Islamic society does not view anger as a negative, nor as a cause for shame. Any attempt to shame people out of their anger and retaliation would be in conflict with Allah's and Muhammad's words, behavior, and commandments—an insult to God and his Messenger.

Islamic education itself fosters anger, hatred, and offense-taking. Muslims are taught that controlling their anger or avoiding a fight is a weakness. As a young student in Gaza schools all I learned were anger, hatred, pride, and retaliation against and condemnation of non-Muslims, especially Jews. That was decades ago, but the same thing still goes on. I recently watched an Arab school play in which some Arab children were dressed as Jewish rabbis and the rest of the students were throwing play rocks at them.

It is hypocritical for Muslims to claim Islam is a religion of peace when imams use the slightest offense against Islam to stir up the worshipers in their mosques to get out to riot, kill, and burn, even in the West. Consider what happened to Danish embassies after the Danish cartoon incident. These are the same Muslims who tell the West not to judge them by the acts of thousands of Muslim terrorists. But when one Danish cartoonist offended Muslims, all of Europe had to suffer horrific anger and terror.

Unlike the Bible, which says: "Anger resteth in the bosom of fools" (Ecclesiastes 7:9), Islamic preaching often describes anger as "holy." It is not uncommon for Muslim groups such as Fatah and Hamas to calls for a "day of rage" close to the Jews' "day of Atonement."[7]

Even at institutions of higher learning in the United States, Muslim student groups such as Students for Justice in Palestine hold protests dedicated to expressing their anger. You can watch a YouTube video of protest leader Hatem Bazian, who starts his speech by shouting to the Muslim crowd, "Are you angry? Are you angry? Are you angry?" and then says, "we need an intifada [a rebellion, coup or revolution] in this country [referring to the U.S.]."[8]

I want to end my discussion of anger in Islam with the first five lines of a long poem written by an American who happened to convert to Islam. This is how Islam inspired him to write:

I am not angry I am anger
I am not dangerous I am danger
I am abominable stress, Eliotic, relentless
I'm a breath of vengeance. I'm a death sentence
I'm forsaken repentance to the beast in his hench men.[9]

Laziness
Self-Reliance vs. Dependency

Laziness is a failure to act and utilize one's talents. Many do not connect the habit of laziness with culture or religion. But one of the most noticeable things to someone who has lived under Islam is how different the West is when it comes to its work ethic, and how Western neighborhoods and communities quickly come together in cooperation and work hard to help one another in hard times and in natural disasters.

Cooperation like that is never seen in the Muslim world, where, when disaster strikes, almost everyone simply waits for help from the government or to be rescued by some powerful person's generosity. It is painful to see Muslims during a catastrophe, stepping on one another to get aid for themselves and not lifting a finger to help the community. Even under normal conditions, it is not uncommon to see hundreds of men sipping Turkish coffee in street cafés while trash is piling up around them on street corners and sidewalks, and they never do a thing to keep their own community clean.

The Bible warns that laziness leads to poverty: "Yet a little sleep, a little slumber, a little folding of the hands to sleep: so shall thy poverty come as one that travelleth, and thy want as an armed man" (Proverbs 6:10–11). "Love not sleep, lest thou come to poverty; open thine eyes, and thou shalt be satisfied with bread" (Proverbs 20:13).

The Bible also points to sloth as an obstacle to spiritual progress.

"The way of the slothful man is as an hedge of thorns: but the way of the righteous is made plain" (Proverbs 15:19). A famous phrase attributed to Edmund Burke—"All that is necessary for evil to triumph is for good men to do nothing"—could never have been produced or made popular in Islamic culture.

Mitt Romney was harshly criticized for saying, during his 2012 visit to Israel, that the GDP per capita differences between Israel and the Palestinian Authority represent a contrast in values, but he was only telling the truth. That is a fact, not just about the differences in wealth between Israel and the West Bank and Gaza, but also about the contrast between Islamic nations and Western nations—with the exception of a few Gulf emirates drowning in oil.

While the West values hard work to improve life on Earth, Islam values jihad to guarantee a life in Paradise. Most Islamic preachers do not see the links between Islamic values, laziness, and poverty. But why would a Muslim man who is continually hammered with the values of jihad be interested in positive hard work for the betterment of society?

It was ironic to see several Muslim leaders recently express their disappointment that everything they own was made either in the West or in Asia, and none of it in Muslim countries. As we have already seen, the top Sunni leader Yusuf al-Qaradawi has accused Muslims of being lazy and lacking a work ethic, especially in comparison with the West. The sheikh betrayed how the ethics of jihad overpower all other ethics in Islam when he said, "The prophet (Muhammad) ordered us to excel in everything, even in killing and slaughtering." The sheikh did not notice the irony here—that the only example for hard work and excelling that he could come up with in Islam was when Muhammad talked about excelling in jihadist violence. Apparently Sheikh Qaradawi does not see the conflict between excelling in killing, on the one hand, and working hard to make the world a better place, on the other.

I once heard a Muslim businessman saying that Muslims do not perform as well when they work under the Islamic system as when they work under the Western system, and he could not understand why. He is correct, and now that I have become a Christian I know why. Islam only rewards jihadists and those who fight for Islam. To land a well-paying job or earn respect in places like Gaza and the West Bank, one must join Hamas or Fatah, organizations that sponsor terrorism. Those who don't support the jihad have no hope for a successful future there. The system in the Muslim world rewards life choices very different from hard and productive work.

As a longtime resident of the Middle East, I was amazed at the lack of initiative and drive in the Muslim population. People were trained to wait for orders to do anything. This is a culture where everyone is relying on someone else to do what needs to be done.

The end result is the Muslim world's stagnant economy, with men and women all pointing at each other about who will do the real work to make a living. Everyone in Egypt wants a cushy desk job, while physical labor is shunned, left to the poor and the desperate.

And Islamic laziness is not confined to shirking from physical work. Sadly, Islam does not value intellectual labor, either. Islamic culture rejects learning that comes from outside Islam, and learning within Islam is subject to crippling limits, too. There are even restrictions on how you are allowed to read the Koran—analysis and questioning are not allowed. Severe punishments against any kind of critical thinking about Islam have forced Muslims into an intellectual laziness that has kept them from discovering even what's in their own books. The happy Muslim is the Muslim who is content not to want to know.

Today millions of Muslims are escaping from the ruins of Islam—the stagnant, lazy, chaotic, and unlivable conditions in most Islamic countries. They seek a more active, vibrant, and orderly life in Western lands, the land of the kafirs—whom the Koran command them to kill. For a while Muslim immigrants thrive, blossom, and enjoy life in the West. But sooner or later, Islam comes back with a vengeance. Second-generation Muslims in the West start sending their kids to the mosque, where they read their Koran and learn from their local imam, a gift of Saudi Arabia, about how jihad is their duty and their pride, about Allah's commandment to rebel against the non-Islamic system.

The cycle of Islamic rebellion then comes full circle, with young Muslims wanting to establish in the West the very system that their parents escaped from. Like Muhammad, they reject the Bible as a book of the enemies and start blaming their inadequacies on others, namely Western culture.

This is how Islam asserts itself. It uses angry unemployed youth to rebel against the non-Islamic values of the Biblically based Western societies that have welcomed Muslims. No society lacks a good supply of young people who would rather blame the system than themselves for their lazy attitude and lack of purpose. These are Islam's best friends—some of them future jihadists. And instead of directing young men like this to assimilate into Western society and become productive citizens, their religious leaders encourage them to embrace their alienation. This is happening under our noses every day, in mosques and jails all across the United States. And you can see the same pattern in every country Muslims flee to. The plan is use the alienation and hatred of disgruntled youth to undermine the wholesome system that has offered Muslims refuge. It's a kind of jihad to conquer Western countries for the sake of Allah.

Greed
Greed as a Sin vs. Greed as a Lure for Jihadists

The Bible wants us to thrive and prosper, but does not want us to be greedy. Greed means being obsessed with accumulating material goods. As the Bible says, "No man can serve two masters: for either he will hate the one, and love the other; or else he will hold to the one, and despise the other. Ye cannot serve God and mammon" (Matthew 6:24). "Mammon" is a word for money.

The word "greed" is mentioned five times in the Koran—though the Arabic words translated that way—"Bukhl" and "Shih"—are really better translated as "stingy" or "withholding" of something for oneself. Essentially, the Koran just advises Muslims not to be stingy. For example this verse encourages spending "in the cause of Allah" and singles out for blame "among you... those who withhold [out of greed]" (47:38). It also tells Muslims to "listen and obey and spend [in the way of Allah]; it is better for your selves. And whoever is protected from the stinginess of his soul—it is those who will be the successful" (64:16). The Biblical sin of greed has a much larger meaning than the Islamic advice not to be stingy. There is not one verse in the Koran that is similar in meaning to Matthew 6:24. Not once does the Koran warn Muslims against greed as a sin that will hurt them and will separate them from God.

The Koran and hadiths often promise material rewards to the Muslim fighters, and to people Muhammad wants to keep in Islam. These rewards are in the form of riches, property, goods, and human slaves taken as spoils of war from defeated and killed non-Muslims: "So enjoy what you took as booty; the spoils are lawful and good" (Koran 8:69). "He rewarded them with abundant spoils... much booty that you shall take" (Koran 48:19). "The booty! O Muslims, the booty!" (Bukhari 4.276).

Muhammad used greed to tempt Muslims with material goods to do what he wanted, whether fighting for him or staying loyal to Islam: "I [Muhammad] give (am giving to) some people, lest they should deviate from Islam or lose patience" (Bukhari 4.276). "The prophet said 'I give to the Quraysh so that they will desire Islam'" (Bukhari 4:374).

And Allah's Prophet also enjoyed material rewards. When disputes over the booty inevitably arose among the Muslims, Muhammad said that he and Allah should get a fifth of the spoils of war: "If people [non-Muslims] are obstinate and refuse to surrender, know that Allah is your Supporter. And know that one fifth of all the booty you take belong to Allah, and to the Messenger, and for the near relatives (of Muhammad)" (Koran 8:40). While, as we have seen, a whole chapter of the Koran is dedicated to the rules for divvying up the spoils of war, not one is devoted to rooting out the seven deadly sins—including greed.

Islamic countries accuse the West of being materialistic, and unfortunately the West believes them. But Westerners should not be ashamed of the wealth they have accumulated from their own hard work. Islam was built on acquiring wealth through the seizure of the material goods of non-Muslims. In Islam there is no guilt or shame about capturing booty, which is described in the Koran as the holy and lawful gains Muslims are entitled to. The Islamic doctrine on the spoils of war in fact does promote the deadly sin of greed.

Gluttony

Gluttony, another one of the seven deadly sins, is an inordinate desire to consume more than you really need. The Bible points out how bad gluttony is for us: "For the drunkard and the glutton shall come to poverty: and drowsiness shall clothe a man with rags" (Proverbs 23:21).

Muhammad did advise his companions and wives not to eat too much, but gluttony is not really a sin in Islam. The Koran describes Paradise as a glutton's dream, with food, fruits, and rivers of wine.

During Ramadan, the Muslim month of fasting, Muslim consumption of basic food products doubles.[10] Muslims are supposed to fast from sunrise to sunset, but then they overeat and overindulge from sunset to sunrise. Islamic fasting, which forbids not only food but also water, is very harsh especially in a desert environment. But while the month of Ramadan is supposed to be holy, Muslims just turn their night into day and day into night, by sleeping all day and staying up all night eating.

And all the year round, with their wealth from oil, Muslims in Saudi Arabia and the Gulf states often indulge in exhibitionist and competitive exhibitions of wealth, including glamorous houses, shiny gold watches, and even gold swords. Saudis are known for a lifestyle of lavish excesses and extravagant gifts. When the late Saudi king Abdullah visited Obama in the White House he gave him gifts worth $1.3 million, prominent among which was a large gold necklace for the American president. The lavish Saudi lifestyle is not a cause of embarrassment for Muslims around the world, on the contrary it is looked upon with great admiration and envy.

The Wages of Sin

The Bible says that the "the wages of sin is death"' so how can Islam get away with embracing the seven deadly sins? When I was a Muslim I never heard a sermon preaching against envy, pride, anger, or even lust or greed in the Biblical sense. I never heard preaching about the importance of uplifting others, but heard a lot of preaching about guarding and defending one's pride and protecting oneself from envy and the evil eye.

I sometimes wonder, *When will the wages of sin eventually catch up with Islam?* I know that Islam as a religion is dying a slow and painful death. If it were not for petro-dollars, Islam would have disappeared in the twentieth century after the end of the Ottoman Empire.

The worldwide phenomenon of Islamic terrorism is not a sign of power but a cry for help by a dying religion. A religion that does not even believe in itself and must lie to survive. But unfortunately the West does not see it this way. Western counties keep trying to appease Muslim culture, rescuing Muslim refugees, and giving honor and respect to a dying religion that has been mired in sin for too long.

9

A REBELLION AGAINST THE TEN COMMANDMENTS

"He that saith, I know him, and keepeth not his Commandments, is a liar, and the truth is not in him."

—1 John 2:4

I n theory, Muslims accept the Bible as true revelation—except that they believe both Old and New Testaments to have been "corrupted" by the Jews and the Christians. In fact, Muhammad rejected the Golden Rule—"Therefore all things whatsoever ye would that men should do to you, do ye even so to them" (Matthew 7:12)—which is the essence of the Bible's moral teaching, and the Ten Commandments, which are summed up by that rule. Jihad is by its very nature a violation of the Bible's commandments. Islam replaced both the Golden Rule and the commandment "Thou shalt not kill" with "Kill your neighbor if he's a non-Muslim."

Jihad by its very nature promotes offensive war and terror against neighboring non-Muslim countries. That has produced bloody wars on the borders between Islam and its neighbors. Such a bloody relationship between Islam and the entire outside world requires a constant string of justifications, false claims, propaganda, and out-right lies—all to convince the West that Muslim violence is justified and to convince Muslims that they are the victims of the West. Arab media and history books are all about justifying jihad.

Love Your Neighbor versus Kill Your Neighbor

The Bible calls humanity to a higher standard. The Ten Commandments are divine commandments establishing the principles under which society and human beings can flourish and prosper. Jesus summed them—and all God's commands to us—up in the New Testament: "Thou shalt love the Lord thy God with all thy heart, and with all thy soul, and with all thy mind. This is the first and great commandment. And the second is like unto it, Thou shalt love thy neighbour as thyself. On these two commandments hang all the law and the prophets" (Matthew 22:37–40).

The endurance of the Ten Commandments is a testament to their wisdom. They are universal values that transcend cultural and historical differences. These Mosaic laws carry values and ideas that were revolutionary for their time. Even today many cultures and people all over the world are still struggling to live by them.

The Arabian culture of the seventh century did not struggle to abide by the Ten Commandments, but it was aware of them. Muhammad knew about the morality of the Bible, but he gave his new religion a morality that is exactly the opposite. While all of the Ten Commandments flow from the requirement that Christians and Jews must love God and their neighbors, all of Islamic law flows from the requirement that Muslims must kill their neighbors until and unless their neighbors submit to Islam. Islam does incorporate a few of the Ten Commandments into its morality, but puts them in service to Muhammad's new morality, which contradicts others of the Ten

Commandments and conflicts with the Bible's moral message on the deepest level.

Some advocates of Islamic Law in America today defend sharia by arguing that it is based on the Ten Commandments. Muqtedar Khan, for example, associate professor at the University of Delaware warns Americans against panicking about sharia because, as the title of his article puts it, "Sharia Is Based on Ten Commandments."[1]

Khan's equation of sharia with the Ten Commandments is incorrect, to say the least. In fact it is an assault on the truth and on the Word of God. If sharia is in harmony with the Ten Commandments and Biblical values, then why does the Koran declare the Bible corrupted and call on Muslims to kill Jews and Christians wherever they find them? Why does Islam declare that the Koran and sharia replace the Bible, if they are the same? It is time for Muslims to answer these questions truthfully and end the charade.

Muslims should be confronted and exposed for spreading lies about their own and other people's religions. Such lies are detrimental not only to the West but to Muslims themselves. It is high time they woke up from their fourteen-hundred-year slumber and self-deception.

Islam's Clash with the Ten Commandments

Sharia books never measure their laws by values of the Ten Commandments, but rather by the Koran and Muhammad's actions, lifestyle, and sayings. The Ten Commandments are mentioned in the Koran, but only as a historical reference to the Abrahamic roots Muhammad wanted to link his new religion to. Instead of adjusting to conform to the values of the Bible, Muhammad reversed them and claimed that Jews and Christians intentionally falsified their Bible. Islamic education has never taught the Ten

Commandments in schools; in fact it totally shuns anything that has to do with the Bible.

Sharia is in fact a breach of the Ten Commandments. The fact that majority Muslim countries are in a constant state of in-fighting, revolutions, and bloody repression, while Western nations are peaceful, is explained by the differences between the religious laws that have shaped the two cultures. Sharia creates constant strife. The Arab Spring failed precisely because sharia is the antithesis of the Biblical Ten Commandments. In every Islamic society there are at least two irreconcilable camps: those who want to strictly follow sharia and force it on everyone else, and those who want to relax it.

After every successful Islamic revolution when the old leader is pushed out or assassinated and a new leader is installed, there is typically a honeymoon period of brief jubilant celebrations. But the excitement and joy are quickly followed by disappointment, as Muslim society slips back to where it started—back into the bondage and tyranny of Sharia.

In his article, Professor Khan accuses Americans of being unreasonable, ignorant, or unjustifiably afraid. This is the accusation of "Islamophobia" that is always thrown at Western critics of Islam. But someone with the professor's level of education should know better. Why is the Middle East, still today, on fire, suffering from horrific civil wars? It is precisely because of sharia. The in-fighting between Muslims today is for the same reason as always—between two camps, those who want to soften sharia to make life more bearable, and those who want sharia to be enforced rigorously. There are no groups in any Muslim country today calling for no sharia; if they once existed they are dead.

What Professor Khan failed to notice is that the Islamic world is on fire over sharia and not over the Ten Commandments.

From the very beginning, Arabia's cutthroat culture clashed with values of the Ten Commandments. Islam came to preserve and not reform Arabian warring values, and that is why the Bible became the enemy of Islam.

Professor Khan's article accusing the West of freaking out about sharia is exactly the opposite of the reality of Islam in history. Muhammed did start by embracing the Biblical idea of one God, but when it came to actually living by Biblical standards and the values of the Ten Commandments, it was Muhammad who freaked out. They clashed with the cutthroat Arab culture Muhammad was committed to. At the very beginning of Islam, that cutthroat culture won out over the Biblical commandments. And even today the whole charade called sharia stands as a legal and religious impediment to abiding by the Ten Commandments, across the Middle East and beyond.

The First Commandment: Loyalty

"I am the LORD thy God, which have brought thee out of the land of Egypt, out of the house of bondage. Thou shalt have no other gods before me" (Exodus 20:2–3). This commandment is of supreme importance to our *personal* relationship with God, which should be based on loving and honoring Him. Jews and Christians are encouraged to become members of God's family and to relate to Him as children relate to their Father in a loving family. "And [I] will be a Father unto you, and ye shall be my sons and daughters, saith the Lord Almighty" (II Corinthians 6:18).

In Islam, the very idea of God as Father is offensive. According to the Koran, "The Jews and Christians say: We are sons of Allah and His loved ones. Say: Why then doth He chastise you for your sins? Nay, ye are but mortals of His creating. He forgiveth whom He will, and chastiseth whom He will...." According to the Koran if he truly loves you, Christians and Jews, and calls you his children, then how come he still punishes you for sin? This passage betrays Muhammad's bizarre views not only of God, but of fatherhood. Essentially he is asking, *Why aren't Jews and Christians spoiled brats, if they are truly the children of God?*

So who is the God of Islam, and what kind of relationship does he tell us to have with him?

The truth is, Allah is not the same as the God of Abraham, Isaac, and Jacob. To begin with, the historical roots of "Allah" have nothing to do with the Bible. It was a name for the chief pagan god of the Kaaba in Mecca before Muhammad. The name of Muhammad's father, who was a pagan himself and died before Muhammad was born, was Abdullah, meaning slave of Allah. And still today Abdullah is one of the most popular names in Islam.

Muhammed linked himself to all the prophets and other Biblical figures not only to gain legitimacy by the connection, but also to bring them down as inferior to him and Islam. In the process, Muhammad shredded the meaning of the Bible. For instance, in the Koran Jesus was just a prophet and not the Son of God. Islam's holy book does not stop there, but refers to Christians as idol worshipers and Jews as the worst of Allah's creation. Islam's view of God as He is represented in the Bible is that of falsifier, a liar, and a corrupter.

Islam's reversal of Biblical values is astounding. In the Bible, loyalty to God springs from love for God, who "loved us first" (I John 4:19). But Islam has no concept of God as loving and compassionate. As we have already seen, Islamic loyalty to Allah is based on fear and submission; the Muslim's relationship to God is that of a slave to his master. That is why the meaning of the word Islam is submission.

Islam does command loyalty to the one God. Those who do not believe in Allah are guilty of "shirk," which means believing in more than one God. Christians are counted as having committed "shirk" because Islam teaches that belief in the Trinity is equal to belief in three gods. Islam does not stop with labeling Christians idolators, but expects and entrusts Muslims to execute the "mushrikin"—the plural for those who commit shirk—if they refuse to convert to Islam (or failing that, Christians must submit to second class dhimmi status and pay the jizya tax, but that option is not available to Hindus and other non-Muslims who don't qualify as "people of the book"). Hence, a Muslim's loyalty to Allah requires that he kill non-Muslims. Thus Islam is enforcing one of the Ten Commandments, "Thou shalt have no other gods before me," by requiring the violation of another commandment, "Thou shalt not kill" (Exodus 20:13).

Islam has no understanding of the Biblical concept of loyalty to God out of love. Islamic loyalty to Allah is out of fear of a distant master who is eager to punish humans. With such a relationship to God setting the tone, Muslims' interpersonal relationships with other human beings are based not on love, but on fear, as we have already seen from numerous examples from the shame-based culture I grew up in.

Loyalty to the God of the Bible is completely compatible with love of friends and neighbors, and also with patriotism and good citizenship in the West. The same cannot be said for loyalty to Allah. In a July 16, 2015, article, Dr. Richard Swier asked, "Can Muslims Be Loyal to Anything Other than Allah?" He gave the example of Muslim Army major Nidal Malik Hasan, who decided to blast away at his fellow soldiers at Fort Hood, Texas, in November 2009, while yelling "Allahu Akbar." Upon joining the Army, Major Hasan had taken an oath of allegiance to defend the U.S. Constitution, to "bear true faith and allegiance to the same, without any mental reservations or purpose of evasion." But despite that oath, Hasan killed twelve of his fellow American soldiers with Allah's blessing. What the West does not understand is that Major Hasan's loyalty to Allah prevented him from being loyal to America and its citizens.

The same thing became clear at the trial of the Times Square bomber, Faisal Shahzad, a naturalized American citizen from Pakistan:

> Judge: "Didn't you swear allegiance to this country when you became an American citizen?"
> Shahzad: "I did swear, but I did not mean it."
> Judge: "You took a false oath?"
> Shahzad: "Yes."[2]

It is important to mention here that taking a false oath under a non-Muslim legal system is entirely legal under Sharia. Committed Muslims know that swearing falsely and lying are proofs of their loyalty to Allah. Islamic loyalty to Allah once again proves to be a twisted form of loyalty that violates another of the Ten Commandments: "Thou shalt not bear false witness against thy neighbor" (Exodus 20:16).

The Second Commandment: Worship

The Second Commandment says, "Thou shalt not make unto thee any graven image, or any likeness of any thing that is in heaven above, or that is in the earth beneath, or that is in the water under the earth. Thou shalt not bow down thyself to them, nor serve them" (Exodus 20:4–5). It forbids us to betray our love of Him by bowing down to meaningless idols. This commandment protects our special relationship with our Creator, who made us in His likeness and continues to mold us into His spiritual image.

Islam does enforce the Second Commandment, like the First—but at the cost of breaking the others, and also with one strange exception that I explain below.

Muhammed started his movement by rejecting idolatry after he was exposed to Jewish and Christian preaching. At first the Prophet did not use violence to convert others to Islam, but that got him nowhere. Eventually Muhammad saw that the only way he was going to be victorious was—as he himself said—through terror. The day Muhammad made the decision to be a warrior and use holy terror to expand his religion was the day he collided with the Ten Commandments and Biblical values.

Muhammad's use of terror devalues human life, which separates him from values of the Commandments. When he ordered the killing and beheading of those who disagreed with him, Muhammad was committing a crime against God.

And strangely, Islam contradicts itself on idolatry: when Muhammad conquered the Kaaba from the "idol worshippers" and claimed it as an Islamic holy site, Muslims retained it as a holy place and even kept one of the idols that was worshipped there prior to Islam: the Black Stone. As John Calvin, the influential French theologian and reformer during the Protestant Reformation, said, "So today the [Muslim] Turks, although they proclaim at the top of their lungs that the Creator of heaven and earth is God, still, while repudiating Christ, substitute an idol in place of the true God."

The Third Commandment: Reverence and Respect

"Thou shalt not take the name of the LORD thy God in vain" (Exodus 20:7). The Third Commandment is about how we communicate our feelings about God to others and how we address and view Him in our thoughts.

We have already seen how so many of the names that Islam gives to Allah describe truly evil behavior: "Deceiver," "Prideful," "the Humiliator," and so forth. Muhammad absolutely took the name of the Lord in vain. In fact, he replaced the true God with an impostor called Allah. Because Muhammad altered the attributes and nature of the God of the Bible to fit Islam, Allah is no longer the same God of the Bible but a fake replacement. That is the ultimate violation of the Third Commandment, which forbids taking the Lord's name in vain.

Muhammad plagiarized the Bible, distorted and denied its true message in the Koran, and claimed the true Bible had been corrupted. He then claimed all the glory of the God of the Bible for Allah and all the holiness of the Bible for the Koran. Even on his deathbed, Muhammad was still commanding his followers to chase and kill all the Jews, who knew about his plagiarism and falsification of their scriptures, all the way to Jerusalem, their Holy Land. Muslims followed his orders, conquered Jerusalem and built a mosque right on top of the ruins of Solomon's Temple.

The Fourth Commandment: Sanctification through Our Relationship to God

The Fourth Commandment requires us to "Remember the sabbath day, to keep it holy":

> Six days shalt thou labour, and do all thy work:
> But the seventh day is the sabbath of the LORD thy God: in it thou shalt not do any work, thou, nor thy son, nor thy daughter, thy manservant, nor thy maidservant, nor thy cattle, nor thy stranger that is within thy gates:
> For in six days the LORD made heaven and earth, the sea, and all that in them is, and rested the seventh day: wherefore the LORD blessed the sabbath day, and hallowed it.

The Hebrews observed a day of rest for all human beings, whom they believed to be made in the image of God. The Sabbath was to be kept holy to renew body and soul.

The Sabbath was yet another revolutionary idea for its time. In other ancient cultures, rest was a luxury reserved to the lucky and wealthy few. The world was divided between a few masters and many slaves, who worked with no rest.

The notion of a Sabbath day of rest to keep holy is not found in the Koran. Islam does make Friday the day when Muslims gather to pray in the mosque. Some Islamic theocracies, such as Saudi Arabia, harshly punish those who neglect to attend Friday prayers, and in less radical countries Muslims who disobey suffer from social shaming and threats. But the Koran states that the Sabbath day of complete rest is only required for Jews (16:124).

Muslims do fight in jihadist wars on Fridays and also during the holy month of Ramadan. In fact, Islamic terror attacks against Coptic Christians in Egypt increase on Fridays. Many Muslims are off of work on Friday, and mosque Friday sermons often call them to do jihadist attacks on non-Muslims. That explains why more attacks happen on Fridays when Muslims leave mosques angry and ready for holy attacks on the enemies of Allah. Jihadist terror is considered a religious duty and a holy act under Islam. Friday is a holy day, so holy acts of jihadist terror fit in beautifully.[3]

The Fifth Commandment:
Respect for Parental Authority

The Fifth Commandment is "Honour thy father and thy mother" (Exodus 20:12). Islam does command children to be "good and dutiful" to parents in many Koran verses. On the other hand, there are Koran verses that encourage Muslim children to disassociate themselves from their non-Muslim parents: "Choose not your fathers nor your brethren for friends if they take pleasure in disbelief rather than faith [in Islam]" (9:23). That in itself is not so different from a few New Testament passages that say that Jesus will bring division (Luke 12:51–53), and warn Christians they may have to choose between family and God: "And every one that hath forsaken houses, or brethren, or sisters, or father, or mother, or wife, or children, or lands, for my name's sake, shall receive an hundredfold, and shall inherit everlasting life" (Matthew 19:29).

But there is nothing in the New Testament like the sharia law that completely undercuts the relationship between children and parents by allowing parents to kill their children with impunity: "a father or mother (or their fathers or mothers) will not be subject to prosecution for killing their offspring, or offspring's offspring" (*Reliance of the Traveller* o1.1-2 p. 584). That law strikes at the heart of love and trust between parents and children.

Thus "honor killing" of family members is a protected right of parents and grandparents under Islamic law. How can a child honor his parents under such conditions, when parents are encouraged by the laws of their religion to care more about their honor than their kids?

The Sixth Commandment: Respect for Human Life

"Thou shalt not kill," says the Sixth Commandment (Exodus 20:13). According to the Bible, taking another person's life is a sin; it is not our right to decide whether they live or die. And Biblical values on the respect for human life go beyond avoiding murder. God requires that we not maliciously harm another human being in word or deed: "Whosoever hateth his brother is a murderer: and you know that no murderer has eternal life abiding in him" (I John 3:15). The

God of the Bible teaches us that life is precious; He wants us to build life and not destroy it.

Western culture takes for granted that all religions share the same basic principles, including considering killing to be a major sin. But the contrast between the Bible and the Koran is most glaring here. It is on the subject of killing that Muhammad's reversal of Biblical values becomes crystal clear. Not only does Islam reject the Sixth Commandment, it actually enshrines killing as the most important form of worship and devotion to Allah. "Killing Jews is Worship that draws us close to Allah" is an Islamic slogan that you can see repeated by members of Hamas on Palestinian television.[4]

Commandments to kill and terrorize are in abundant supply in the Koran, hadiths, and sharia, as we have already seen. Those who murder under the title of holy jihad are honored as "shahid" for the sake of Allah—like my thirty-five-year-old father, sent by the Egyptian government on a mission to "slay and [be] slain," as the Koran says (9:111), when I was eight. He killed Jews, and he got killed in the process. Meanwhile, suicide is not permitted under Islamic law—with one exception; if it is done in a "martyrdom" operation. In other words, as long as the person committing suicide kills others for jihad.

Islam has totally inverted the Sixth Commandment. While Christians and Jews are bound by their covenant with God not to kill, Muslims are under a covenant to do war, "Fighting is prescribed for Muslims" (Koran 2.216). As we have seen, Allah even reprimands Muslims who stay home to avoid fighting: "Not equal are believers who sit home and receive no hurt and those who Fight in Allah's Cause with their wealth and lives. Allah has granted a grade higher to those who Fight with their possessions and bodies to those who sit home. Those who Fight He has distinguished with a special reward" (Koran 4:95).

Muslims often have no choice but jihad because those who flee from fighting are promised Hell—and sometimes killed by other Muslims. The Koran says, "If you march not forth, He will punish you with a painful torment and will replace you with another people, and you cannot harm Him at all, and Allah is able to do all things" (9:39). "Refusing to perform jihad and fleeing from combat with unbelievers" is not just a sin, though, but also a crime against Islam (*Reliance of the Traveller* w52.1, 369–70). As Muslim authorities teach, even today, and even in countries where Muslims are a minority: "Those who reject jihad are considered infidels."[5]

Relentless commandments to fight and kill are all over the Koran: "fight with the ringleaders of the unbelief.... Will you not fight against those people who have broken their oaths, conspired to expel the Messenger and were the first to attack you? Do you fear them? Nay, it is Allah Who is more deserving of your fear.... Fight them; Allah will punish them by your hands and humiliate them. He will grant you victory over them and heal the hearts of a believing people." (9:12–15). "Fight those people of the Book (Jews and Christians) who do not believe in Allah and the Last Day... until they pay Jizya (protection tax) with their own hands and feel themselves subdued" (9:29).

Let me list the different commandments to kill the different classes of people who are named as targets by Muslim scriptures, with citations to the Koran verses and hadith passages that command the killing:

1. Kill idolators wherever you find them (9:5, 22:19–22)
2. Kill Jews everywhere and anywhere, even if they hide from Muslims (Bukhari 4:52:177)
3. Kill Christians if they violate the dhimmi treaty or don't pay jizya tax (Koran 9:29)
4. Kill apostates, that is Muslims who leave Islam (Koran 4:89 and o8:4, and Bukhari, 4.52.260)

5. Kill (and torture) non-Muslims who resist Islamic jihad: "The only reward of those who make war upon Allah and His messenger and strive after corruption in the land will be that they will be killed or crucified, or have their hands and feet on alternate sides cut off, or will be expelled out of the land. Such will be their degradation in the world, and in the Hereafter theirs will be an awful doom" (Koran 5:33)

6. Kill non-Muslims who preach the gospel to Muslims, or otherwise lead them away from Islam (p. 609, o11.10)

7. Kill homosexuals (Abu Dawud, 4447), burn and throw them off of buildings alive (Mishkat, vol. 1, p. 765)

8. Kill those who commit blasphemy against Muhammad or Allah—even if they repent—including all of the following:

    - Reviling Allah or his Messenger
    - Being sarcastic about "Allah's name, His command, His interdiction, His promise, or His threat"
    - Denying any verse of the Koran or "anything which by scholarly consensus belongs to it, or to add a verse that does not belong to it"
    - Holding that "any of Allah's messengers or prophets are liars, or to deny their being sent"
    - Reviling the religion of Islam
    - Being sarcastic about any ruling of the Sacred Law (sharia)
    - Denying that Allah intended "the Prophet's message…to be the religion followed by the entire world" (*Reliance of the Traveler* pp. 59798, o8.7)

As we know to our sorrow, Allah's command to Muslims to murder is not a relic of the bloody past. We have already seen that one Islamic preacher has recently promoted stabbing while wielding a knife and yelling "Stab!" Another Islamic cleric, Abu Hamza al-Masri, said to his followers, "Killing a Kafir who is fighting you is OK. Killing a Kafir for any reason, you can say, it is OK—even if there is no reason for it. You can poison, ambush and kill non-believers. You must have a stand with your heart, with your tongue, with your money, with your hand, with your sword, with our Kalashnikov. Don't ask shall I do this, just do it."

"Glory kneels before you" were words spoken at the funeral of two Arab terrorists who recently boarded a bus in Jerusalem with a gun and a knife and murdered Haviv Haim (age seventy-eight), Alon Govberg (fifty-one), and Richard Lakin (seventy-six).[6] This is how Islam rewards those who kill the enemies of Allah and places them on a pedestal. There are many verses in the Koran that are specifically designed to relieve Muslims of any kind of guilt for killing Allah's enemies. The Koran comforts killers by saying it is not your hands that are doing the killing but Allah's: "It is not ye who Slew them; it is God" (8:17).

Khalid Sheik Mohammed, the 9/11 mastermind, told American authorities after being captured: "See, I told you, I cut Daniel's throat with these blessed hands." The God of Islam considered the hands of KSM blessed for cutting the throat of Daniel Pearl.[7]

The Seventh Commandment: Purity in Relationships

The Bible, as we have already seen, condemns adultery for both men and women, while in Islam it is almost always only women who are declared guilty, caught, and punished for sexual sins. The Seventh Commandment simply says, "Thou shalt not commit adultery"

(Exodus 20:14). It forbids the violation of the marriage covenant by willful participation in sexual activity with someone other than one's spouse. Adultery leads to the corruption of the institution of marriage, which is established by God as between one man and one woman (Genesis 2:24 and Matthew 19:5).

The Bible promotes loyalty between spouses, something that is impossible in Muslim marriage because of the polygamy and sexual slavery permitted in the Koran and sharia. Allah told Muhammad: "O Prophet! surely We have made lawful to you your wives whom you have given their dowries, and those whom your right hand possesses out of those whom Allah has given to you as prisoners of war..." (Koran 33.50). The phrase "those whom your right hand possesses" means slaves.

Muslims look at loyalty in marriage and adultery in a totally different way from Christians and Jews. Adultery is a crime punishable by death or stoning in Islam. Muhammad himself ordered the stoning of adulterers: "Two people guilty of 'illegal' intercourse are brought to Muhammad, who orders them both stoned to death." Apparently their act was out of love, since the verse records the man as trying to "shield the woman from the stones" (Bukhari 6:60:79). Adultery is easy to detect in women, who must be loyal to one husband, but it is a totally different story for men. Loyalty to one wife is not required in Islam. In addition to allowing polygamy, there are many legal loopholes in sharia, as we have already seen, that allow men to have sex with women who are not their (permanent) wives.

Most victims of honor killings in the Muslim world are women. There are at least five thousand *reported* honor killings of Muslim women annually for the crime of having sex outside of marriage.[8] The unreported cases could be even higher. Here again, Islam seems to obey one of the Ten Commandments—but only by breaking another one: "Thou shalt not kill."

The Eighth Commandment: Honesty

The Bible says "Thou shalt not steal" (Exodus 20:15). In Islam, stealing is also a sin. But not always. In fact, Muslims have a right to seize the kafirs' property.

In the West, where society's rules were formed by the Bible, the Eighth Commandment safeguards everyone's right to acquire and keep property they own legitimately. Without a strong respect for other people's property, society would be chaotic.

In Islam, stealing is a sin punishable by the amputation of limbs. Muhammad said, "The hand should be cut off for stealing something that is worth a quarter of a Dinar or more" (Bukhari 81:780). Muslims still practice amputation for stealing today.

But let us not be fooled by Islam's harsh punishment for stealing into thinking that Islam is serious about stealing under any conditions. Just as with murder and lying, Islam only forbids stealing under certain conditions—namely, when a Muslims steals from other Muslims.

Killing and stealing are interconnected in Islam. Because after killing non-Muslims in jihad Muslims are encouraged and awarded with their property, their homes, businesses, women, and children. As we have already seen, these are called legitimate spoils of war or booty. Thus forcefully taking the property of unbelievers is not considered stealing under Islam but a legitimate right: "And He caused you to inherit their land and their houses and their wealth, and land ye have not trodden. Allah is ever Able to do all things" (Koran 33:27).

In the Koran, Allah himself gave Muhammad the right to take the property of the Jews after he beheaded between six and nine hundred Jewish men in two days: "What Allah has bestowed on His Messenger (and taken away) from them [the Jews]—for this ye made no expedition with either cavalry or camelry: but Allah gives power to His messengers over any He pleases: and Allah has power over all things" (59:6).

Even today, a leading imam who is also a professor at Rhodes College in Memphis, Tennessee, has said, "Muslims have the right to take the property of filthy Christians and Jews." That is Yasir Qadhi, who was described by the *New York Times Magazine* as "one of the most influential conservative clerics in American Islam."[9] Qadhi justifies stealing from Jews and Christians as "a means to establish monotheism on the land." He quotes Muhammad saying "I have been commanded to fight the people until they" convert and explains that "if they don't, their life and property are halal [free for the taking] to the Muslims."[10]

So the excuse for allowing Muslims to steal from non-Muslims is for the purpose of spreading monotheism! It seems that Islam never got the news that Judaism and Christianity were always monotheistic religions, way before Islam came into existence. But even if they were not, is converting people a legitimate justification for stealing in a major world religion? Apparently it is.

The Prophet Muhammad bragged, "I have been given five things which were not given to any one else before me. 1. Allah made me victorious by His terrorizing my enemies. 2. The earth has been made for me. 3. Booty has been made lawful for me yet it was not lawful for anyone else before me. 4. I have been given the right of intercession. 5. Every Prophet used to be sent to his nation only but I have been sent to all mankind" (Bukhari vol 1: 331).

ISIS in Iraq and Syria is openly stealing not only from non-Muslim minorities, but also from believers in other sects of Islam, such as the Shiites. They are also stealing antiquities from museums, and what they can't carry away they destroy. Reuters reported on December 28, 2015, that the Islamic State has set up departments to handle "war spoils," including slaves, and the exploitation of natural resources such as oil.[11]

The following is an excerpt from a televised sermon by prominent Egyptian sheikh Abu Ishak al Huweini, waxing lyrical about the benefits of stealing from non-Muslims:

> … Jihad for the sake of Allah is a pleasure, a true pleasure. Mohammed's followers used to compete to do it. The reason we are poor now is because we have abandoned jihad. If only we can conduct a jihadist invasion at least once a year or if possible twice or three times, then many people on Earth would become Muslims. And if anyone prevents our dawa [proselytizing] or stands in our way, then we must kill them or take as hostage and confiscate their wealth, women and children. Such battles will fill the pockets of the Mujahid who can return home with 3 or 4 slaves, women and, children. This can be a profitable business if you multiply each head [slaves] by 300 or 400 dirham. This can be like financial shelter to a jihadist, in time of financial need, can always sell one of these heads [slaves]. No one can make that much money in one deal (from hard work….[12]

The Ninth Commandment: Truthfulness

In the Bible, lying is a sin: "Thou shalt not bear false witness against thy neighbor" (Exodus 20:16). In Islam, lying and slander are a religious obligation—if they're for the benefit of Islam.

The Ninth Commandment tells us that our lives, thoughts and behavior should be anchored to truth. If we truly love people then we must not lie to or otherwise deceive them.

There is no hesitation or double talk about the importance of truth in the Bible. "And ye shall know the truth, and the truth shall make you free," says Jesus (John 8:32). He describes Himself as "the way, the truth, and the life" (John 14:6). The Psalmist asks, "Lord, who shall abide in thy tabernacle? who shall dwell in thy holy hill? He that walketh uprightly, and worketh righteousness, and speaketh the truth in his heart" (15:1–2).

As with stealing, Islam has many loopholes and contradictions regarding lying and speaking the truth. We already saw in chapter three many of the Islamic sources permit lying or even require it as an obligation.

A religion that is not clear about what is sin and what is not with regard to such a basic moral issue as lying versus telling the truth does a great deal of harm to any society where it holds sway. In Islamic countries, one Muslim may gain respect and rewards for lying to non-Muslims to protect Islam, while another may be harshly punished for telling the truth—for example, the many journalists who have been jailed and even executed because they told stories the government wanted to suppress. These are the fruits of Islam, which has produced a society that is uncomfortable with the truth, and more comfortable lying.

How can Muslims trust a God who is proud to call himself the greatest deceiver? How can they emulate a prophet who lies, kills, and steals? If Allah allows them to lie to expand the power of Islam, then how do they know Allah and Muhammad weren't doing the very same thing in the Koran itself—in other words, how can they even trust that Allah and Muhammad are who they claim to be?

The day Islam gambled with its own credibility and reputation by obliging its followers to lie for the purpose of expansion, was the day it condemned itself to perpetually trying to cover up previous lies and justifying and defending itself to a world that has no trust and only fear of Islam. Islam is in a constant stressful and draining race to cover up and camouflage its lies and hide and disguise its true goals and intentions.

Various Islamist groups—not just Al Qaeda and ISIS—instruct their members on how to conceal themselves to avoid being detected in their efforts to spread Islam and sharia to the West: avoid mosques, shave your beard, and even wear a Christian cross in order to blend in.[13] Several Arab students who attacked my views when I spoke on college campuses were wearing crosses to give the impression that they were Middle East Christians who support Islam. But their anger at my criticism of Islamic law left no doubt in my mind that they were Muslims and not Christian Arabs.

This kind of Islamic deception is going on all over our university campuses in America. Islam has been trying to build itself up in the U.S. by using deception.

Meanwhile, in the Middle East, Islam has been proving—by trying to build stable and successful societies and governments with no success—that a foundation of lies is a shaky foundation for a society. Instead of repenting, reforming, and asking for forgiveness for its history of lies, Islamic society has been fighting the truth for fourteen hundred year and counting.

Americans know that their country is the land of the free and the home of the brave, but how many fully understand why? As long as the U.S. sticks with Biblical values, including the truth, it will always be free.

It is a miracle of the Holy Spirit that I was saved from the jaws of a religion that punishes truth-tellers. I consider myself a living example of what the Bible means when it says that "the truth shall make you free" (John 8:32)

The Tenth Commandment: Contentment

The Tenth Commandment says, "Thou shalt not covet thy neighbour's house, thou shalt not covet thy neighbour's wife, nor his manservant, nor his maidservant, nor his ox, nor his ass, nor any thing that is thy neighbour's" (Exodus 20:17). The focus of the Tenth Commandment is on our hearts and minds. It tells us not to covet, meaning desire or crave the possession of something that belongs to somebody else. Not all desires are immoral, but coveting is an improper longing for what is not rightfully ours. It can lead us to greater sin, and that is why God warned us against it. Instead of coveting, the Bible advises us to do the opposite—to rejoice when other people are blessed.

By asking us not to covet, the Bible encourages us to look deep within ourselves to uncover our thinking and motivation. That self-examination turns us to repentance and God's grace in a wonderful process for cleansing ourselves from the kind of thinking that can lead us to sin and guilt.

The Tenth Commandment is utterly alien to Islamic values and the example of Muhammad. Muhammad was a very intelligent man, but not analytical or a deep thinker. He never commanded Muslims to do a self-examination of their minds and hearts to stop them from thinking along lines that could lead them into evil acts of sin. In fact Muhammad lured his followers by promising to fulfill their covetous desires.

Muhammad took pride in doing precisely what the Tenth Commandment forbids. The Prophet's life is a series of examples of coveting without restraint. He called those he coveted his enemies and the enemies of Allah to justify his improper desires. Muhammad literally charged into stripping his enemies of their possessions, homes, property, trading caravan goods, women, and children. And he called this killing, raping, and ransacking a divine service and worship of God.

Muhammad did not just covet the possessions of his non-Muslim enemies. When he desired the wife of his adopted son Ali, he came up with a new revelation making it legitimate and holy for Ali to divorce his wife and for Muhammad to marry her.

Muhammad was extremely envious of the Jews of Medina, especially when they refused to convert to his new faith. After Muhammad beheaded all the male members of the Jewish tribe, he had his first pick of the young wives. He forced one of them to have sex with him the very night he beheaded her husband. This horrifying behavior is all documented in Islamic books on the life story of Muhammad, which never refer to it with shame, but instead with pride. That is the tragedy of Islamic values—Muslims are prevented by their religion from telling good from evil.

The whole concept of jihad is a brazen violation of the Tenth Commandment, because it means conquest over non-Muslims and taking what they have. Jihad has taken Muslims into some very dark places, allowing them to commit horrible crimes to achieve the objects they covet: forced sexual slavery, beheading, flogging, torture, terror, lying, and so forth.

Even after he had conquered all of Arabia, Muhammad still coveted more. His desire for conquest of other people and their possessions had no limits. After his death, his followers continued to conquer and plunder the wealth of other civilizations, such as Egypt and Persia.

Muhammad's Appropriation of the Bible

But Muhammad didn't just take what he coveted from other civilizations. He also stole from other religions—namely Christianity and Judaism, the religions based on the Bible.

Muhammad coveted the honor and glory of God Himself. He coveted the moral authority of Jesus, the Son of God. So Muhammad called the Bible corrupted and replaced Jesus with himself as God's legitimate representative on Earth. The Koran claims that Jesus will come back as a Muslim, deny the Bible, and proclaim Islam the correct religion for humanity. And Muhammad used the authority he had stolen to set up a morality that is in opposition to the Ten Commandments, and that authorized him to act on his own lusts and greed. But to oppose the Ten Commandments is to oppose God, His blessings, the truth, and reality itself. That is where the uncontrollable darkness of coveting, envy, lust, and sin led one man—and is now leading 1.6 billion Muslims, nearly a quarter of the world's population.

10

MENTAL HEALTH IN THE BIBLE VS. MENTAL HEALTH IN ISLAM

R eligion should provide its followers with comfort, guidance, and a sense of order and meaning in life. Religion should be able to help its followers develop sound thinking and healthy choices; in other words, a sound religion will be in harmony with mental health.

One thing that felt amazing to me once I started to read the Bible were the many verses that talk about a sound, sober, and healthy mind, emotions, and heart: "For God hath not given us the spirit of fear; but of power, and of love, and of a sound mind" (II Timothy 1:7); "And be not conformed to this world: but be ye transformed by the renewing of your mind, that ye may prove what is that good, and acceptable, and perfect, will of God" (Romans 12:2); "Set your affection on things above, not on things on the earth" (Colossians 3:2); "Let not your heart be troubled" (John 14:1).

A sound mind is a low priority in Islam. The psychological profile of Muslim society that we have seen in previous chapters is not a healthy one: cursing, anger, hatred, vindictiveness, controlling and punishing others, and no value for self-control. Islamic culture punishes truth-tellers and rewards those who lie and slander. It discourages openness and forces Muslims to live in a mental fortress.

What is considered mentally unhealthy in the West is often considered good in Islamic society. For instance Islam does not admit any conflict between beating women and honoring them. A Saudi family therapist has explained why wife-beating is a good thing.[1] Another Saudi authority, Dr. Abdul-Rahman al-Sheha, has said, "Submissive or subdued women...may even enjoy being beaten at times as a sign of love and concern...."[2]

The relationship between Muslims and their God is not healthy. As portrayed in the Koran, it is like a dysfunctional family relationship, characterized by resentment and recrimination. Allah often looks down on his creation as ungrateful and thankless followers: "Most Men thank Not" (Koran 2:243). "[E]ven after that, We pardoned you in order that ye might give thanks" (Koran 2:52). A common refrain from Allah throughout the Koran is "laalakum tashkurun" meaning "wouldn't you give thanks [to Allah]?"

Like Allah Muslims often accuse others of being thankless and ungrateful. It is not uncommon for family members and parents to angrily accuse even little children of being thankless and ungrateful—something I heard many times, both in my own home and in other Muslim families. The psychological impact of being addressed that way when I was only eight years old was horrendous.

It is not uncommon to see Muslims offer someone help, then shortly afterward brag about it to others and accuse those they offered the favor to of being ungrateful. Some Muslims even offer others favors for the sole purpose of being regarded as givers to thankless people. Allah set the example for this unhealthy passive-aggressive behavior in the Koran.

My feelings of guilt from being called thankless as a child took a long time to heal. The God of the Bible is the reason for my full healing and recovery. The God of Abraham, Isaac, and Jacob saved me from Allah's constant condemnation.

As someone who knew nothing about the Bible before I came to America, I am almost in a constant state of wonder at how precious it is to feel God's acceptance, love, and grace. It is an incredible honor for God to tell us, the terribly needy humanity on this Earth, that He is pleased with His creation, that He wants to find the good in us and help us bring it out, and that He sent His Son in the flesh to save us through His grace and not our works. The God of the Bible lifts us up and rejoices over us: "The Lord thy God in the midst of thee is mighty; he will save, he will rejoice over thee with joy; he will rest in his love, he will joy over thee with singing" (Zephaniah 3:17).

But one does not even have to be a devout Christian to be blessed by Biblical values and to benefit from the principles of good living and a sound mind that they support. As an outsider who came to this country after thirty years in the Muslim world, I can see very clearly just by living in the U.S.—even if one is an atheist who hates the Bible—that the benefits of a healthy culture shaped by the Biblical Fruits of the Spirit are everywhere, plentiful for the taking.

Islamic Doctrines That Undermine Mental Health

The values of Islam stand in stark contradiction to the basic principles of mental health that are accepted throughout the West. Islamic culture cannot comprehend what a free mind can do.

There are some features of Middle East society that are attractive, and even comforting, to certain aspects of human nature, but judging from my own personal experience and the experience of the millions of Muslim refugees flocking to the West, life under Islamic culture is challenging to mental health.

Islam teaches that jihadist expansion is the number one goal of a Muslim, and everything is sacrificed for jihad: family happiness and physical and mental health and well-being. In pursuit of jihad, Islamic culture has to use brainwashing and mind control tactics similar to those used by totalitarian regimes. And Muslim leaders boast that jihad—hurting and killing others to spread Islam—has become an addiction to them.[3]

Everything that the God of the Bible tells us to do is for our benefit. Following His commandments will not damage anyone; it will only improve our mental health. Forgiveness of one's enemies, for example, is beneficial to the one who forgives. On the other hand, many of Islam's commandments and laws tell Muslims to do things that will surely hurt them and hurt others.

"Targhib wa tarhib," for example, is an Islamic doctrine that means "seducing (luring) and terrorizing." It sanctions the use of lure and terror as a tool for "dawa" (Islamic evangelism) and in Islamic education. It amounts to manipulating the instinctive parts of the human brain with extreme opposing pressures—highly rewarding, then severely punishing—to brainwash people into compliance with Islam.

Most ordinary Muslims are unaware of this doctrine, but books have been written about it.[4] Mainstream Muslim sheikhs such as Salman Al Awda have discussed it on Al Jazeerah TV. On a show called *Sharia and Life*, he recommended "to Exaggerate" "Reward and Punishment, morally and materially" "in Both Directions" and said, "The use of terror under this doctrine is a legitimate sharia obligation."[5] People in the West think of terror as something that Islamic jihadists inflict on non-Muslims, and it is. But terror is also the mechanism for ensuring compliance within Islam. Terror is the threat that keeps jihadists on their missions, and that makes ordinary Muslims obey sharia.

An online course for recruiting jihadists contains this description:

> Individual Da`wa depends on eliciting emotional responses from recruits (and building a personal relationship. Abu `Amr's approach illustrates a recruitment concept called al-targhib wa'l-tarhib, which is a carrot-and-stick technique of extolling the benefits of action while explaining the frightening costs of inaction. The concept was introduced in the Qur'an and is discussed by many Islamic thinkers exploring the best way to call people to Islam (several scholars, for example, have written books titled al-targhib wa'l-tarhib). According to Abu `Amr, recruiters should apply the concept throughout the recruitment process, but emphasize the benefits of action early in the process and the costs of inaction later.[6]

In other words, recruiters of jihadists should start by emphasizing the "lure"—the future glory, supremacy and fulfillment of every lustful wish, such as for virgins in heaven. Later, they should threaten the recruits with "terror" and shame—the consequence if they fail to participate in jihad.

Part of the "tarhib" or "terrorizing" side of this doctrine is to make a cruel example of those who do not comply with the requirements of Islam. That is the reason Muslim countries such as Saudi Arabia, Iran, and ISIS intentionally hold ceremonial public beheadings, floggings, and amputation of limbs. Countries like Egypt, Jordan, and Turkey are more discrete, but they are tolerant of honor killings, the killing of apostates, torture and murder in their jails, and the beating of women and children. The doctrine of "targhib" and "tarhib" is alive and well, not just in Islamic theocracies but also in the so-called "moderate" Muslim countries.

Islam has been using torturous brainwashing techniques and cruel and unusual punishment from its inception until today. While the Bible is in harmony with and nurtures human nature, Islam does the opposite—it uses the human instincts for survival and self-preservation to break the will of human beings and brainwash them into slavish obedience.

Like the majority of Muslims, I never heard of this foundational Islamic doctrine when I was growing up. But even though I have only learned about this doctrine in the last few years, I did suffer from its presence in my life, in the Islamic preaching I heard, in day-to-day life in a Muslim country, in my family relations, and also in how the government operated and how people of authority, in general, treated the people under them.

"Al-wala' wal bara'," meaning "loyalty and enmity," is another Islamic doctrine with detrimental effects on the mental health of Muslims. Islam dictates to Muslims who their friends and enemies should be. The lines are clearly marked. Muslims are required to conduct their relationships, loyalties, and hostilities according to Islam's rules, to befriend some and to assign permanent animosity to others, under penalty of treason to their religion.

This Islamic doctrine tells Muslims who their permanent friends are and who their permanent enemies are. This is essential for jihad, in order to keep Muslims from ever softening toward non-Muslims. Muslims must be eternally unforgiving and unfriendly toward non-Muslims, until they covert to or submit to Islam.

Osama bin Laden once wrote,

> As to the relationship between Muslims and infidels, this is summarized by the Most High's Word.... "We renounce

you. Enmity and hate shall forever reign between us—till you believe in Allah alone" (Koran 60:4). So there is an enmity, evidenced by fierce hostility from the heart. And this fierce hostility—that is, battle—ceases only if the infidel submits to the authority of Islam, or if his blood is forbidden from being shed (a *dhimmi*), or if Muslims are (at that point in time) weak and incapable (of spreading *sharia* law to the world). But if the hate at any time extinguishes from the heart, this is great apostasy!... Such, then, is the basis and foundation of the relationship between the infidel and the Muslim. Battle, animosity, and hatred—directed from the Muslim to the infidel—is the foundation of our religion.[7]

Notice that Islam condemns Muslims whose hatred for non-Muslims "extinguishes from their heart" as apostates. That means that the death penalty awaits Muslims who no longer hate non-Muslims.

Islam has neatly divided humanity between the innocent, sin-free, and good Muslims and the wicked, misguided, unclean, and doomed non-Muslims. Below are some Koran verses that support this doctrine as expounded above by Osama bin Laden:

- "Do not take Jews and Christians as friends or protectors" (5:51)
- "Do not take My [Allah's] enemies and your enemies as allies, extending to them affection while they have disbelieved.... If you have come out of jihad in My cause and seeking My approval, take them not as friends.... You show friendship to them in secret, while I am All-Aware of what you conceal and what you reveal" (60:1)

- "Verily, we are free from [have disowned] you and whatever you worship besides Allah, we have rejected you, and there has started between us and you, hostility and hatred for ever, until you believe in Allah Alone" (60:4)

The apparently perpetual Arab-Israeli conflict is one result of Islam's assignment of non-Muslims, and particularly Jews, to the status of permanent enemies of Muslims. Muslims call Israel the little Satan and America the great Satan for the same reason. It is also why Middle East Christians and other minorities can never find true friendship and equality in Muslim countries.

Even when Muslims move to non-Muslim countries their preachers, their holy books, and their religious laws tell them that their loyalty must remain with the "ummah" (the worldwide Islamic community) rather than go to the new kafir country they move to. That law of loyalty to Islam is an absolute duty, under penalty of apostasy.

In a discussion on the impossibility of unity between Hindus and Muslims, Bengali poet and philosopher Rabindranath Tagore (1861–1941) said, "...under no circumstances is it permissible for any Mohammedan, whatever be his country, to stand against any Mohammedan."

The doctrine of "loyalty and enmity" should be a warning to the West, which is absorbing large numbers of Muslim refugees. The unity of any country that absorbs Muslims will sooner or later be threatened.

The doctrine of "loyalty and enmity" stands in the way of the healthy functioning of society at all levels. It has had very negative effects on interpersonal relationships between Muslims as well. This is because such extreme hatred for anyone eventually afflicts the human heart with harshness, unforgiveness, and lack of empathy, even for the people one is supposed to love.

In Muslim society, distrust is common and friendships are guarded. Alliances and loyalties among Muslims are never guaranteed to last; they can flip on a dime. This is because friendships are not based on personal choice or genuine affection. That's true not just between Muslims and non-Muslims, but also within the Muslim community, where relationships depend on who each person is in the order or hierarchy of the family and society.

Principles of loyalty and enmity are so strong in Islamic interpersonal relationships that they are often used as a tool to punish, disgrace, or manipulate one person to another person's advantage. Withdrawing friendship from a family member is perhaps the most vindictive way to punish a person because social status in the Islamic world is linked to family acceptance and honoring.

I have also seen the loyalty and enmity doctrine enabling those who want to take advantage of people Muslims are not allowed befriend, such as Christians, who are offered false acceptance or friendship only to be set up for later disappointment when it is discovered that the purpose of the pretended friendship was only for personal gain.

For me personally, friendships under Islam were difficult, lacking in trust and sincerity. Muslim friendships often have a hidden agenda or are based on appearances instead of being genuine friendships. The real point of the relationship is to show Islamic strength in unity—"us against them." Islam thrives on every opportunity to show off that unity, as in the public prayers of the Muslim community, which we have already discussed. This is very different from the Biblical values of inclusiveness, lifting up others, and treating one's neighbor as one would want to be treated.

The spirit of Islam is renewed in an "us against them" atmosphere. The Islamic community gets a special boost of exuberance from showing off unity and loyalty to Islam in the West. The fact is that majority

Muslim societies in the Middle East now have few non-Muslim minorities left, so their unity under the "loyalty and enmity" principle has come to seem somewhat stagnant. Muslims in the Middle East are left with little to unify in opposition to; they end up in a destructive search for unity and loyalty directed against their own governments and fellow citizens, in the form of revolutions and counter-revolutions.

Strangely, by opening the doors of the West to Muslims escaping Islam's hopeless stagnation, the West has given a life line to a culture starving for the internal loyalty and external enmity from which it draws its energy. So Muslims' confrontation with Western culture gives Islam new energy.

The Islamic doctrines of "lure and terror" and "loyalty and enmity" have produced a culture of toxic extremes: pride and shame, generosity and selfishness, caution and carelessness, seducing and terrorizing, loyalty and backstabbing.

Muslim leaders are put on a pedestal, treated like gods, and given great honor. But most go on to experience a horrific reversal of fortunes—sometimes involving tragic and humiliating ends at the hands of the same people who used to kiss their hands. Think of Saddam Hussein, dragged out of his "spider hole" and executed, or Muammar Gaddafi brutally killed in a civil war and his body put on show for days. But also consider the somewhat less dramatic stories of Hosni Mubarak, the Shah of Iran, Anwar Sadat, and even Mohamed Morsi, out of power after just one year in office and jailed by the government that replaced him.

Mental Health and Islamic law

Islamic law is repulsive to most people, because they intuit that it does harm, not only to the victims of its excruciating punishments, but also to the one who inflicts them. Here are some Islamic laws that

Muslims must abide by and that are damaging to the sound human mind:

1. Muslims are commanded to perform jihad—do offensive battle against non-Muslims—and those who escape from jihad or refuse to support it are to be executed.
2. One of the main duties of a Muslim head of state is to do jihad against neighboring non-Muslim countries.
3. Oath-breaking, slander, and lying, particularly to non-Muslims, is an obligation if it is for the benefit of Islam.
4. Islam commands Muslims to conceal sin and gives some immunity from sin.
5. There is no minimum age limit for a girl to be contracted into marriage.
6. Muslims will not be prosecuted for killing adulterers and apostates.
7. A husband has the legal right to beat his wife.
8. Loyalty in the marriage is expected from the woman but the man has the right to marry up to four wives.
9. Parents have the legal right to perform female genital mutilation on under age daughters.
10. A man has the legal right to have sex with slave girls he owns, in addition to four wives.
11. A man has the right to a temporary pleasure marriage that can last for only a few hours.
12. In court, the testimony of a woman has half the value of a man's.
13. To prove rape, a woman must provide four male witnesses.

14. A woman must cover every inch of her body, which is considered "awrah" meaning it is as offensive as a sexual organ. Some sharia books allow the face, only, to be shown.

15. A woman needs male permission to leave her house and travel.

16. Divorce is entirely in the hands of the man, even if he has three other wives.

17. There is no prosecution for parents or grandparents for slaying their offspring, for example in an honor killing.

18. A Muslim head of state can legitimately come to power through force.

19. Questioning or criticism of Islam, and especially of Muhammad, is punishable by death even if the person repents.

These Islamic laws not only conflict with Biblical values, but they also have a horrific effect on the human psyche.

That does not mean that all Muslims are crazy, of course, but it does mean that most Muslims, especially those who live in a majority Muslim country, must adapt every aspect of their life to accommodate a cruel and unusual legal system. Even rich and powerful Muslims, who have the luxury to relax Islamic standards to a large extent behind closed doors, are subject to a lot of stress at least in their public lives, as they keep up the appearance of obedience to sharia.

Critics of Islamic sharia law are correct to fear it. I often wonder how a Muslim man can preserve his sanity with over 164 verses in the Koran commanding him to do jihad—killing and getting killed, terrorizing and committing genocide on infidels (29:6, 29:53, 22:52, 2:191, 9:5, 4:47, 8:67, 7:4, 8.17, 8:60, 3:151, 9:111, to give just a few examples); giving men the right to marry and have sex with pre-adolescent girls (65:4), rape infidel women conquered in jihad (24:13), and to own and have sex with slaves (4:24, 2:178); to torture and terrorize those who reject Islam (22.19–22, 2:191, 9:5, 4:47, 8.67, 7.4, 8.17, 8.60, 3.151); to beat their wives (4:34); to whip fornicators (24:2); to extort jizyah from the dhimmis (9:29); and, to rob and steal from victims of jihad (all of chapter eight, on the spoils of war).

The Islamic refugee crisis we are seeing today is not just from wartorn Syria. Refugees are fleeing the intolerable conditions in almost all Islamic countries. Modern technology allows Muslims to see for themselves Western freedoms that go against their indoctrination, and that leads them to ask questions. I never experienced that kind of exposure to Western culture in the sixties and seventies. Muslim leadership is no longer able to conceal and distort the truth about the lives of the infidels, as they have done for centuries.

I continually get desperate emails from people in Egypt and other parts of the Muslim world, often entitled "help me" and expressing the writer's anguish and frantic desire to get the hell out of Islamic society. But unfortunately Muslims are often confused about *why* so many people want to leave the Muslim world these days (sometimes it seems that virtually everyone who lives there, except perhaps for the residents of the oil-rich Muslim states, would prefer to be somewhere else). But few are able to connect their desperation with Islam or its laws. This is not good news for the West, which is absorbing a large number of refugees who have fled Islamic society—but are bringing Islamic values along with them.

Because of the mental trauma most Muslim refugees have experienced, they tend to second-guess their instincts. They often continue listening to the same sheikhs and Islamic leaders, who seduce their children with the same jihad propaganda. Thus second generation American Muslims grow up under the same indoctrination and dysfunctional values their parents grew up with in Islamic countries. They are told that jihad is their chance to make Allah happy. The chaos and violence in the Muslim world is always blamed on bad leaders, historical injustices to Muslims, and even on the foreign policy of the U.S. Anything and everything is blamed except sharia or Islam itself. This allows Muslims the false hope that Islam can finally have the chance to succeed in the West. Thus many Muslims end up not assimilating.

Few of the refugees fleeing trauma in the Islamic world are able to extract themselves from the values and brainwashing that caused their trauma in the first place. They end up sending their kids to Islamic schools, and ironically the kids become the future Muslims who carry the banner of sharia in America.

It is unfortunate that Western multiculturalists think they are doing Muslim immigrants a favor when they don't expect them to assimilate and abandon their sharia indoctrination and pathologies.

The Two Faces of Reality in Islam

One of the worst of those pathologies is Muslims' entrenched habit of holding two contradictory beliefs in their minds at the same time.

Recently, for example, Ahmed al-Tayeb, the grand imam of Al Azhar Islamic University in Cairo, made two conflicting statements about the clear-cut Islamic law on apostasy. Before a German audience in March of 2016, Sheikh al-Tayeb stated unequivocally that religious freedom for apostasy is guaranteed by the Koran. But a few days earlier in Egypt he had said just the opposite—that apostates must either renounce their apostasy or be executed.[8]

This kind of double talk, sometimes in the same breath, has become a normal, honorable, and even expected form of communication and debate in Islam. And the root cause of this distortion of reality goes back to the Koran itself and the character of Muhammad. The Koran is so full of contradictions that the only way to make any sense of it is the Muslim doctrine of "abrogation," which, as we have already seen, means that later Koran verses simply cancel out the earlier verses they contradict—but the earlier verses are still in the Koran for the convenience of Muslims who want to cite them in arguments with non-Muslims, to pretend, for example, that Muslims still believe there is "no coercion in religion." Thus abrogation is very convenient in apologetics for Islam, and it's also necessary to reconcile the Koran's many contradictions. Muhammad did not follow what he preached, and he often gave himself special privileges not allowed to ordinary Muslims. For instance, as we have seen, Muhammad limited polygamy to four wives, but he had eleven.

Thus many Muslims have developed an ability to believe in two opposite ideas at the same time and feel perfectly comfortable with them. In Islam, winning the argument is more important than reason and truth.

By Western standards this dual thinking creates a major deficiency in the credibility of Islam. But by Islamic standards, it is the norm and the convenient, expedient, and right thing to do. Most Muslims never noticed the contradictions in Islam until recently, when Westerners started asking questions.

One prominent example is from the public discussion after 9/11. The fact is that "jihad" in the Koran refers to fighting and war 97 percent of the time it is mentioned. But after thousands of Americans were killed in a jihad attack on 9/11, defenders of Islam insisted that jihad only meant an "inner struggle" rather than violence. They convinced Western politicians and media, and they even seem to have convinced themselves—at least in that part of their mind that doesn't know perfectly well that the Koran commands violent attacks on non-Muslims until they convert or at least submit to Islam.

Dual thinking is rife in Islam, as you can see from the following pairs of contradictory beliefs that Muslims manage to hold in their heads at the same time:

- Allah is most gracious and merciful versus Allah will torment and never forgive the kafirs
- Islam is "din al haq" (the religion of truth) versus Muslims are obliged to lie and slander if it is for the benefit of Islam
- A man has the right to beat his wife versus Islam honors women
- Islam is a religion of peace versus Muslims should kill and be killed for Allah
- There is freedom of religion and speech in Islam versus Muslims must execute apostates and blasphemers
- We mourn the death of Palestinian children who die by Israeli missiles versus we are proud to sacrifice our children's lives in order to kill Jews
- We honor Christians and Jews as "the people of the book" versus the Bible was intentionally falsified by the kafir Jews and Christians

Islam, a major world religion, has gotten away with forsaking reason and holding on to contradictions, double talk, and triangulation for centuries. It is unfortunate that most Muslims have adapted to such contradictions, become comfortable with double talk, and lost their ability to think clearly about Islam.

"Yes" Can Mean "No," and "No" Can Mean "Yes"

Islam's cruel punishments and its use of lure and terror on its followers have led many Muslims to exhibit behavior characteristic of trauma victims. One of those characteristics is a fear of saying "yes" or "no" truthfully, or a habit of saying "yes" when they mean "no" and "no" when they mean "yes."

This custom pervades all levels of Muslim society; it took me many years to outgrow it after I came to America. One common example is the custom of answering "no thank you" when your host offers you food. Even if you are hungry and would like to say "yes," you have to say "no" the first time—or even several times—before you can accept the offer. So it is customary for the hosts to insist, offering food multiple times, before a guest can finally say "yes."

In Egypt, even poor hungry people say "no" first when food is offered. It still hurts me today to remember our gardener telling my mother "no thank you" when she offered him a meal. Thankfully, she did insist that the obviously hungry man take the food home to share with his family. Centuries of oppression of the poor—who are essentially treated as slaves—have trained many poorer Egyptians to say "no thank you" when food is offered.

It took me several years in America to train myself to say "yes" and "no" when I meant them. It also took me several years to stop insisting, the Middle Eastern way, on offering food to my guests repeatedly. My kids who were all born in the U.S. never understood why I insisted on pressing food on them, their friends, and everyone that stepped into the house! I finally explained to my kids that not taking no for an answer was a cultural thing I had developed in my upbringing.

It was not until I invited my pastor Jim Tolle and his wife Alice to an Egyptian dinner that I learned about the wisdom of the Bible regarding saying "yes" and "no." When I joked about my old habit of insisting on offering food because "no" didn't mean "no" in my culture of origin, Pastor Tolle mentioned Mathew 5:37: "But let your communication be, Yea, yea; Nay, nay: for whatsoever is more than these cometh of evil." In other words, let your "yes" be "yes" and your "no" be "no."

The evil one did come six hundred years after Jesus was raised from the dead in the same Middle East that brought us the Bible truth. And he has been chasing that truth out of the Middle East ever since.

Raising Children the Muslim Way

The most common child-rearing method in most cultures is rewarding good behavior and penalizing bad behavior. But Islamic culture takes that rule to a whole new level.

In addition to frequent and severe corporal punishment, Islamic culture resorts to shame and pride to achieve compliance. Children who obey are rewarded with public approval and often compared favorably to other children, including their siblings, to boost their pride and feelings of supremacy over others.

Children who do not obey are shamed, embarrassed, and even humiliated by being beaten in public. In elementary school in Gaza, we were supposed to memorize poetry about jihad and martyrdom and to recite it, expressing our wish to die in jihad. Teachers and school officials praised and favored girls who were quick to memorize these poems, but those who did not learn them by heart were shamed before the whole class. I remember being beaten with a ruler on my hand at age seven for not memorizing my jihad poems properly.

The Islamic doctrine of "lure and terror" is not just used for dawa (proselytizing) but has permeated every aspect of Islamic life, including interpersonal relationships, and especially child rearing.

Islamic schools are famous for horrific corporal punishment. There are horrific videos on YouTube showing teachers in Egypt, Gaza, and Iran beating their entire classes full of children, often on the face. In one video, the Muslim teacher beats and humiliates the children—then forces them to slap one another on the face.[9]

Muslims defend this Islam-sanctioned child abuse by saying that children are also abused in the West. But there's a huge difference: In the West, those who physically harm children go to jail. In Muslim culture, child abuse is the accepted norm.

Western authorities—and the whole society, which has been shaped by Biblical values—stand firm on the side of the abused child, but in the Muslim world it is the exact opposite. Islamic societies double down on abused children, who are often treated as if they have brought the violence upon themselves. Even victims of honor killings receive no compassion from society. The general reaction is not "how could that happen?" but "they must have done something really bad!"

The Muslim child often grows up extremely sensitive to criticism, with a desperate need for approval and acceptance.

When the *Wall Street Journal* reported on Anwar Ali—the Pakistani boy who cut off his own hand after he accidentally raised it when his imam asked who didn't love the Prophet Muhammad—the paper pointed out that the story "underscores the deep, dangerous and often overlooked threat posed by radical Islam—its assault on the mind."[10]

The extreme shame that this boy felt led him to mutilate himself rather than live with shunning and rejection. And after the incident the boy was actually praised for his devotion to Allah. It is this same "lure and terror," pride-and-shame dynamic that leads Muslim fathers to kill their own daughters for honor—by gruesome methods like stoning. Fear of shame, disgrace, and rejection is behind many of the ills of Muslim society. And it all flows straight from the heart of Islam. Allah himself repeatedly threatens people with extreme shame, humiliation, and disgrace in the Koran. His threats have become a reality and a curse in Islamic society.

The horrific violence in the Koran, and in Islam generally, also endangers Muslim children's mental health.

The internet is full of videos of Arab kids singing about and role-playing how to be jihadists, throwing rocks at rabbis and Israeli soldiers, saying they will never compromise or stop the jihad. In some cases they are taught how to behead little toys and teddy bears. A mosque in Canada put on a children's play where bigger kids acted out beheading small children; one little boy was on his knees waiting to be beheaded.

Some Islamic schools, especially in Saudi Arabia, teach children the Islamic principle of "torment and terror in the grave." Children are shown horrific images of what happens in Hell to the bodies of the kafirs and to disobedient Muslims. This is the sort of description that children hear in Islamic schools:

> O servants of Allah! The state in the grave of a person whose sins are not forgiven is more horrifying than death itself. Fear its (the grave's) narrowness, its squeezing, its imprisonment and its loneliness. Verily the grave calls out daily: "I am the house of loneliness, the house of terror and worms." The grave is like a garden of Paradise for a good-doer, while it is like a dungeon of hell for the evil-doer. Allah tells His enemies He will send ninety-nine serpents in their graves that will tear their flesh and smash their bones, and this punishment will continue till the Day of Judgment. If one such serpent exhales towards this earth, all the plants and trees will be destroyed.[11]

Animal Cruelty in Muslim Countries

There has been a fourteen-hundred-year ban on dogs from the homes of Muslims. It goes back to how Muhammad viewed dogs. A hadith encourages Muslims not to enter a house if there is a dog in it:

It was narrated that Aishah said: "Jibril promised to come to the Messenger of Allah...but he did not arrive. He (the Messenger) had a stick in his hand which he threw down and said: 'Allah does not break His promise....' Then he turned and saw a puppy beneath a bed. He said: 'O Aishah, when did this dog get in here?' She said: 'By Allah, I do not know,' He ordered it be taken out, and Jibril came. The Messenger of Allah said: 'You made an appointment with me and I waited for you but you did not come.' He said: 'I was prevented by the dog that was in your house. We do not enter a house in which there is a dog or an image.'" (Muslim 5511)

The influence of that hadith is still felt across the Islamic world, where fatwas are regularly issued to remind Muslims of this prohibition: "Do not keep pet dogs at home.... Prophet Mohammed once said: 'Angels do not visit homes where there are dogs and paintings.'" Dogs are rarely ever seen as pets in Muslim homes, and in countries like Iran dog owners are threatened with fines or lashing for practicing vulgar Western customs.

As a result, Muslims have no clue about the relationship a dog and a human being can have. All they know is to avoid dogs. They consider them "najas," or unclean, and believe any contact with them contaminates the purity of Muslims, especially before prayers. If a Muslim is touched by a dog, he must wash, or else his prayers will not be accepted by Allah. And Muslims must pray five times a day, so it is practically impossible for them to own dogs.

For years I avoided owning a dog and was even scared of them. If my children had not begged me to get a dog, I would never have owned one. And now I am a dog lover. Islam deprives Muslims of so much—not only friendship with the kafirs, but also the joy of the special relationship with man's best friend.

One of the most denigrating insults in Islamic society is to call someone "son of a dog." Islamic culture deprived Muslims of the joy and companionship a human being can experience from owning a pet and turned this relationship into a filthy curse on a Muslim. Islam has turned the dog into yet another enemy of man in a world that is desperate for loving relationships.

Unfortunately, this shunning of dogs in the Muslim world shades over into the inhumane treatment of animals. It is very sad to see a whole culture desensitized to animal cruelty, which is a fact of life on the streets of Muslim countries. Few Muslims are bothered by it.

I have personally witnessed horrific cruelty to dogs, cats, pigs, and donkeys in the Muslim world. There are hundreds of heartbreaking YouTube videos of dogs, donkeys, and other animals being pushed off cliffs, tortured, whipped, and set on fire, all in Islamic countries. This terrible abuse goes unpunished in many areas of the Muslim world.

It was in America that I was blessed with understanding and appreciating the love of animals. I now look at my dog and wonder how did I live half my life in Egypt without ever experiencing this unique special relationship between a human being and a dog. I sometimes wonder why did Islam have to deprive human beings of such a relationship, and dogs of a caring human family.

Then I realize that Islam has deprived Muslims of many other loving relationships, not just with dogs. Loving relationships are a low priority in the jihad culture.

Crazy Islamic Fatwas

The Arabic word "fatwa" means an Islamic religious ruling, a scholarly opinion based on Islamic law that is issued by a recognized Islamic authority.

Because of modern technology, Islam is no longer able to conceal or block information on its embarrassing and outrageous rulings and fatwas that even most Muslims were unaware of for fourteen hundred years. Below are a few of these crazy fatwas ranging from silly to the aborrent. They're not the best evidence for the mental stability of the Muslim world:

1. In a 2000 Fatwa entitled "The Transmitted and Sensory Proofs of the Rotation of the Sun and Stillness of the Earth," Saudi Arabian Grand Mufti Sheikh Ibn Baaz asserted that the earth was flat and disk-like and that the sun revolved around it.

2. Women are prohibited from watching soccer and football in the Arab world, because supposedly all they really care about is looking at men's thighs and not watching the game.

3. Men must wear clothes to cover their thighs.

4. A Malaysian fatwa banned girls from acting like tomboys as violating Islamic tenets. And a fatwa was issued against tennis player Sania Mirza for not wearing proper clothes during her games, thus corrupting Muslim youth.

5. A fatwa was issued forbidding Pakistani children from immunizations because the clerics claim that vaccines are a Western conspiracy to make Muslims sterile.

6. Egypt's Grand Mufti Ali Gomaa said that drinking the urine of Muhammad is deemed a great blessing. After a public outcry, the Mufti recanted, saying it was only his "personal opinion."

7. In 2007 Ezzat Attiya issued a fatwa saying that an adult female can breastfeed an adult male coworker in

order to defuse sexual tensions in the office. This ruling is based on the Islamic belief that if a woman
breastfeeds a baby that is not hers she automatically
becomes a foster mother to the child.

8. The former dean of Al-Azhar University, Rashad Has-
san Khalil, issued a fatwa saying that a marriage would
be considered void if the couple had sex in a naked
state.

9. When a woman was raped by her father-in-law, instead
of punishing him, a fatwa said that her husband had
now become her son!

10. In 1988, the publication of Salman Rushdie's novel *The
Satanic Verses* led Iranian revolutionary leader Ayatollah Khomeini to issue a fatwa of death with a huge
bounty against Rushdie.[12]

11. Turkey's top religious authority, the Diyanet, issued a
fatwa answering the anonymous question, "Is It Reli-
giously All Right to Lust for My Daughter?" The
Diyanet explained, "There is a difference of opinion
on the matter among Islam's different schools of
thought.... For some, a father kissing his daughter
with lust or caressing her with desire has no effect on
the man's marriage." But in the Hanafi school of
Islamic thought, the *mother* would be "forbidden" to
such a man. And the girl would have to be "over nine
years of age."[13]

Modern Psychology Owes Much to the Bible

A 2013 study in the *Journal of Religion & Health* found links
between a "punitive God" and emotional problems. It showed that

people who believed in an angry and vengeful God were more likely to suffer from social anxiety, paranoia, obsessional thinking, and compulsions.[14]

The cruelty and contradictions of the Islamic God stand in the way of mental health. According to the jihad principle, Muslims have divine rights over non-Muslims, straight from Allah. Islam fosters the dysfunctional idea that *I can do whatever I want to you, the kafirs, but if you do something to me that I think is wrong or "un-Islamic," then I can kill you.*

It is not a coincidence that the field of modern psychology was birthed, established, and evolved in Western Biblically based cultures. Could anyone imagine someone like Sigmund Freud or Carl Jung emerging from Saudi Arabia, Egypt, or even Turkey? Free thinkers like that are beheaded or assassinated as apostates before anyone can hear about their theories.

It is a miracle that two thousand years ago principles of the healthy mind and soul were brought to humanity by the Bible. As someone who was immersed in Islamic culture for much too long, I am convinced that the Bible provided the fertile ground that nourished principles of mental health and allowed them to thrive.

The Bible tells us how to discover our gifts, how to have purpose, how to build each other up. It promotes self-awareness, by asking us to look first at the wickedness within. It tells us to live by the truth, to confess our sin, to live in harmony with others, and to seek redemption. The Bible also gives us luxuries to live by that were unheard of two thousand years ago: integrity, love, gentleness, joy, patience, kindness, faithfulness, and self-control. Today these are still unknown luxuries in many parts of the world, especially the Muslim parts.

Before the invention of modern psychology, the Bible told us that humans could not be free or happy without living by the truth: "And ye shall know the truth, and the truth shall make you free" (John

8:32). "Sanctify them through thy truth: thy word is truth" (John 17:17).

While the Bible was expanding the horizons of humanity, helping the human race to see the healthy side of living and to answer deep philosophical questions, the Koran was moving from one contradictory idea to another to meet the immediate needs of Muhammad on a particular day—whether he found it convenient to revoke the "no compulsion in religion" teaching, or to be able to marry his adopted son's wife.

Before modern psychology existed, the Bible taught that trust and love are among the most essential factors in our relationships with God and with others. The West teaches boundaries because the Bible respects boundaries. But in Islam there are no boundaries and no respect for privacy. Muslims feel entitled to spy on others, and if they catch them sinning or acting inappropieately they feel entitled by Islamic law itself to punish them.

Islam burdens its followers with never forgetting past vengeance, including especially Muhammad's unfinished business against the Jews. Muslims today are still living in past hatreds and will never let go, because Allah has entrusted them with vengeance on his behalf until the day of resurrection.

Muslim countries borrow mental health principles from the West, but they fail to fully implement them because such healthy values conflict with Islamic culture. Islam by its very nature cannot accommodate healthy functioning of human nature, which involves such principles as freedom of speech and religion, telling the truth, taking responsibility for your own actions and your own happiness, and loving people in general. Islam's purpose and priorities for people are in sharp conflict with the principles of happiness and freedom. And it can't change, because the very survival of Islam is in doubt if the

Muslim mind were ever allowed to heal from the psychological slavery of the religion.

Allah's priority in the Koran is never life, or liberty, or the pursuit of happiness. His goal is always the expansion of Islam—which absorbs all the dedication and purpose of his followers, down to the last man, woman, and child, and requires the punishment of everyone else. With such goals in Islam, it is hard to imagine Islamic leaders eagerly sending their followers to anger management classes, advixing them to read self-help books, or recommending that those who need help see a psychologist.

The very little psychiatry and psychology that is taught in the Muslim world is imported knowledge from the West. The fact is, psychological theories about the healthy mind conflict with sharia, and so they are taught by teachers educated at Western universities and do not have roots in Muslim culture.

Both the Bible and the Koran have an understanding of human nature. But each book works on a different side of that human nature—our deepest and truest needs, on the one hand, and our basest instincts, on the other. The choice between mental health and dysfunction, happiness and misery, could not be clearer.

11

FAMILY

On the surface, the Bible and Islam appear to have similar family values. Like Christianity, Islam expects for children to obey their parents and men to be the providers for the family. Both religions prohibit sex outside marriage.

But as we have already seen on the issue of adultery, the underlying reality is very different. Christianity and Islam have starkly contrasting priorities and goals, with the result that the understanding of the family—and of the roles of men, women, and children—in the Muslim world and the West are not at all the same.

The Bible talks about modesty for women, but Islam has taken this concept to an extreme. In Islam, modesty is taken so far that it robs women of their identity and isolates them from normal human interaction.

Muslims pride themselves on their strong family loyalty, which is very noticeable, especially in comparison with the average secular Western family. But in the Muslim world loyalty and obedience to the family is not an option, but a legal obligation—reinforced by the Islamic values of honor, pride, shame, and submission. Violations of family loyalty are harshly punished, in many cases by honor killing.

Islamic culture and law are tolerant of domestic violence, even in public. While many Muslims are unaware that sharia law clearly states that parents and grandparents cannot be prosecuted for killing their offspring, that law poisons their family relationships.

One of the cultural differences I noticed when I moved to the U.S. was parents knocking at the door of their children's bedrooms before entering. Such family etiquette is rarely used in Muslim culture, which has little respect for boundaries and privacy between family members.

It is not uncommon for Muslim parents to pick spouses for their children, both male and female, but especially for females. If a daughter rebels against her parents' choice, the results are family strife, domestic violence, and in some cases honor killing.

The Islamic doctrine of "loyalty and enmity" takes Muslim family loyalty to a whole new level that is very different from Biblical family loyalty. Muslims who violate family loyalty are often shunned, threatened, and coerced. Their rebellion against family ties is a serious breach of Islamic law.

Relationships in the West, whether between family members or friends, are very different from the coercive relationships in Islamic society. In the West, both friendships and family relationships are not based on blind loyalty, but on mutual respect, because people have freedom about how close they want to be to other people. There is also no strong cultural taboo against befriending people of different religions. And there is no gender segregation at weddings, family gatherings, and at parties.

Family relationships and friendships are less complicated in America. They are based on love, which is the heart of the teachings of the Bible, but not of the Koran. They are not determined by a fixed hierarchy that defines whom to be "with" and whom to be "against."

Family Values vs. Jihad Values

The Christian family is the best testimony for the world of Biblical values. Men and women with Biblical values make their priorities God, family, church, country, and work. In Islam, after believing in Allah, the number one priority for a Muslim believer is not family; it is jihad. That changes the whole dynamic of the family—its functions and priorities, and the roles of each member.

As we have seen, Muhammad and Allah value the jihadist more than any one else. The number one goal of Islam is expanding the power and domination of Islam to cover the whole world through the establishment of an Islamic government called the caliphate. As we have also seen, Islamic preachers describe jihad as worship.

So a Muslim man's devotion and loyalty must be first and foremost to the establishment and expansion of Islam, not to his wife and family. Until Islam conquers the whole world, anything and everything, including sacred family relationships and the life of the jihadist himself, must be sacrificed if necessary.

One hadith shows the Islamic perspective on jihad and family: "Somebody asked, 'O Allah's Messenger! Who is the best among the people?' Allah's Messenger replied, 'A believer who performs Jihad with his life and wealth.' They asked, 'Who is next?' He replied, 'A believer who stays in one of the mountain paths worshipping Allah and leaving the people safe from his mischief'" (Bukhari, p. 391, vol. 1). Notice that Muhammad gave men two choices, either to fight or hide in a mountain away from other human beings. He did not say if you don't fight then go home and take care of your wife and children. Muhammad has no other job for men besides fighting. He has no advice or encouragement for the ordinary hard-working man of integrity who wants to serve his God, his family, and his community. The Islamic paradise, unfortunately, was not created for such a man, the good, loyal, and loving husband and father.

One Man and One Woman vs. One Man and a Harem

In fact such a man of integrity and devotion to family, wife, and children is a major threat to Islam. The last thing Muhammad wanted was a happily married and devoted husband of one woman, a committed father to his children who loves his life on earth. A man like that will not want to do jihad, to get killed while killing Allah's enemies. He will not be seduced by the juvenile fantasy Muhammad promised of an obscenely lustful Islamic Paradise. He will not be lured by the rewards the Prophet offered—up to four wives in this life, plus sex slaves taken in jihadist wars, plus, after death, sexual orgies with big-breasted virgins (houris), beautiful little boys "like pearls," and enhanced sexual powers.

Islam wants a gang of fighters ready to sacrifice everything for jihad: the family, the sacred bonds of love, and even the joy of life on earth. It is common belief that women are the sacrificial lamb of Islam, but men are the first target of the use and abuse of humanity by Islam. Jihad destroys a man's happiness and his life in exchange for promises in the afterlife; Islam then destroys the woman and the wife, her natural priorities, security, and dignity; it destroys children, who are often orphaned and are sometimes even strapped with explosives and sent to kill Allah's enemies. Everyone is sacrificed by Allah.

The Purpose of Children in Islam

In several hadiths, Muhammad stresses that his fighters should "Marry women who are prolific" so that the Muslims will outnumber their enemies (Bukhari 11:2045).

The Islamic value of breeding for the sake of jihad is still preached today by Islamic leaders. PLO chairman Yasser Arafat once boasted, "The womb of the Arab woman, is my strongest weapon." Houari Boumedienne, the ruler of Algeria, said in 1974, "One day, millions of men will leave the Southern Hemisphere to go to the Northern Hemisphere. And they will not go there are friends. Because they will go there to conquer it. And they will conquer it with their sons. The wombs of our women will give us victory." The Ayatollah Khomeini called for Muslims to produce more fighters: "An Islamic Regime must be serious in every field... including the field of breeding). More Muslims means more power. More Muslims means more soldiers."[1]

The Koran advises Muslims not to let their children get in the way of more important things, like jihad: "And know that your possessions and your children are a test, and that with Allah is immense reward" (8:28).

According to Islamic scholar Allama Ibne Hajar, every Muslim should make the intention that he would offer his sons to be jihadists: "If a person holds this intention, while having sexual intercourse with his wife, that if he is given a male child he would make him Mujahid, he would gain the reward for his intention even if it does not occur."[2]

Sacrificing the Family at the Altar of Jihad

When I first read the above recommendation from the Allama (all-knowing, in Arabic) I did not know whether to laugh or cry. His advice is ridiculous, but it is tragic how Islam sacrifices the family—including my own—for jihad.

By making jihad the single most sacred act of worship, Muhammad made Islam an expansionist genocidal ideology rather than a religion. The jihadist is rewarded with Allah's Paradise for wreaking havoc on people on earth. By commanding fathers to prepare sons for jihad even before conception, Islam has established its priorities.

Family ties are naturally tricky; relatives often clash with one another. The way the Bible handles the challenges of family life is to place love at the center of family relations. With love, even for one's enemies, the Bible has elevated human society to a level never seen before in human history.

But unfortunately family love is not a priority for Islam. In fact, as we have seen, Islam commands believers to withhold their love and friendship and even to disown family members who are not Muslim.

The Koran does not stop at this commandment to shun and disown non-Muslim family members, but also threatens, wait until you see what Allah will do to you after you die if you don't obey: "If your fathers, and your sons, and your brethren, and your wives... are dearer to you than Allah and His messenger...then wait till Allah brings His command to pass" (9:24).

The duty to shun non-Muslim family members has deeply corrupted Islamic family relations—because it is not applied just to those who actually reject Islam. Muslim family members often judge other Muslim family members harshly as being not good Muslims. Those who do not meet that standard are subject to being shunned and disowned. A woman who refuses to marry the person the family has picked for her, for example, is often disowned, as is a man who does not want to go to jihad.

Biblical family values are by their very nature a threat to Islam. Muslims often envy the citizens of the West, wondering, *How come Western governments value the lives of their citizens but ours don't?* and *Why do women in the West enjoy the loyalty of their husbands and respect in the political system?* The answer is Biblical values.

The way Islamic culture handles this threat is by lying to Muslims. The defenders of Islam claim that it honors women and that Western women are loose and sex-crazed. They have created and spread the myth that Islam honors women, even that Muslim women are treated better than Christian and Jewish women. Muslim women are supposedly *more* respected because they are protected under their garb and in their homes.

Protecting Family "Honor," Not the Family

Honor, not love, is the central concept in Islamic family values. Honor supersedes family trust. Islamic honor values are the cause of friction, distrust, and disputes in Muslim family relations. Islamic society judges on appearances rather than on the content of people's character—and it judges very harshly, leading men to feel extremely vulnerable and insecure, especially about how their female family members appear to others. A Muslim man's honor and self-esteem are thus at the mercy of how his female family members behave and dress. And Muslim society tells men that the proper way to react to women's "misbehavior" is through aggression and domestic violence. From early childhood on, the Muslim little boy is brought up to regard women who are not covered as sluts who are asking for it. In fact this kind of brainwashing of little boys goes on in Islamic schools even in the West.

Family relations—especially between fathers and daughters—are strained because of the father's fear and shame if his daughter should, God forbid, smile at a man in the street, have a boyfriend, or—the ultimate fear of the Muslim father—if his daughter should lose her virginity before she gets married.

Islamic law actually declares such women deserving of death when it protects parents and grandparents from being prosecuted if they kill them for disgracing the family honor.

Muslim men can have no respect or dignity in Muslim society unless they protect their honor, often by physical abuse of women in their family or even honor killing. In the movie *The Stoning of Soraya M.*, which is based on a true story, the father and the son of an accused wife and mother threw the first stones.

The concept of honor applies not just to men but also to mothers, whose personal honor depends on the honor of their children, and vice versa. An Iraqi mother spat on her own son in public because he fought with the Iraqi Army against ISIS,[3] and an ISIS member executed his own mother in public in the Syrian city of Raqqa because she had encouraged him to leave the group.[4]

It's clear what Islamic priorities are regarding the family.

Looking back on my life under Islam, I don't remember ever hearing even once an Islamic preacher giving a sermon against honor killing or beating women. But it is not just women who are ill served by Islam, but men and children as well. Families in the Muslim world will never be happy and healthy until men are freed from the immense pressure of Islamic shaming for honor.

Islamic Law and Women

One major difference that we have already seen between Biblical and Muslim marriage is that the Muslim marriage contract requires loyalty only from the wife to the husband, while the husband has no obligation under the Islamic law to remain loyal to one wife. Of course that does not mean that there are no loyal Muslim husbands. But those who choose to be loyal are under no legal or moral covenant to do so. In the Muslim marriage contract, the man is asked to give the names and addresses of wives number one, two, and three, if any.

That means that in the marriage ceremony the groom gives no vows of loyalty to his bride.

Married Muslim women live under a number of humiliating laws:

1. Rebelliousness (disobedience in any form) on the part of the wife nullifies the husband's obligation to support her and gives him permission keep her from leaving the home.
2. A husband has the right to beat his wife and does not have to say why to her family or police.
3. Divorce is only in the hands of the husband and is as easy as saying: "I divorce you"; it becomes effective even if the husband says he did not intend it.
4. There is no community property between husband and wife, and the husband's property does not automatically go to the wife in case of the husband's death.
5. In fact the wife is entitled to only a small portion of the husband's estate, after the biggest share is given to male children, parents, and brothers.
6. A woman's rights are half those of a man in inheritance and in many other matters.
7. The testimony of a woman in court has half the value of a man's.
8. Marriage is a contract between buyer and seller, in which the man pays the woman's family a dowry in exchange for sexual rights over her body.
9. A man is allowed to have sex with three additional wives, slave women, and women captured in battle; and if a married woman becomes a slave her marriage is annulled.
10. A woman loses custody of her children if she remarries.

11. To prove rape, a woman must have four male witnesses.

12. A rapist may only be required to pay a dowry.

13. A Muslim woman must cover every inch of her body, which is considered "awrah," as shameful to show as a sexual organ.

14. A Muslim man will not be prosecuted for killing his wife if she is caught in the act of adultery. The opposite is not true.

15. The Koran also says to punish women "guilty of lewdness" by confining them to the house "until death takes them" (4:15) and "cutting off their inheritance" (4:19).

As you can see, Islamic laws promote the sadistic repression of women, depriving them of their humanity and dignity, and keeping them from being heard or seen. This is the system that the defenders of Islam claim protects and honors women. In reality, Islamic law leaves women extremely insecure and in a much weaker legal position than men. That harsh inequality creates and deepens hostilities between the sexes.

The Muslim wife also feels insecure about her children, their security, and future, in case her husband decides to get a second, third, and fourth wife and have other sets of children with them.

Islamic values have a corrupting impact on the husband even if he is basically a decent person. In times of trouble the Islamic sheikh will often advise a man to beat his wife, like the Koran says, or to get a second wife as a solution to marital problems—very different advice from the kind that the Christian man gets at his church.

As a child I remember being at the home of relatives and overhearing an argument between a married couple. The wife was begging the husband to "please have as many mistresses as you want but don't marry on me." That was a very sobering lesson in the realities of Islamic marriage.

I have personally seen women, among them my own family members and friends, suffering not only from the fear that their husbands would marry other women but also from physical and mental abuse at the hands of husbands and other male family members—all the result of a corrupt and oppressive legal system that no religion should ever advocate.

The difference between the status of women within the family in Islam and in the Bible is like night and day. The legal oppression of Muslim women speaks for itself. But that does not stop Muslim defenders from defying reality and telling the world that Islam honors women more than any other religion.

Why on earth would a religion that was birthed in the same Middle Eastern region as the Bible come along six hundred years after Christianity and reverse all the wholesome family values brought to the world by the Bible? The answer is that a man who is devoted to his wife and children in a monogamous marriage is a threat to jihad. Men who love their families as number one after God will not want to die in jihad in order to kill the enemies of Allah. So because jihad should be the Muslim's number one priority after pledging loyalty to Allah and Muhammad, a Muslim man's relationship with his wife and family had to be sabotaged. Muslim men must never be allowed to develop true love and loyalty to their wives. So marriage in Islam is essentially a relationship of ownership, in contrast to marriage in the Bible, where the man and woman become one flesh. That way the jihadist is free to leave for jihad anytime and is promised more women in Paradise if he dies. Thus Islam basically reduced the loving relationship of marriage to sexual slavery.

Sex Slavery Yes, Love No

One of the cartoons in the French magazine *Charlie Hebdo* that inflamed the anger of many Muslims depicted a Muslim man with four wives all dressed in black Islamic hijabs, one of them short and small—a child. In the back behind the women was an uncovered sex slave. And the Muslim man was pointing at a young Western couple sitting on a bench and saying about the couple in love, "This is immoral, this is against Islam."

The cartoon's commentary on Islamic values is sad but true. It is the truth that got Muslims offended, and it was exposing the truth that got the French cartoonists at *Charlie Hebdo* killed.

Islam has substituted love of jihad and martyrdom for love of family. And in order to make it easier for men to prioritize jihad over family, the Muslim man is allowed the use of women as sex slaves while discouraged and shamed for being devoted, loyal, and loving to one wife. Even in Heaven, Islam does not allow a man to reunite with his earthly wife or wives. Instead it promises men more promiscuity than on Earth; in heaven he gets seventy-two virgins.

Islam discourages men from falling in love but encourages them to treat women as sexual objects. Sex slaves are prizes to jihadists as part of the spoils of war. And as we have seen, even sex slavery is not the depth of depravity to which Muslim values on relationships sink: one fatwa went as far as to permit incest for the jihadists.[5]

ISIS advertised the return to open Islamic sexual slavery markets with this announcement: "Memo: Brothers wishing to buy slaves should register their names with the administrator of the battalion. Regarding brothers currently in service, if they want to be a part of the auction, they should be released within 10 days. If a brother is not registered, he is not allowed to be present at the slave market. Bids should be given in a sealed envelope and whoever wins, he is obligated to buy. Success comes from Allah."[6]

Anything but Love

In Saudi Arabia and other sharia-compliant countries, celebrating Valentine's Day is banned. Shops are prohibited from selling red flowers and other gifts dedicated to celebrating love between a man and a woman.

The expression of love even between spouses is considered offensive; it is often ridiculed and discouraged. Loving a woman is a threat to jihad, so it must be stamped out.

Islamic values and Biblical values about what being a man means are totally different. Islamic manhood means pride and honor, and that honor is directly linked to subjugating and controlling women. If Muslim society were to treat family happiness and the best interests of men, women, and children as priorities, the jihad would collapse and Islam's political expansion would end. That is why the oppression of women and jihadist political Islam go hand in hand.

I spent my youth in Egypt, mostly in a miserable home atmosphere where pleasing society was more important than the internal life of a person. I never saw what true love meant, especially between a man and a woman. Movies in Egypt often showed how women are shamed, abused, and even killed for a love relationship with a man. Love was often associated with deep guilt and shame.

I grew up hearing the Arabic word "hurma" to describe women but never thought much of its meaning. It means "forbidden." And it explains a lot about how women are viewed in Islamic society—as an untouchable alien piece of property.

Some Islamic sources describe women as "not human."[7] For fourteen hundred years, Arabic culture has not been able to settle on what to do with women: cover them, confine them to their homes, or treat them as less than human.

Such Islamic values have poisoned any chance of a healthy and loving relationship, a meeting of the mind and heart, between a man and a woman. It is a miracle that some Muslim marriages are happy and successful—despite Islam, not because of it.

12

FEMINISM: BIBLICAL, SECULAR, AND ISLAMIC

Bible-based cultures are the envy of the world, especially when it comes to women's freedom and quality of life. Freedom from bondage for both men and women is all over the Bible. That is one reason why wherever the Bible went the status of women improved tremendously.

The Bible limits men and women equally in their sexual behavior, restricting both to within the boundaries of a monogamous marriage. Under Islamic values a man is not required to be responsible and control his sexual impulses. The Bible does not favor men or give them all kinds of sexual freedoms over women, as Islam has. Before Jesus restricted marriage to a holy covenant between one man and one woman, polygamy was a common form of marriage based on inequality between the sexes. Inevitably—as we can see both in the Old Testament stories of Jacob, Rachel, and Leah and in the Islamic world today—polygamy creates strained, hostile, and chaotic relationships between men and women. Monogamous marriage became the foundation upon which the Bible-based civilization was built.

The Bible placed boundaries of commitment, loyalty, holiness, and respect for family, especially on men—boundaries that had never been seen in human history before. With monogamy, the Bible exalted the woman and gave her a sense of security and dignity within the family. It also gave security to children, resulting in a wholesome family life, in which every member of the family could thrive.

With monogamy, the Bible also placed responsibility on the man to be in control of his sexual impulses for the sake of peace, family health, happiness, and law and order. Under the Bible, human civilization was on its way to a new beginning to be built on a solid foundation.

In the macho culture of the Middle East two thousand years ago, who could ever have imagined God telling men: "husband of one wife" (I Timothy 3:2); "For this cause shall a man leave his father and mother, and cleave to his wife; And they twain shall be one flesh: so then they are no more twain, but one flesh" (Mark 10:7–8).

This is a groundbreaking divine commandment. If we were to apply modern-day terminology, Biblical marriage should be considered the number one, the one and only true "feminist" movement— brought to us by the one God of the Bible. But unfortunately most secular Western feminists do not recognize that the Bible is what set them free.

I often wish that angry American feminists could only see what I see. The difference between who I was in Islam and who I am today in Christ is like night and day. And the Bible is the source of my freedom from Islamic oppression. My freedom, equality, and dignity as a woman in America today is due to the Bible, not the result of the sixties feminist movement.

As I was adapting to and enjoying my new-found freedoms in America, I was extremely alarmed to hear several Islamic leaders in America demand sharia as a religious right. Well-organized and funded Islamic groups were popping up all over the U.S. with the blessings and financial support of oil-rich Arab countries, especially Saudi Arabia. What was even more alarming was how the American public had no clue about what sharia and Islamic values are.

I feared that the same Islam that I escaped from was now chasing me in America. After driving the Bible out of the Middle East and into the West, Islam is now coming to the West to finish the job.

Six hundred years after Christ, the culture of the Arabian Peninsula reversed the achievements of the Bible regarding marriage, women, and monogamy in the Middle East. The core of what the Bible advocated was what threatened Arab culture the most: setting people free, especially women.

Why the Suppression of Women Is Necessary in Islam

While there are even female defenders of sharia who advocate to the West that "Muslims are the true feminists,"[1] the fact is that Islam fears women. It fears their normal healthy role in a man's life, especially under the Biblical form of marriage. A man's love and loyalty to his family are without a doubt in conflict with the call to sacrifice his life in jihad against the enemies of Allah. Family happiness is not what Islam wants for a man.

Allah is in competition with women for the heart and mind of the man. Under Islamic law, the woman is always the loser.

The number one role of a man in Islam is to be trained to be a jihadist and the role of all citizens, young or old, male or female, is to train, bless, finance, support, and stand on the side of the jihadist who is at the center of Islamic values.

Since Islam is asking men to literally love death, nothing that the jihadist wants is denied to him. He is lured with the highest honors, plenty of money, and all the women he could want. He is even forgiven if he no longer obeys important commandments of Islam, such as to pray, fast, and so forth. The Muslim man is thrown into the wilderness of lust by Allah, who in exchange wants nothing less than his life, to be sacrificed for the expansion of Islam. The goal is what is good for Islam, not what is good for the man.

The lure and seduction of men to their deaths in jihad beggars the imagination. Allah's promises of sexual promiscuity and infinite pleasure in the Islamic holy books were originally aimed at the most sexually deprived men in the most rugged and merciless area of the world, the Arabian Desert. Islamic law showered sexual privileges on them. The Arab male took the bait, but at what a cost!

Islam turned marriage from a holy covenant based on love, devotion, and loyalty between one man and one woman into a hostile relationship where women have to compete with Allah himself for a man's devotion. And Allah always wins.

There is a very telling hadith about Muhammad's hostility toward happy marriage: "During the lifetime of the prophet, we used to avoid chatting leisurely and freely with our wives lest some Divine inspiration might be revealed concerning us. But when the Prophet had died, we started chatting leisurely and freely (with them)" (Bukhari, 7:62:115).[2]

In other words, during Muhammad's life, his fighters were too scared to chat with their wives even in their leisure time—because if they did Muhammad was bound to come up with a Koran verse reprimanding them for being nice to their wives. Only after Muhammad's death were they finally able to talk normally with their wives.

These are the same fighters Muhammad encouraged to rape women captured in war and promised a hundred times the virility of a hundred men and the enjoyment of many "houris"—gazelle-eyed virgins whose beauty was never seen on earth—in Paradise. Muhammad clearly viewed a normal marriage as an impediment to jihad, and he thus discouraged his men from being thoughtful, kind, loyal, and loving to their wives.

The wholesome and loving Biblical marriage between one man and one woman is an existential threat to Islam. If Muslim women fully understood the huge difference in the concept of marriage between the Bible and the Koran, they might rebel. But women in the Islamic world don't get to see what Biblical marriage is like. They are restrained, suppressed, used, and abused under the harsh rules of Islamic law so that men are freed for the business of Allah: jihad. Islamic law was created to limit human rights, and especially women's rights, for the purpose of facilitating jihad.

Thus there is a strong correlation in Islamic culture between Muslim manhood and devotion to Allah, on the one hand, and the mistreatment of women, on the other. It is not uncommon for a Muslim man who is loyal to one wife and treats her with love and respect to suffer ridicule for not being man enough. In fact, a Muslim woman whose husband actually loves her is often accused by her in-laws of having put a spell of some kind on him. It is not a coincidence that Islam puts pressure on men to denigrate women and treat them as property, especially in public. A man who allows freedom to the women in his family can end up being treated as a pariah in Muslim society, where pride and people's opinion is everything. If a woman "shames" a man, Muslim society requires him to "cleanse" his "honor." This is where the expression "honor killing" comes from: a man is subjected to intolerable social shaming until he takes care of his dishonor by beating, denigrating, or even murdering his wife, daughter, or sister.

While Muslim men cannot tolerate any hint of infidelity, Muslim women must accept their husbands' disloyalty during jihad, when they are given the right to rape women won in war. Sadly, as we have seen, some Muslim women have completely bought into this mentally sick system. To give one more example, a top female Islamic scholar in Al Azhar University, Suad Saleh, recently stated that captured enemy women could be punished with rape by jihadists.[3]

What Islam demands from women is inhumane and intolerable. It has a devastating effect on the healthy psyche of the whole family.

Even today, my ninety-six-year old mother still expresses her pride in her sacrifice when my father lost his life to jihad sixty years ago. In a recent interview on Egyptian TV entitled "Mustafa Hafez, the Shadow Man," Egyptian TV dedicated a show to the great old jihadist heroes and their triumphs over the Zionist entity. My mother, who was an honored guest of the show, proudly showed old photos and letters she received from my father when he was in the 1948 Arab war against Israel. Watching the interview was overwhelmingly sad for me; it opened old wounds.[4]

Under Islam, women have abandoned their roles as givers and protectors of life and been reduced to cheerleaders for jihadists, who are not playing a football game, but literally gambling with their lives and the lives of their family. Islam has no respect for women's nature. The Koran and hadith are replete with derogatory descriptions like these:

- "Women are deficient in intelligence and religion" (Koran 2:282)

- The Koran regards "Satan's tricks as weak, but the guile of women as great" (Koran 12:28 and 4:76)

- "Muhammad said: I saw that most of the inhabitants of Hell-fire were women" (Bukhari 1:2: 28)

Women are also described in Islamic scriptures and preaching as untrustworthy, harmful to men, the devil's gateway, and like dogs. If they are not properly covered the Islamic way, they can be accused of seducing men and would be responsible for their own rape. This is a sample of the depraved advice given to men in mosques: "Women on Earth is cursed and bad because she makes herself beautiful, but the virgins in heaven are OK to show their full breasts and be as beautiful as men want."[5] This hadith clearly asks men to resist women's attraction on earth, which is described as bad; but in heaven women's exposing of their breasts to lure men is okay.

Women are to adapt their lives to fulfill the needs of jihadists. Often they must accept second, third, or fourth place in the order of their husbands' priorities. That is their badge of honor, and those who don't conform will learn the hard way. And defenders of Islam call women who sacrifice themselves for jihad "true feminists"!

The Rebellious Woman under Islam

Islam forbids women from any kind of rebellion, and even from complaining about sharia's oppression, especially to non-Muslims. Being punished for complaining of abuse is perhaps the cruelest form of slavery. A true feminist movement in the Islamic world is thus out of the question because it would require women to unite and rebel.

The "nashiz" or "rebellious" woman is mentioned by name in sharia law, which authorizes her husband to beat her, stop his financial support, and imprison her in the home. Sharia courts issue orders declaring women "nashiz," after which their husbands are allowed to implement these punishments.

As soon as a woman is married, the husband has the right to pick and choose her friends, and husbands often limit their wife's friendships to devout hijab-wearing women. Women who show any inclination to rebelliousness are shunned not only by society at large but also often by other women.

Such severe religious and legal obstacles to rebellion by women make it almost impossible for women to unite, meet to communicate freely, congregate, or protest. In fact, to do so is a crime under Islam, even today.

Amnesty International recently announced that Iran intensified its repression of women's rights activists during the first half of 2016 by threatening, interrogating, and imprisoning women connected to collective initiatives relating to women's rights. Dr. Homa Hoodfar was recently arrested in Iran. Many other women in the Muslim world have suffered imprisonment and even death for campaigning or other concerted feminist activities that are deemed criminal under sharia.[6]

Complaining to the police is useless. Muslim women rarely report domestic violence, sexual harassment, rape, or any kind of abuse by males. Women in Egypt say that they don't resort to the police for protection from men because the police will mistreat instead of rescue them.

There was an opportunity for Muslim women to rebel against sharia during the Arab Spring of 2011. But when I looked at all the posters and signs carried by women in Tahrir Square in Cairo, I could not find one sign carried by a woman demanding equality under the law, or even calling for laws against domestic violence.

Why was that? Even during the Arab Spring, a Muslim woman could not risk being labelled "nashiz." Remember, a "rebellious" woman can legally be beaten and confined to the house—for the rest of her life, until she dies.

Under Islam, a woman is expected to martyr herself, but in a different way from a man. While he goes to literally sacrifice his life, she must never complain, but willingly sacrifice everything. Even if her husband dies she must be a sacrificial lamb who expresses her pride to the community by saying she will now dedicate her life to her children and, if necessary, give all of them to jihad.

A woman like that is placed on a pedestal by Arab media, given a life-time pension, and often rewarded with a distinguished position in the government of a Muslim nation. They mingle with the powerful in their society. Such women tell the media they are happy and privileged to live under sharia and that Islam honors them.

The worst kind of oppression is when the victim is forbidden from complaining, rebelling, or even identifying the oppressor by name. And that is exactly what Islam has accomplished: Muslim women are afraid even to name the oppressor.

Islamic Feminism

"Islamic feminism" is different from Western secular feminism in many ways. While Western feminism is an anti-establishment and anti-Biblical rebellious movement, Islamic feminism is pro-establishment and pro-Islam.

The majority of Muslim women, even the educated ones, are in denial about the oppression of women in the Koran and sharia. They choose to blame the oppression of women in Muslim societies on misinterpretations, or on bad guys who have hijacked Islam. For example, Muslim activist Linda Sarsour, the director of the Arab American Association of New York, has said, "I am a feminist and the reason I am a feminist is because I am a Muslim."[7]

Musdah Mulia, a Muslim professor who also claims to be a feminist, maintains that Islam is a religion of equality. She has said, "blame Muslims, not Islam, for gender inequity." According to Muslim anthropologist Ziba Mir-Mosseini, "The problem [for women in Islam] has never been with the text (the Koran), but with the context."[8]

Saudi Arabia and Gulf states highly reward "Muslim feminists" who defend Islam to the West with well-paid government or academic positions. Like Muslim men who are proud of their jihad, these women are proud of their hijab and wear it with pride, as an expression of their support of sharia. These defenders of sharia who claim "I feel free in my veil" are a powerful class of Muslim women who project a holier-than-thou aura. What is written in the Koran about the punishments for disobedient or rebellious woman doesn't seem to concern Muslim feminists; it is as though they feel it does not apply to them, but applies to other women, who probably deserve it. Such attitudes often create hostility between women in the Muslim world.

As Palestinian Media Watch reported, a survey in Gaza showed that a high percentage of women felt that domestic violence is justified on certain occasions: "41% of the women agreed that violence was justified if the woman leaves home without notifying her husband, while 74% agreed that violence was justified if she neglected her children."[9]

In Britain, the first female sharia law judge has issued a brazen warning that flies in the face of UK law, stating that "the government cannot ask Muslims not to have more than one wife." This is a prominent and intelligent Muslim woman defending polygamy.[10]

Centuries of severe oppression have taught Muslim women to mold and adapt themselves to fit the sharia requirements, at least in public. Like men, women have learned that sacrificing their own happiness and that of their families is the only way to achieve a degree of respect, power, and dignity in Muslim society. Some women even go as far as becoming more radical than men in support of sharia, the very laws that oppress women. That is the assured route to acceptance and respect in Muslim culture. Everyone must sacrifice for Allah, especially women.

It is not uncommon to see seasoned older women report on and turn in misbehaving younger women and girls; such reporting is considered a badge of honor for committed Muslim women. ISIS created an all-female brigade for the purpose of apprehending women who did not follow the harsh interpretation of sharia law—something similar to the virtue police in Saudi Arabia, except that this is by women against women. The all-female force arrests women and school-girls, keeps them locked up for hours, and even subjects some to whipping and humiliation for reasons such as showing hair, or wearing a thin veil that does not meet proper Islamic standards.[11]

Islam has succeeded in turning women against one another. Instead of joining together to uplift and improve one another's lives, powerful Muslim women unite with men in authority to enforce sharia against other women.

There are no Saudi or Egyptian women's groups formed to support or rescue Christian and Yazidi women who are being raped by Muslim jihadists. Muslim women are not even there for their fellow Muslim women, such as Kurds, who are also being killed and raped.

There are dozens of volunteer Western Christian and Jewish women's outreach groups and missionaries in the Muslim world but hardly any volunteer aid work by Muslim women. Western female American missionaries Dayna Curry and Heather Mercer were imprisoned and then miraculously freed by American forces. A ten-member Christian medical team headed by a British female surgeon was executed by the Taliban in Afghanistan in 2010.[12] While female volunteers from the West are helping the war-torn Muslim world, hijab-wearing Muslim women are seen busy shopping in Paris, London, and Rome. It is not at all a part of Islamic culture for women to go and help other women. Women helping women is a Western phenomenon that grew out of Biblical culture.

Perverted Feminism

Strong women do exist in Islam. In fact because of the tremendous pressure from life under sharia, Muslim women have developed a perverted form of feminism: a kind of coping mechanism like Stockholm syndrome. Like kidnap victims identifying with their kidnappers, women in the Islamic world have learned to defend sharia and be protective of Islam's reputation. Many are proud and assertive in their defense of Islam, especially to a Western audience. They claim they are not oppressed. But in a world where jihad is above life itself, life is cruel and such cruelty produces many aggressive women, who turn their aggression on those who are dependent on them—in private and away from public display.

Muslim women are well trained. They know that if they want to enjoy a certain level of power and respect, they must never defy sharia but embrace it. The rewards for compliant Muslim women may explain why most of the Muslim college professors in Saudi Arabia and other Muslim countries never criticize sharia but claim it to be harmless.

Muslim culture has produced women with such a high tolerance for oppression that most don't even recognize it as such. Growing up in Egypt, it never occurred to me that Islamic laws are unfair to women. I never even made the connection in my mind between Islam and the tolerance for domestic violence there.

Living under the warped and twisted conditions that Islam has created, women take pride in their own bondage. They have developed learned helplessness, not only with respect to themselves but also to other women. Muslim women's thinking about Islamic oppression of women seems to be: *If you can't beat 'em, join 'em.*

I once gave a lecture at Wellesley College in which I criticized the polygamy and mistreatment of women in Islam. A number of very assertive female Muslim students were extremely hostile to my criticism. They defended sharia, polygamy, and male-only divorce rights. They even dismissed my criticism of the child marriage of girls, saying it does not really happen much, even if it is legal on the books.

The fact is, Islamic feminism has to be sharia-compliant.

In fact, "Muslim feminists" seem to spend a lot more time and energy promoting sharia than they do defending women.

In London, Muslim women wearing full black niqabs and carrying signs protesting British law and supporting sharia warned Europe of another Holocaust and another 9/11. Here in America, the angry mother of the Tsarnaev brothers responsible for the Boston Marathon bombing threatened, "America will pay," instead of apologizing for what her sons had done. These are the kind of women that Arab TV uplifts and places on pedestals. The message to Muslim women is that this is the only kind of feminism Islamic society will tolerate. "Muslim feminism" is essentially the feminine form of jihad: women defend sharia, promote jihad, and even emulate the Islamic virtue police against other women.

The Development of Western Feminism

The suffrage movement in the early twentieth century gave women voting rights and fostered their personal growth and economic power. The fight for women's voting rights in America was a bloodless one; in the U.S., feminists met very little opposition. The fact is, Western culture and Biblical values never opposed improving the lives of women and giving them freedoms.

As a result of the achievements of American women, the feminist movement grew around the world. Even Muslim society experienced some changes. But they were more cosmetic than substantive. Women in the Muslim world enjoyed the most freedom during the time after the Ottoman Empire had ended and before petro-dollars helped Islam recover from the long period of ensuing weakness.

In the sixties a different kind of feminist movement emerged in America. I was a teenager in Egypt at that time, and it was fascinating to watch the feminist protests. We Egyptians could not understand the sexual revolution, since we considered Western women as already having achieved all the cultural and legal freedoms that we girls in the Middle East could only dream of.

After seeing a glimpse of America's sixties feminist movement on Egyptian TV, I remember flipping the channel to watch an Egyptian movie about the honor killing of "bad" women who had sinned sexually. That movie, entitled *Bedaya wa Nehay*, *Beginning and an Ending*, quickly brought my mind back to the reality of women's lives under Islam.

The cultural difference between two opposite worlds on the same television set was phenomenal. What was more amazing to many Muslim observers was the calm and respectful reaction of the American public and legal system to the feminist revolution of the 1960s. There were practically no ugly confrontations and no real suffering by the women protesters—essentially no opposition at all. Certainly there was no "honor killing" of women who were burning their bras in public. To the contrary, feminists like Gloria Steinem became instant celebrities, media darlings, and popular culture icons.

Even though the sixties feminists' movement rebelled against the Biblical values of modesty and monogamous sex within marriage, there was no bloody confrontation. This was a demonstration of how the Bible, unlike Islam, allows people freedom.

Nineteen-sixties feminism has been largely discredited. But its negative effects can still be felt in American culture, which has adopted values that are anti-male, anti-family, anti-Bible, and pro-abortion.

The feminist movement that promoted the sexual revolution in the 1960s was arrogant and reckless. And even today, proponents of that kind of secular, leftist feminism are still dedicated to destroying their political opposition. Conservative women are mercilessly attacked while leftist women are given carte blanche to use their femininity as a shield of protection. That is not genuine feminism; it has become feminine tyranny.

Western Secular Feminism

Defining marriage as a God-created covenant between one man and one woman was in itself the most powerful feminist advance ever. And Christianity is the most revolutionary feminist movement. True liberty in Christ was meant for both men and women.

But secular Western feminists do not see the Bible's blessings to women and the family. Instead they blame the Bible for what they call the "patriarchal" family. As a result their movement is anti-Bible and anti-men.

Western feminists have decided to throw the baby out with the bath water. They deny the revolutionary freedoms the Bible has given women, men, and the family and consider as "oppressive" Bible verses such as "Wives, submit yourselves unto your own husbands, as unto the Lord" (Ephesians 5:22). Such a narrow reading of the Bible ignores verses such as Galatians 3:28—"there is neither male nor female: for ye are all one in Christ Jesus"—and Ephesians 5:25—"Husbands, love your wives, even as Christ also loved the church, and gave himself for it."

There is no doubt that when the New Testament was originally written it limited men a lot more than it limited women. The impact of the Biblical values limiting sex for *men* to within a monogamous marriage benefited and honored women at a time when women were regarded as property. But Biblical marriage was not meant to favor one gender over another; it provides the best conditions for a wholesome and loving family, in which men, women, and children can all thrive.

The Bible teaches distinct divinely ordained roles for men and women, not on the basis of preferential treatment to promote ulterior goals (as Islam does with jihad), but to give both men and women freedom to achieve their full potential. For the man to conform to God's command to be loyal and devoted to one wife and not commit adultery even in his mind, he must constantly be aware and in control and fight his natural male urges. The Bible asks a man to love his wife sacrificially, laying down his life for the woman he loves.

And it asks a woman to be understanding and supportive of the man who loves her and puts her on a pedestal, obeying his lead. That is not in any way demeaning to women, but Western feminists do not seem to appreciate this kind of mutually loving relationship between men and women. They deny both sexes any specific physical or psychological needs and measure everything in terms of absolute equality and pure rights.

I will never forget the horrific campaign that secular feminists waged against the Promise Keepers movement. These were godly men who wanted to promise their wives to be better husbands, to share what is in their heart and mind, to share in housework and changing diapers. But this healthy movement was totally assaulted by the leftist feminists, with the help of the media. There was no logical explanation for their assault on the Promise Keepers—unless secular feminists are an angry group of bitter women who hate to see men and women happy under the values of Biblical marriage.

And now their agenda has become much clearer, and it is truly outrageous. It is to eliminate all differences between the sexes, even in the use of the bathroom. They are now pushing unisex bathrooms on the public, rewarding businesses and states that go along with the latest step in the sexual revolution, and punishing those that don't.

But Western feminists want to have their cake and eat it too. They insist on absolute equality, but they also insist on preferential treatment for women. For example, women should be able to have any job a man can have—including soldier or firefighter—but the physical requirements of those jobs have to be changed for women, to accommodate the obvious physical differences between men and women. Far-left female politicians demand special treatment, too. They can humiliate their male opponents, who must not respond in kind without being called bigoted sexists.

How Feminists Have Failed Muslim Women

When I first started speaking against sharia and its oppression of women, I naïvely thought that secular feminists would be eager to take up the cause. Unfortunately, they showed no interest whatsoever. They ignored Islamic crimes against women: the legal tyranny, kidnapping, sexual slavery, and the stoning and flogging of women in the Muslim world.

Rather than objectively researching Islamic laws regarding women, marriage, and family and evaluating both the pro-sharia and anti-sharia viewpoints, secular feminists have chosen to take the official Islamic side propagated by Islamic governments and Muslim feminists.

American feminists have made their choice. They have chosen to stay silent rather than expose Islamic misogyny, even in the West—such as rapes of European girls, child marriage, honor crimes, domestic violence, and female genital mutilation. And they are certainly no friends of outspoken former Muslim women.

When several formerly Muslim women, including Wafa Sultan, Ayan Hirsi Ali, and I, started speaking publicly on the dangers of Islamic values and laws—and on the plight we were in on account of having left Islam—we still had no support from feminists. To them we did not exist. Even feminist student groups refused to sponsor us when we spoke on college campuses, and many have called us "Islam-ophobes," a term of opprobrium suggesting an irrational fear of Islam.

How can we be accused of an *irrational* fear of Islam when we live under Islamic threats and fatwas of death? None of us can visit any Islamic country, including our countries of origin, because if we did we would be killed. And our killers would be considered heroes.

Secular progressive feminists, just like Muslim female defenders of Sharia, clearly have no interest in criticizing sharia. They appear to have no sympathy for the women who are suffering under Islam.

But guess who sympathized with our plight, listened to our stories, and gave us support? It was ordinary Americans, and especially Christian and Jewish women and men of faith. To them, Islamic tyranny was as clear as black and white—while progressives view Islam in shades of gray. Surely they must see that women are oppressed in the Muslim world. But that appears to be outweighed, for them, by the opportunity to respect and even celebrate a culture that is a contrast and a challenge to the Western, Bible-based culture that they hate. I am grateful for the ordinary Americans, who are free from enslavement to political agendas and motivated instead by human decency and Biblical values.

Are Secular Feminists the Heroes They Claim to Be?

American popular culture and media regard the sixties feminists as heroes. But the secular feminist movement's image as the saviors of women and the champions of their rights has crumbled before the eyes of those of us who can see that they have nothing to say about the institutionalized oppression of women in Islam and the current epidemic of rape of Western girls by Muslim males in Europe.

The question now is, if sharia's oppression of women even inside Western borders cannot capture the interest of feminists, then what is their cause? It cannot be women, as they claim.

The truth is that feminists have a kind of respectful fear of Islam because Islam could not care less about feminism. Islamic society will not hesitate to react violently—with terror—to any kind of rebellion by women. Western feminists are not exactly the brave bunch they claim to be. They would rather fight the Bible than fight Islam—Christians won't hurt them!

Another important reason why Western feminists will not touch Islam and its harsh treatment of women is because Islam shares secular feminists' disdain for Biblical family values. Like feminists and the rest of the ultra-Left, Islam has more important goals that are in conflict with the health of the family unit.

In the case of Islam, it is the expansion of the Islamic state through jihad that comes first, before women, men, and children. As for Western feminists, they too have lofty goals—to change the nature of sexual relationships, to eliminate any gender differences, and to enforce all of that through a stronger government and less individual freedom—and the end of the Biblical family that is the tradition in the West.

Secular and Islamic Feminism Converge

There are many commonalities between Western feminists and the defenders of Islam. Their common enemy is Biblical values, and especially the lifelong marriage covenant between one man and one woman. Both belief systems are ruthless about sacrificing family happiness for what they see as loftier goals.

While the ultra-Left feminist carries a sign that says, "I am proud of my abortion," the Muslim feminist says, "I am proud to sacrifice my son and husband to jihad." Both ideologies obviously stand against the nature of women and what is best for them.

Under a pretense of being pro-woman, both secular and Muslim feminism have sold out the best interests of woman for the sake of their ideological agenda. And that agenda feeds their egos. The bottom line for many activists in both camps is maintaining personal power and preferential treatment for themselves. They believe that they are better and more deserving than the other women, who are not like them. Just look at how secular feminists treat conservative women, and how Muslim feminists ignore the rape of women at the hands of jihadists.

Leftist women who were supposedly appalled at Mitt Romney for using the word "binders" to describe a list of qualified women are the same feminists who defended Bill Clinton against accusations of sexual abuse and even rape. These are the same women who stood by Hillary Clinton when she muddied the reputation of her husband's accusers, who were called "trailer trash."

Western secular feminists and elite Islamic feminists have been coming closer in recent years. Several assertive Muslim women, some hijab-wearing and some not, have risen to high positions in the American political system, especially under the Obama administration. Dalia Mujahid was the first veiled woman adviser in the White House and Huma Abedin was Hillary Clinton's deputy chief of staff and also served as vice chairwoman of Hillary Clinton's 2016 campaign for president. Abedin, who is a practicing Muslim, said that she leaned on her faith during the sex scandals involving her husband, Anthony Weiner. The connection between leftist feminist Hillary Clinton and a devout Muslim feminist such as Huma Abebin is a development worth paying attention to.

The Obama administration also followed the lead of Islamic governments, which single out hijab-wearing women for special respect and attention. Olympic fencer and hijab-wearing Muslim Ibtihaj Muhammad, for example, garnered attention in the U.S. after teaching the First Lady Michelle Obama how to fence. She also appeared on *The Ellen Show*, was chosen as one of *Time* magazine's one hundred most influential people of 2016, and met President Obama at the White House.

Even CNN jumped on the bandwagon, promoting the Muslim athlete as more deserving to hold the American flag of the opening ceremony of the Olympics than Michael Phelps, the most decorated Olympian of all time.[13] Despite all her popularity in America, the Muslim athlete does not sound particularly grateful to be living in the United States. During the Rio Olympics she told the world that she doesn't feel safe because of anti-Muslim sentiments in America.

Meanwhile secular Western feminists like Unni Wikan, a professor of social anthropology at the University of Oslo, Norway, regularly pander to Islamic values, blaming Westerners for problems actually caused by Muslims. In 2001 she called Norwegian women who had been raped by Muslim immigrants "blind and naïve": "I will not blame the rapes on Norwegian women, but Norwegian women must understand that we live in a multicultural society and adapt themselves to it.... Norwegian women must take their share of responsibility for these rapes. For example, by not inviting into their homes Muslim men with little knowledge of Norwegian culture."[14]

Another sign of the confluence between Western feminism and Islamic values was an article posted by CNN entitled "I Am a Feminist and I Converted to Islam," in which the author speaks positively about converting to Islam, wearing a hijab while at the same time preserving her feminist way of life. This Muslim feminist convert still lives in America, enjoying freedoms under the U.S. Constitution that she would not have under the Islamic law she should embrace if she is truly a devout Muslim.[15]

Why Secular Feminists Will Not Fight Islam

Why are Western feminists buying Islamic propaganda on how Islam honors women?

Western secular feminists have succeeded in convincing many Americans that the impediments to women's rights were Western patriarchal culture, Biblical values, and men. And that is how they want to keep it. Their enemy must always be family Biblical values. If secular leftist feminists decided to take on Islam with its outright misogynistic laws, then the feminists' theory about their own cause against Western Biblical values would collapse.

Fighting Islam's oppression of women—even just opposing acts of legalized violence in the Middle East, or Muslims' rapes of Western women in Europe—would open a Pandora's box for Western secular feminism.

So feminists in the West have chosen to limit their defense of women to the fight against Western Biblical values and Western men. They will never admit that Biblical values are the true reason why they are enjoying freedoms never enjoyed by women in any other culture in the world and that the American legal system, Constitution, and Bible are no impediments to women's freedom and happiness.

It is difficult to predict where feminism is heading. But one thing that feminists need to understand before it is too late is that the only thing standing between them and the wrath of Islam is the Holy Bible.

13

"MY KINGDOM IS NOT OF THIS WORLD" VS. ISLAM AND THE CALIPHATE ARE ONE

It should not be a surprise that very different kinds of governments emerge in Islamic societies and in societies that have been shaped by the Bible. Government is a fruit, a product, and a reflection of the values of society. And we have seen, Islamic values and Biblical values are mirror opposites. Consequently, the governments they produce are also mirror opposites.

The Bible emphasizes the sovereign authority of God over human beings, rather than the sovereignty of the state or the authority of man over man. The God of the Bible never abdicated His authority to the state, to a king, or to any man.

In the Bible Jesus said: "My kingdom is not of this world" (John 18:36).

Societies based on Biblical values do not give absolute power to fallen human beings. They have built-in mechanisms to protect against human wickedness, tyrannies, dictatorships, and totalitarian rule. There are no guarantees, of course, because it is ultimately up to human beings to protect their Biblical values and even fight for them if necessary. Majority Christian nations are made up of people who could fall into sin and self-destruction if they abandon Biblical values or take them for granted. But a constitutional republic like the United States, with its checks and balances, and its rule of law not men, is structured to limit the chances of tyranny by limiting human power.

Islam, on the other hand, is inherently totalitarian. It can never accept any limitations on government power to enforce Allah's commandments. Islam requires total submission of the individual to the Islamic government—the caliphate—for the sake of jihadist expansion. Here too, there are no guarantees. Not all Muslim nations adhere equally to sharia, so there is more freedom in some than in others. But the difference is not because sharia and the Koran are more tolerant in one nation and less in another. The Koran is the same book everywhere, and all the schools of sharia demand that Muslims be governed by Islam's tyrannical laws.

Islamic values will never lead a nation to liberty, democracy, or political stability. Those things cannot happen without major violations of sharia and the rejection of Islamic values. That was exactly what happened in the case of Turkey, when Kemal Ataturk veered away from Islamic values in the early twentieth century and linked his country to European culture. But Turkey's deviation from sharia was hard to maintain if the country was to continue considering itself a Muslim nation. Sharia clearly states that any Muslim leader who brings novel ideas that are not based on sharia would be considered an apostate and should be forcefully removed from office. Many Muslims today consider Ataturk an apostate who destroyed Islam in

Turkey. After living with Ataturk's deviations from sharia for many decades, Turkey is slowly moving back to its Islamic roots, which means back to tyranny and political instability.

Islamic leaders are proud of using coercion, terror, and tyranny in order to keep Islamic governments faithful to sharia. We have seen how top Sunni authority Sheikh Yusuf Qaradawi said that without the death penalty for apostasy, Islam would cease to exist. Abu A 'la Mawdudi, the most influential Islamic theologian of the twentieth century, proudly stated that Islam is a totalitarian system and a form of fascism, just like Nazism and Communism, that would destroy all personal freedom.[1]

This is how Mawdudi described the ideal Islamic state (caliphate): "It seeks to mold every aspect of life and activity.... In such a state no one can regard any field of his affairs as personal or private.... such a state should be run only by those who believe in the ideology on which it is based and in the Divine Law which it is assigned to administer. The administrators of the Islamic State must be those whose whole life is devoted to the observance and enforcement of this Law."

That is true, as we have seen to our horror, about "the Islamic State," the caliphate set up by ISIS. But it is also true about any and every genuine Islamic state. Even Muslims who do not support ISIS and are repulsed by the atrocities in the Islamic State know that any true Islamic state would have to be ruled by Muslims who would enforce sharia.

And, as Mawdudi said, the caliphate would also be committed to jihad: "Jihad is both offensive and defensive at the same time. It is offensive because the Muslim Party attacks the rule of any opposing ideology, and it is defensive because the Muslim Party is constrained to capture state power in order to protect the principles of Islam in space-time forces."[2]

Biblical Self-Government vs. Islamic Tyranny

Since all men are sinners, the Bible teaches self-control rather than the authority of man over man. Jesus did not wish to take control of the government: "And he said unto them, Render therefore unto Caesar the things which be Caesar's, and unto God the things which be God's" (Luke 20:25). But the Bible has inspired and influenced the state, fostering the self-control that makes self-government possible. That is why without Judeo-Christian values a constitutional republic or democracy cannot work. The Bible stresses the importance of governing self and family first as the foundation for good governance (Matthew 18:15–18, Galatians 5:16–26, I Corinthians 6:1–11, I Timothy 3:1–5, Titus 2:1–8).

Islam does not trust citizens to choose freely to uphold Islamic values. Thus capturing state power in order to force submission to Islam and its principles is the main goal of Islam. The above statements of Mawdudi and Qaradawi should put the West on notice that the goal of Islam is always to capture government power and control it absolutely, in order to put an end to people's freedom to resist the religion of Allah.

Wherever Islam goes, the goal is to control government in the country it invades. Islam did not expand through peaceful missionary work. While Christian missionary families volunteered to live modest lives in some of the most dangerous parts of the world to preach the Gospel, Islam expanded through conquering nations—by "futuhat," the Arabic word that literally meaning splitting nations open.

As Mawdudi explained, "The objective of Islamic Jihad is to eliminate the rule of an un-Islamic system, and establish in its place an Islamic system of state rule.... Islam wishes to do away with all states and governments which are opposed to the ideology and program of Islam."[3]

In short, Islam needs jihad in order to enforce its moral vision on the world. The purpose of Islamic fighting is "To put an end to the sovereignty and supremacy of the unbelievers [non-Muslims] so that the latter are unable to rule over men. The authority to rule should be vested in those who follow the true faith [Islam]; unbelievers... should live in a state of subordination."[4]

Without government control Islam is impotent and powerless. Even the most fervent Muslims lack confidence in the validity of its teachings, the justice of its sharia, and the loyalty of its followers. That is why it has to be enforced through tyrannical government control.

Without Islamic control of the government, citizens would not be forced to submit to sharia, jihadist wars against non-Muslim countries would not be waged, and the legal oppression of non-Muslims and the collection of "jizya" penalty taxes could not go on. But above all, without control of government the Islamic blasphemy and apostasy laws would not be enforced, and Islam would end.

While Christianity expands from the bottom of society up, Islam is forced on the society from the top down. After conquest by the sword, the new Islamic government forces Islam on the people until after decades and centuries of life under terror, nations like Egypt have no memory of their Biblical past.

Islamic Government: Immune to Criticism

Western and Biblical values rely on reason; thus Jews and Christians do not fear criticism of their religion. But the fact is, no religion or ideology should be immune from criticism. The freedom to speak out against a religion is especially important if the government and the laws people are forced to obey are determined by that religion.

Islamic sharia dictates that government should fall under the total control of Islam and its laws. And since Islamic law bans the criticism of Muhammad, Allah, and Islam itself, that immunity to criticism is extended and transferred to the Islamic state (the caliphate).

Under Islam, there is no escape from tyranny. Sharia makes the preservation and spread of Islam the number one duty of the caliphate: "the Islamic community needs a ruler to uphold the religion, defend the sunna. . ." (*Reliance of the Traveller* o25.2).

Islamic law is dictator-friendly as long as the head of the Islamic states rules by sharia. According to the sharia manual *Reliance of the Traveler*, the caliphate must be ruled by a Muslim male. It is invalid to appoint a non-Muslim to authority, even to rule over non-Muslims (o25.3). In fact, if the Muslim ruler (caliph) ceases to be Muslim or imposes "bid'a," Arabic for a novel idea that conflicts with sharia, on the people, then he loses his authority. At that point, he should not be obeyed. In fact, it becomes the obligation of the Muslim public to rise against him and remove him from office (o25.3). The forceful seizure of power from such a caliph at any point in his term of office is thus a valid and legitimate form of change of government under sharia (o25.4). But as long as the caliph is a believing Muslim, it is obligatory upon citizens to obey the commands and interdictions of the caliph, even if he is unjust (o25.5). So essentially the caliph is free to be a dictator, and the people can do nothing about it. The only way he can lose his right to rule is by deviating from Islam.

In other words, Muhammad made sure that if at any point the Islamic government veers away from sharia, Muslim citizens have the right to forcibly take out the leader and replace him with another who would enforce it. Sharia clearly states that a Muslim head of state can come to power through seizure of power, meaning through force. Allah made sure that his Muslim helpers on earth would forcibly take out any leader who would not enforce sharia. The almighty Islamic government must never be ruled except by sharia enforcers.

Under sharia, the caliphate has absolute, total control and power over citizens. In the eyes of a Muslim, Allah and state enforcement of sharia are one. That is the reason why wherever Muslims go they feel lost without a sharia-controlled government. Muslim immigrants sooner or later start demanding to live under an Islamic government that enforces sharia. Without such a government, Muslims feel that they have betrayed Allah.

Islamic Revolutions: All About Government Control

Islam is not a belief system concerned with influencing hearts and minds. Instead the ultimate goal is to unify the world under a universal Islamic state, the caliphate. To Islam, that political goal is much more important than anything Christians or Jews would recognize as a truly religious or spiritual goal.

The Islamic world has always been torn by civil unrest, revolutions, and counter-revolutions for control of government. These Islamic civil wars have typically been between two camps who want a stricter and a less strict version of sharia law. Recently it is usually a military dictatorship on one hand and an Islamic terror group that wishes to impose full sharia on the other hand. These are the only two groups that can be serious contenders for power in a majority-Muslim country, where democratic values cannot exist.

Islamic wars with the outside world are also about bringing government under the fold of Islam and sharia. Any neighboring country that is not Islamic or does not follow sharia is a target of Islamic jihad. It is the duty of the Muslim head of state to attack it and never befriend it. Muslim leaders who befriend un-Islamic states are considered apostates who deserve to be killed. That's precisely why Egyptian president Anwar Sadat was assassinated—because he was working for peace with a non-Islamic entity.

God Does Not Relinquish His Power to Government vs. the Caliphate Assumes the Power of Allah

The God of the Bible never abdicated his throne to man: "Which in his times he shall shew, who is the blessed and only Potentate, the King of kings, and Lord of lords; who only hath immortality, dwelling in the light which no man can approach unto; whom no man hath seen, nor can see: to whom be honour and power everlasting" (I Timothy 6:15–16).

The God of the Bible warned his followers against judging people. Christians are supposed to judge only the sin, and never to hate the sinner. The God of the Bible says that "Vengeance is mine; I will repay, saith the Lord" (Romans 12:19). That phrase has a much deeper meaning than you might think. It covers much more than just the obvious. It has taught Christians a wonderful lesson—to mind their own business.

Allah, on the other hand, told Muslims that "vengeance has been prescribed for them" (2:178) and entrusted his followers with enforcing sharia on one another. So minding your own business is not an Islamic value. Muslims consider other people's business as their own to judge and punish if it deviates from sharia. So in a sense Allah has abdicated his power to Muslim leaders and the Muslim public, to do vengeance, retaliation, and enforcement of Allah's law against sinners, whether Muslims or non-Muslims.

When the ISIS fighters behead, torture, rape, set fire, and drown people in cages, they truly believe that this is a commandment and power given to them by Allah. Muhammad himself acted the very same way, so who will convince them that they do not have this authority from God?

That transfer of power from Allah to the Islamic government totally changes the equation of the Islamic political system, government, and social structure, making them completely different from the West. Sharia itself and its enforcement on man by man have given human beings divine power over their fellow humans beings. Muslims feel authorized by Allah to make life-and-death decisions over those who sin, and not necessarily just over criminals. Sharia punishes not only the crimes of man against man, such as murder and theft, but also crimes against Allah—in other words, sins. That might explain why ISIS and Islamic governments such as those of Saudi Arabia and Iran execute, behead, torture, and stone sinners against Allah. When Western governments ask terrorists, *Why are you doing this?* the answer is typically *I got that authority from Allah in the Koran.*

Any Islamic state thus has the authority from Allah to be the representative of his godliness on Earth. And sharia crowns the government with Allah's power. The relationship between Allah and the Islamic state is thus intertwined in reality and also in the minds of Muslims. That is one reason why Islamic revolutions and political assassinations never solve the problems of the Muslim world or end by establishing good government.

The Government Serves the People vs. the People Serve the Government

The Bible emphasizes servanthood, not political power. "And whosoever of you will be the chiefest, shall be servant of all. For even the Son of man came not to be ministered unto, but to minister, and to give his life a ransom for many" (Mark 10:44–45).

From the beginning, Muhammad produced a religion to fit his huge appetite for power and control and his endless lust for wealth and pleasure. The Bible was an inconvenience, to say the least. Muhammad's fears of rejection, of losing control, and of being stripped of powers he had seized by the sword became the driving force behind Islam itself. To preserve Muhammad's power and perks, there had to be divine orders from Allah himself to convince Muhammad's followers that sacrificing their lives on earth was worth it. Everyone—men, women, and children—had to voluntarily give themselves as slaves to the Islamic state, which is the representative of Allah on earth. The reward for all serving the state (and Allah) was never a promise to be finally set free, but a promise of endless sex in Heaven. Millions of Muslims took the deal.

That was the carrot. But there was also a stick. Islam designed a whole social structure and system of government where citizens are to serve Allah and the Muslim state in exchange for—being allowed to live. Fear of execution for the smallest deviation from Islam is the driving force behind Muslim obedience to Islamic governments.

Serving the Islamic state is synonymous with serving Allah. Opposition to or criticism of an Islamic leader who rules by sharia, even if he is unjust, is a crime punishable by death. Rebellion is allowed only against leaders who deviate from sharia. Total dedication and servitude to the sharia state and its jihad goals is the highest form of worship in Islam.

To preserve such a pyramid scheme from ever being exposed by smart Muslims, the Islamic state has to stay in control over the Muslim mind, keeping it isolated from and paranoid against societies that allow freedom and have respect for the individual. For fourteen hundred years Islam has preserved its power over its citizen slaves through relentless and constant hate propaganda, fear-mongering, slander of Jews and Christians, and outright lies and distortions.

Expressions such as human rights, women's rights, child abuse, voting, constitutional republic, democracy, and "government of the people, by the people, for the people" were never heard by the citizens of Islamic states until Western technological advances brought them to the Muslim world. The old war between Islam and the West was re-ignited—but this time as an ideological war. Islam right now is in a fight for survival, but the West unfortunately does not know that.

Instead of thwarting Islam's constant need to expand in order to survive, the West rolled out the red carpet to Islamic expansion and gave Islam new respectability and hope. By welcoming Islam to America and Europe, the West gave the religion of Allah a new license to survive and thrive. The West saved Islam from imminent self-destruction, intentionally or unintentionally giving it a life line to stay in business longer. But its survival could mean the end of Western Biblical civilization.

In Harmony with Human Nature vs. Working against Human Nature

Western policies in the Middle East are based on the hypothesis that Muslims are just like everybody else and want the same things in life: freedom, democracy, a job to take care of their family, and so forth. In other words, they want life, liberty, and the pursuit of happiness like everyone in America. But are these the values of Islam? The answer is no.

This is why whenever the West tries to help the Muslim world the project fails. When the West works with and supports Islamic leaders, the Muslim public blames the West for supporting dictators. On the other hand, when they take out Muslim dictators—Saddam Hussein, for example—Muslims accuse the West of overstepping its boundaries, meddling in Islamic internal affairs, and occupying Muslim lands. When it comes to dealing with Islamic nations, the West will always be blamed, because Muslim citizens are trained to blame their oppression on outside forces and never on Islam and sharia.

As individual human beings, Muslims in their heart do yearn for the natural needs that we were all born with. They have the same desires that nature has given to us all. But what both the West and the Muslim world refuse to understand is that the natural needs of human beings will never be met under the Koran and sharia law. Human rights and democracy are incompatible with Islamic values. Any effort to import them to the Muslim world will be harshly dealt with by the Islamic sword.

Allah never promised Muslims life, liberty, and the pursuit of happiness, but he surely promised them lots of sex in Paradise if they do jihad. What Muhammad wanted the most from his followers was for them to challenge the sovereignty of non-Muslim nations with jihad and sacrifice their life, liberty, happiness, and family. Ridding the world of the kafirs was more important than giving Muslims what they are missing—that is, love, peace, forgiveness, and being saved right here on earth.

Instead, Islam bans Muslims from putting their natural needs, desires, and even human rights above jihad until an Islamic state controls the whole world. So Muslims will never be able to achieve happiness, or even basic human rights, until Allah's utopia, the caliphate, is achieved on Earth. Muslims are left chasing a mirage, doing jihad to keep the killing of non-Muslims and the expansion of Islam going. And all they get is an IOU from Allah, an admittance ticket to the supposed Islamic Paradise.

Regardless of how Muslims may feel about their human rights, Allah's plan does not include life under a democracy. The priority of any genuinely Islamic state is jihad and not the protection of human rights.

Endowed by Our Creator vs. Endowed by Our Islamic State

The human rights recognized today in the West have their origins in the Bible. The U.S. Declaration of Independence states, "We hold these truths to be self-evident, that all men are created equal, that they are endowed by their Creator with certain unalienable Rights, that among these are Life, Liberty and the pursuit of Happiness." Human rights are called inalienable because they were given to humanity by the God of the Bible. They were not created by any government, and they cannot be taken away by any earthly ruler. The role of government in a society based on the Bible is to protect these human rights, given to all citizens by God.

But *all* religions are given equal rights under the U.S. Constitution. And the migration of Islam—which claims to be a religion, but is really a totalitarian political ideology—to the West has caused some confusion on this point. The rights in the Declaration of Independence do not seem "self-evident" to many Muslims, who are in pursuit of something very different from happiness. Their goals are jihad, the expansion of Islam, control of the government, and enforcing sharia. And if their goals are achieved, the Bill of Rights and the U.S. Constitution will be crushed. Under Islam, the only rights citizens have are the rights allowed them by sharia and the government.

One day American Muslims could demand a different constitution and bill of rights. They could claim that their rights do not come from the God of the Bible, but from Allah—which means that all Americans would have to live under a caliphate or Islamic state.

If Islam succeeds in America, such a constitutional disaster will be a matter of when, not if. That has happened in all nations that took in many Muslims. India for example, had to split itself into two states, Pakistan and India, in order to avoid permanent civil war. And even with that, Muslims in Pakistan continue to threaten India with terror.

Allah does not endow his creatures with human rights or extend his grace to all human beings like the God of the Bible. All men are not created equal under Islamic law: as we have seen, Allah calls non-Muslims his enemies and tells Muslims that non-Muslims do not deserve to live on this Earth.

The West must challenge political Islam and sharia law as soon as possible. Islam does not define itself as just a religion; we should take Muslims' word for it. The influential Islamic scholar Mawlana Abu'l-A`la Mawdudi said of the ideal Islamic state, "Its sphere of activity is co-extensive with human life.... In such a state no one can regard any field of his affairs as personal and private."[5] He called the caliphate "the very antithesis of secular Western democracy.... Considered from this aspect the Islamic state bears a kind of resemblance to the Fascist and Communist states."[6]

What the West Needs to Know

While Islamic law will accept nothing less than the total control of the government and the legal system of a country, defenders of Islam continue to deceive the West by claiming that sharia is in harmony with the U.S. Constitution.

Muslim jihadists are fully aware that the U.S. Constitution protects the free exercise of religion, and they also know that sharia does not allow the free exercise of any religion other than Islam and Islam alone. Since Islam calls itself a religion it is thus legally protected to be freely preached and practiced in the U.S. on an equal footing with the Bible. That ensures that we will see future civil unrest in America.

When the U.S. Constitution was written, Islam was not practiced in America, but now it is. Millions of Muslim immigrants are pouring into the West, welcomed with open arms by Western political leaders. This is while Christians and Jews are being liquidated in the Middle East. Sooner or later the nature of Islam will win even over the so called "moderate" Muslims in the West, and demands for an Islamic government and laws will be heard loud and clear.

 The only way for America to protect its system from Islam is not just to outlaw sharia, but more importantly to define the word "religion" in the Constitution. According to American values, no ideology should be awarded the privilege of being called a religion if it executes apostates, bans human rights and freedom, and demands control of the government. These should be the minimum conditions for any belief system to be recognized as a religion under the U.S. Constitution.

Though today the percentage of Muslims when compared to the U.S. population is still minuscule, the Islamic fight to penetrate and control the American government is already underway. During the Obama administration a large number of practicing Muslims and even Muslim Brotherhood sympathizers, succeeded in getting appointed to key positions in the administration, in the judiciary, and in other parts of the government.[7]

And today it is not just Muslims who argue that no one has the right to criticize or slander Islam or Muhammad. The United Nations is trying to ban criticism of religion—in effect extending sharia blasphemy law to the entire non-Muslim world.

The UN attempt to ban criticism of religion was supported by Obama in a speech in which he said, "The future must not belong to those who slander the prophet of Islam." President Obama had no comment when an Egyptian court sentenced four teenage Christian boys to prison for a video mocking ISIS.[8]

14

ISLAM: A REBELLION AGAINST THE BIBLE

In the first thirteen chapters of this book I have laid out the differences between Islam and the Bible. I first began to notice them when I came to the United States after growing up in Egypt under Islam. The Bible-based culture of America and the sharia-based culture of the Middle East are like night and day—or, rather, like day and night. The Bible led me out into the light after I had been living in darkness for the first thirty years of my life.

The longer I lived in a culture formed by the Bible, the more I compared everything here in America to everything I knew growing up in the Islamic world. And the more clearly I saw how Islam is a direct contradiction of the Bible on virtually every significant point. While the Bible frees Christians' hearts and minds, Islam traps Muslims in slavery to pride, shame, and fear. While the Bible forbids lying, Islam commands it. While the Bible condemns lust and greed, Islam promises to reward them. While the Bible fosters loving, happy family life grounded in the mutual fidelity between one man and one woman, Islam demands faithfulness only from the woman—on pain of death—and fosters family strife, with up to four wives (plus sex slaves) competing for the man's attention for themselves and their children, and encourages the man to look forward to acting out his basest lustful fantasies with other women in the next life. While the Bible teaches confession and forgiveness of sins and warns Christians to "Judge not," Islam teaches Muslims to hide their own sins and ferret out and punish the sins of others. While the God of the Bible loves everyone He has created, the God of Islam hates non-Muslims. While the overriding theme of the Bible is the redemption and happiness of believers, the overriding theme of Islam's holy book is punishing non-believers.

It is truly astonishing. The Bible and Islam are like mirror images of each other. But how did it happen that almost a quarter of the world's population has embraced a religion that is a perfect contradiction of the Bible's teaching on nearly every important point?

To understand, you have to go back to the life of Muhammad and his situation on the Arabian Peninsula fourteen hundred years ago.

A Counter-Revolutionary Faith

Abul A'la Maududi called Islam "a revolutionary faith."[1] It would be more accurate to describe the Muslim faith as counter-revolutionary—a backlash against the revolution that the Bible had created in human society.

The Bible, given to man by God, was the original revolutionary book. It told the human race to follow the path of Jesus, Who would lead us through a miraculous transformation of redemption and healing. And the transformation in Christians' born-again hearts changed the course of human civilization. This supernatural and revolutionary transformation could never have developed through the natural wisdom of man alone.

Historian W. E. H. Lecky called Christianity "an Agency... which all men must now admit to have been... the most powerful moral lever that has ever been applied to the affairs of men."[2]

Christ did not come to make enemies. He did not have hidden goals and selfish priorities that required His followers to sacrifice their lives, to kill and get killed to enslave other human beings. Jesus did not come to command us to hate, destroy, and terrorize. The Earth already belongs to God, so what kind of God would command his followers to engage in holy expansionist wars to conquer the world? And what kind of religion would make the sword its symbol?

Following Jesus was never going to be easy. Christians' power does not come from the sword. The Bible says, "If any man will come after me, let him deny himself, and take up his cross, and follow me" (Matthew 16:24).

Those who chose to follow Jesus through the narrow gate were few. "Enter ye in at the strait gate: for wide is the gate, and broad is the way, that leadeth to destruction, and many there be which go in thereat: Because strait is the gate, and narrow is the way, which leadeth unto life, and few there be that find it" (Matthew 7:13–14).

But those who follow Jesus are the ones who will have the light of life: "I am the light of the world: he that followeth me shall not walk in darkness, but shall have the light of life" (John 8:12).

Muhammad refused to take the narrow road behind Jesus. And he didn't just quietly reject the Bible. Instead, he launched a ferocious rebellion against it and everything it stood for. Islam is a negative religion, consumed with subversion. It is a rebellion and a counter-revolution against the Biblical revolution.

It is not just happenstance that Islamic values are the opposite of Biblical values. Muhammad rejected Christianity as an alien belief system that would have subordinated Arab culture—his culture—to outsiders' principles and the outsiders' way of life. Muhammad's answer to the challenge that the Gospel posed to his culture was a new, specifically Arab religion. He borrowed a lot from the Bible—including monotheism. But he was not going to allow Arabia to be transformed by the good news of Jesus. Instead, he wanted the Arabs' culture to be preserved in stone—and conquer the world.

Muhammad custom-tailored his own monotheistic faith to make it the perfect opponent of Biblical faith. He was not only going to reject the Bible, but was going to fight its followers—Christians and Jews—whom he called enemies of his Allah. And today, the Islamic counter-revolution against the Bible is growing strong all over the world.

Muhammad built Islam on a foundation of lies: that the Bible was corrupted, that Allah (not the God of the Bible) is the true God, that Jesus is only a prophet and not the Son of God, that Christians are polytheists because they believe in the Trinity. The credibility of Islam depends on discrediting the Bible.

To see why Muhammad had to make a new religion that would lie about, contradict, and fight the Bible on every point, we need to go back to the starting point for Islam: Mecca, a small city on the Arabian Peninsula, six centuries after Jesus.

Starting from Mecca

Different cultures in the Middle East, the birthplace of the Bible, reacted differently to the Biblical revolution. Following the Bible was going to require major individual, social, and cultural change and adaptation. Some cultures struggled with the Bible and some adopted and converted to Christianity quickly. One example of a culture that took the latter path was Egypt, which became a Christian nation and remained one for six hundred years.

But one culture in particular, that of the Arabian Peninsula, resisted the Bible for several centuries at a time when most of the Middle East was part of the Christian Byzantine Empire.

Finally, in the seventh century AD, there came a point when pagan Arabs started feeling the strong influence of the people of the book, many of whom lived in Arabia. The Arabs were at a crossroads. They felt the pull of monotheism, which they had learned about from Christians and Jews and the Bible they believed in. The Arabs came very close to embracing the Gospel.

But in the end the proud, cutthroat, and rebellious desert culture of Arabia mustered the most ferocious rebellion against the Bible that the world has ever seen. Muhammad started a vicious counter-revolution against the Bible, and his followers have never let go of it to this day.

Mecca was a religious and commercial center in Arabia, important mostly because of the Kaaba, a pre-Islamic religious monument. As we have already seen, before Islam the Kaaba was a pagan shrine. Over three hundred and sixty gods were worshipped there. Muhammad's father was the head of the Quraish tribe, which had control over the Kaaba. That gave Muhammad's family a special status among the Arab tribes.

But by Muhammad's time, Arabia was already softening to monotheism. There were respected and wealthy tribes of Jews locally, and Christians had their little corner among other religions in the Kaaba. Finally, Arabian culture was on the very cusp of being transformed by the Gospel, as virtually every other culture in the Middle East already had been.

Muhammad knew that if the Bible won Arabia over, it would be the end of his tribe's power. If the Arabs became Christians, pilgrims would no longer flock to the Kaaba from all over Arabia. Instead they would go to the north, to Jerusalem. Accepting the Bible would also mean that the Arabs now shared a religion with the Byzantine Empire, which was the major power in their region. And that did not sit well with fierce Arab pride. Muhammad wanted to fight the Byzantine Christians, not fall within their orbit. And there were also Muhammad's personal desires. Accepting the Bible would mean accepting Christian morality, which forbids lust, greed, and violent hatred.

Muhammad knew it was only a matter of time before the Arabs would embrace major cultural and religious transformation that was going to touch every aspect of their lives—and strip his own tribe of its source of power in Mecca, threaten the independence of all the proud Arab tribes, and interfere with his own personal ambitions for power and pleasure. Believing in the Bible would have upended the entire culture of Arabia. The Bible would have replaced the unceasing violence of Arabia with peace and the culture of pride and shame with a new culture of freedom and happiness. It also would have turned Muhammad's own life upside down.

So he had to move quickly to offer an alternative: to unite Arabia under a purely Arabian monotheistic religion that would challenge the authenticity of the Bible. Islam was a strategy to use Arab pride as a defense against the appeal of Christianity, a movement to prevent Arab culture from being transformed by Biblical values. And it was very effective. Arab pride veiled the eyes of Arabia against the gospel.

Muhammad's plan was not fully formed at first. There were many twists and turns along the way, as Islam slowly took the form we know today. When the Prophet began, he needed to bolster his credibility with approval from the people of the book. So to appeal to Christians and Jews, he linked his new faith to Abraham. He also started praying toward Jerusalem, hoping that that would influence Jews and Christians to convert to his new religion. When they

declined, Muhammad flipped. He declared that the Bible was intentionally corrupted by the hypocrite Jews and Christians, and started
praying toward Mecca, which was still a pagan city at that time.

No Arab was allowed to convert to Christianity on Muhammad's watch—on penalty of death. That is still the law in Islam
today. The Koran itself commands Muslims not to befriend or deal
with Jews and Christians, but to convert them, and if they refuse
enslave them or kill them. The doctrine of "loyalty and enmity,"
which we have already looked at in detail, is a tactic that was first
used by Muhammad and is still used by Muslims today to keep
Muslims from getting close enough to Jews and Christians to learn
what the Bible really says.

Muhammad's plan, as we have seen, was to conquer Jerusalem,
build a mosque on top of the ruins of Solomon's Temple, and turn it
into Islam's second holiest city. That plan succeeded after Muhammad's death. Jerusalem was conquered by Arabs, and to this very day
Muslims consider it their second holiest city. The purpose was to take
it from Jews and Christians, and never to allow them to be first.

Muhammad was on a sacred mission to save Arabia from loss of
power, and the Arabs from any diminution of their pride. So he came
up with a holy book—like the one the Christians and Jews had, but
with crucial differences. Like the Bible, this new holy book taught
monotheism. But the monotheistic religion that it taught was uniquely
Arab. The God it preached was a combination of the Meccan moon
god "Allah" with some confused Bible stories. The Koran is full of
confusion and contradictions—perhaps because of the haste in which
Muhammad's new religion was created, in the few years before its
Prophet died.

The end result was a book that constantly has to be defended by
Muslims—less by reasoned arguments than with threats of terror. It
is no surprise that Jews and Christians could not make sense of the

Koran and rejected it—when they were free to do so. They considered it an abomination, and it was.

Even Arabs were not convinced by the Koran; they converted only after Muhammad's use of terror. In fact Muhammad did not know how to evangelize the pagans of Mecca; instead of reaching out to win their hearts, he insulted and cursed them and called them infidels.

His anger mounted as Arabs continued to refuse to convert to Islam. When curses and threats did not work, Muhammad tried to bribe them with promises of wealth, booty, and power from the conquest and subjugation of others. According to Islamic records on the life of Muhammad, the Prophet's uncle brought Muhammad and Meccan leaders together to talk about their grievances over Muhammad's abuse of their gods. At that meeting, both Muhammad and his uncle made the possibility that the Meccans under Muhammad would conquer others and enrich themselves a selling point for Islam. Muhammad's uncle promised that "if you follow him in his religion, you shall be the kings of the Arabs and the non-Arabs" (Al-Tabari, 142–43). Muhammad himself promised that the Meccans "will rule over the non-Arabs" and said, "Uncle, I want them to utter one saying. If they say it, the Arabs will submit to them and the non-Arabs will pay the jizyah to them."[3]

Muhammad's pitch to the leaders of Mecca says it all. The Prophet enticed them to convert to Islam by promising them power and wealth. He promised them everything: to be "kings" over both Arabs and non-Arabs, who would bow and submit to them, plus riches from the extortion of protection money, jizya, from Jews and Christians.

Muhammad's offers to the Meccan leadership were rejected over and over again. Peaceful negotiations failed Muhammad. At that point, he resorted to the sword. Suddenly Allah flipped to commanding Muhammad to do violence: "fight and slay the pagans (mushrikiin) wherever ye find them, and seize them, beleaguer them, and lie in wait for them in every stratagem (of war)" (Koran 9:5). The Meccan leadership that had opposed Muhammad was viciously killed, and their holy Kaaba was converted to Islam by the sword. Muhammad's dealings with the Meccans is a perfect example of an Islamic tactic we have already looked at closely: "lure and terror."

Islam became the shield of Arabia against the impact of the Bible and against the transformation that Christianity had been on the verge of bringing to the Arabs. Instead of adopting the Bible, Arabia chose to become enemy number one of Jews, Christians, and the values of the Ten Commandments.

Preserving Arab Pride and Shame

Adopting Christianity would have meant losing Arabian culture, with its brutal tribal customs of pride and shame. Muhammad knew that monotheism was coming to his people sooner rather than later, and he had to move quickly. He had to lead his people away from the Bible and unite them under a new monotheistic religion. By declaring that Christians and Jews had intentionally corrupted the Bible, he created a rift of distrust between the Bedouins of Arabia and the people of the book. And then he was able to sell the Arabs on his own competing monotheistic faith, complete with its own moral values, laws, and concepts of right and wrong.

Muhammad's pride was not going to let Arabs take orders from foreign leaders in Constantinople or Rome. Distrust of the outside world prevented Muhammad from accepting a foreign holy book, regardless of how desperately his people needed it. Islam was Muhammad's solution to the problem of how to preserve what he felt were Arabia's cultural superiority, political independence, and power. He was not going to allow his nation to become just another province of the Byzantine Empire.

To this day, Muslims know that their counter-revolution will lose to the Bible if the jihad ends and people are allowed to choose freely what to believe. To keep the rebellion against the Bible going, the state of war must be permanent. Because Muslims do not trust their religion to survive on its own, the holy land of the Jews and Christians must remain a torn war zone, held hostage as ransom. It has to be re-conquered by the Muslims, so that it will stay subsidiary to Mecca, and there will be no revival of the threat that the Bible once posed to Arab culture in the region.

Islam was founded on the values of pride, greed, envy, and power. Muhammad knew he could not achieve his incredibly devilish plan peacefully, and he was more than okay with his followers living in a constant state of horrific terror and violence. He convinced his followers that anyone who stood in his way was an enemy of Allah and must be eliminated. Fear, public humiliation, slavery, rape, and terror became Islam's permanent winning formula, the foundation upon which Muhammad's new religion was established.

Muhammad and the Jews

Muhammad never truly respected Jews and Christians, even though at the beginning of his mission he praised them. In fact his true feelings toward Jews and Christians were colored with deep envy. Muhammad expressed this envy not by becoming Christian or Jewish, but—as we have seen—by plagiarizing what he could from the Bible and linking his new religion to the history of the people of the book to gain legitimacy.

But Jews and Christians disputed Muhammad's claims, misrepresentations, confusions, and errors in reporting Bible stories. So, as we have seen, Muhammad responded by accusing Jews and Christians of falsifying their Bible. He pretended that the original uncorrupted Bible was like the Koran and agreed with Muhammad.

Even though Muhammad knew that all the Biblical prophets were Jews with no connection to the history of Mecca, he still continued to link himself and the Kaaba to Abraham.

Muhammad's deep envy and rage when his fellow monotheists, the Jews, rejected his new religion, knew no bounds: "Among the Jews are those who distort words from their [proper] usages and say, we hear and disobey.... But Allah has cursed them for their disbelief, so they believe not, except for a few" (Koran 4:46). The Koran is an extremely hateful, angry, anti-Semitic book. In *The Legacy of Anti-Semitism in Islam*, Andrew Bostom has detailed and documented indisputable evidence of a uniquely Islamic anti-Semitism, a specific Muslim hatred of Jews that has been expressed continuously since the advent of Islam.

The Koran describes Allah as a hater of whole groups of people, particularly the Jews. Non-believers in Islam, especially Jews, are condemned and cursed. To express his devotion to Allah, a Muslim must torture and murder Jews until the Day of Judgment. Many verses of the Koran describe Jews as apes and swine and threaten them with horrible punishments: "Become apes—despised and disgraced!" (7:166); "Be apes—despised and hated by all" (2:65); "They are those whom Allah has cursed; who have been under His wrath; some of whom were turned into apes and swine"(5:60); "Allah has cursed them on account of their unbelief" (2:88); "Allah is the enemy of the unbelievers; The punishment of those who wage war against Allah and His apostle and strive to make mischief in the land is only this, that they should be murdered or crucified or their hands and their feet should be cut off on opposite sides or they should be imprisoned" (5:33); "they shall have disgrace in this world, and they shall have a grievous chastisement in the hereafter" (5:41); "Amongst them we (Allah) have placed enmity and hatred till the Day of Judgment" (5:64).

At Muhammad's deathbed the Jews and Christians were still on his mind. He commanded his followers not to leave either Jews or Christians in Arabia. Muhammad also commanded them to kill the Jews wherever they went, even if they hid from the Muslims. This was Muhammad's deathbed wish, and so far the unfinished business with the Jews and Christians has lasted for fourteen hundred years. Non-Muslims are banned from ever entering Mecca and Medina, an originally Jewish city. No Christian or Jew today calls Saudi Arabia home, though some live there on temporary permits.

War on non-Muslims wasn't the only conflict Muhammad's successors had on their hands after his death. When the Prophet died, Arabian tribes abandoned Islam and went back to their old gods. But Muhammad's successor, Abu Bakr, wanted to preserve Muslim power, so he launched the brutal and bloody two-year "war of apostasy" to bring Arabia back to Islam. Islamic history is proud of these wars, which are documented in detail—including how tens of thousands of Arabs were burned, beheaded, dismembered, and crucified. It's not very different from what ISIS is doing today.

After Arabia was solidly under Muslim control, Christians and Jews across the Middle East lost to Islam also. The Byzantine Empire lost to Islam, and under sharia, the jizya tax, and the dhimmi system the remaining Christian and Jewish populations in the entire region that Islam had conquered gradually shrank. Those who managed to survive and kept their faith had to pay protection money in addition to living humiliated in second-class status. They have been living in survival mode ever since, and their ability to grow and thrive within their faith in the Bible has been stunted. Christians and Jews in the Muslim world are prohibited from practicing and expressing their religion publicly and denied the right to build churches, lecture, dialogue, debate, or even share religious books.

Islam is all about depriving non-Muslims of self-government and the right to practice their faith, not about nourishing and reviving the internal life of Muslims. According to Sayyid Qutb, leader of the Muslim Brotherhood in the '50s and '60s: "The foremost duty of Islam is to depose the government and society of unbelievers (jahiliyyah) from the leadership of man."[4]

Expansion

Muhammad was animated by an obsessive need to capture, seize, and expand. This is an attribute of the predatory desert tribal culture of Arabia. Even today, the motto of ISIS is "baqiya wa tatamaddad," which means "remaining and expanding"—the jihad principle of constantly staying in, fighting to keep what you have, and being in a constant outward motion against cultures that do not want to convert to Islam.

Muhammad was probably the ultimate ethnocentric. He rejected the Biblical transformation and renewal for his people rather than surrender his power and pride. Islam was his shield and sword against the Bible.

Muhammad's ambitions were limitless. He was not just going to be the final prophet, but also a warrior and the political leader of a constantly expanding Muslim state, "the Ummah." For that purpose no grisly deed was off limits, and anyone and everyone could be sacrificed for Allah and Muhammad's sake. As Muhammad himself said, "I have been sent with the shortest expressions bearing the widest meanings, and I have been made victorious with terror, and while I was sleeping, the keys of the treasures of the world were brought to me and put in my hand" (Sahih Al-Bukhari, Volume 4, Book 52, Number 220).

Muhammad claimed superiority over all the Abrahamic prophets, including Jesus, whom he insisted was just a prophet. The hadith report that Muhammad said, "I have been given superiority over the other prophets in six respects: I have been given words which are concise but comprehensive in meaning; I have been helped by terror (in the hearts of enemies): spoils have been made lawful to me: the earth has been made for me clean and a place of worship; I have been sent to all mankind and the line of prophets is closed with me" (Sahih Muslim, Book 004, Number 1062, 1063, 1066, 1067).

To make sure Arabian culture would be closed to any change, the Koran commands Muslims not to befriend non-Muslims or to make peace, except when Muslims are weak. That may explain why Islam's borders with non-Muslim nations have always been to be bloody.

Islam is not about transforming hearts and renewing minds; it is about conquering lands and enslaving minds. That was all that was on Muhammad's mind, even when he was on his deathbed, when he said, "No two religions are allowed in Arabia" and ordered the forced conversion, expulsion, or ethnic cleansing of Jews and Christians and the murder of pagans.

After his death, Muhammad's successors continued the very profitable business of conquering non-Muslims and seizing their wealth. They conquered the Middle East with incredible speed. Expansion became a way of life, a business, and the holy right and duty of every Muslim individual, leader, army, and government.

To this day, the world still suffers from Islamic jihad. And as we have already seen, not one Islamic leader has taken responsibility for the centuries-old culture that created 9/11, Al Qaeda, and ISIS. Instead, Muslim media, politicians, and the Muslim education system continue to blame the West, Israel, historical injustices against Muslims, colonialism, American foreign policy, and Israeli overreaction to Arab shelling and terror. When there are no other excuses, they resort to name calling, and the slurs of "racist" and "Islamophobia" work to silence any critics in the West.

Confusion is the name of the game. "Moderate" Muslims and Muslim governments blame the so-called "radicals." The Muslim Brotherhood claims to be moderate and blames Al Qaeda. Al Qaeda blames ISIS. And ISIS blames U.S. foreign policy and the inhumanity of Israeli soldiers.

The sad thing is that many in the West are taken in by this charade. Only a miracle from God will rescue the West from its delusions about Islam.

The Original Culture Clash

The fact is, the original culture clash between Muslims and Bible believers had nothing to do with Europe or America. It originated and erupted inside the Middle East, with a rebellion in the Arabian Peninsula against what Islam called "the people of the book"—Jews and Christians.

The Jews and Christians of the Middle East lost this first culture clash, were forced to submit to Islam, and had sharia law and second-class dhimmi status imposed on them. Then, as we have already seen, centuries of this Muslim abuse destroyed Christian communities across the Islamic Muslim world. Once Bible believers were pushed back to Europe, Muslims attacked them there. The Christians in Europe managed to fend off the jihad, and in modern times the technological achievements of the West kept Islam at bay. But in the last few decades the ferocious Islamic jihad against the Bible has been reignited with a vengeance all over the world, but especially in Europe, America, and Australia.

Theodore "Teddy" Roosevelt (1858–1919) predicted that if we do not fight we will lose to Islam the same way the people of the book in the Middle East lost to Islam in the seventh century: "Christianity is not the creed of Asia and Africa at this moment solely because the seventh century Christians of Asia and Africa had trained themselves not to fight, whereas the Moslems were trained to fight. Christianity was saved in Europe solely because the peoples of Europe fought. If the peoples of Europe in the seventh and eighth centuries, and on up to and including the seventeenth century, had not possessed a military equal with, and gradually a growing superiority over the Mohammedans who invaded Europe, Europe would at this moment be Mohammedan and the Christian religion would be exterminated...."[5]

Perpetrators Posing as Victims

Islam must conquer and expand, but today, when—thanks to the influence of Biblical values—most people believe in peace and human rights, Muslims must cover up their violence and create confusion about their intentions.

Most human beings do not want to live in a permanent state of hatred, hostility, and literal war with others. The classic Islamic tactics of "lure and terror" and "loyalty and enmity" have been very effective at keeping Muslims on board with jihad at the expense of their safety and security, their family lives, and their happiness. But there is also another tactic in the Islamic arsenal. Nothing works—like magic—on the human psyche better than the picture of yourself as a victim. Keeping Muslims in a constant state of paranoia is Islam's most powerful motivational tool for jihad.

My friend the cartoonist Bosch Fawstin, a former Muslim originally from Albania, explains the victimhood myth that Muslims have bought into in an article entitled: "The Muslim World Is a World Where the Bad Guy Won." As Fawstin explains, Muslims need to understand that their own religion is at war with them (as well as with the rest of the world).

In reality, Muslims are victims of Islam. And yet they have been convinced that somehow they are the victims of the people Islam wants to conquer.

After all, the best defense is a good offense. It's much easier for the defenders of Islam to accuse the rest of the world of victimizing Muslims—however little basis that claim has in the facts—than to explain away the actual violence that jihadists are perpetrating on the non-Muslim world.

The Muslims-as-victims-of-the-West myth defies the reality of history, not to mention the present-day Islamic genocide on Middle East Christians, Jews, and other minorities such as Yazidis. It also contradicts the facts about the victimization of some Muslims—the Kurds, for example—by other Muslims, whether for ethnic reasons or because of hostility between different sects of Islam.

Even actual acts of Islamic terror are used as evidence of the Muslim victim myth. After every act of terrorism by a Muslim, Muslims explain it away as a reaction to being victimized and insulted by the West. Islamic logic is *You made me do it.*[6]

Unfortunately, the non-Muslim world has bought into this myth as well. Western politicians and media keep repeating such obviously false Islamic claims. During a 2016 Democratic primary debate, Hillary Clinton accused Donald Trump of angering ISIS: "They are going out to people showing videos of Donald Trump insulting Islam and Muslims in order to recruit more radical jihadists." In fact there were no ISIS recruitment videos featuring Trump at that time.

Three speakers at the fourteenth annual Muslim American Society-Islamic Circle of North America (MAS-ICNA) convention on December 2, 2015, allied themselves with the Black Lives Matter movement, claiming to be oppressed and calling for a revolutionary movement inside America similar to the Arab Spring. Khalilah Sabra said: "We are the community that staged a revolution across the world. If we can do that, why can't we have that revolution in America?"[7] This is the modus operandi of Islam wherever it goes. It claims, *Muslims are your victims, thus we must rebel and destroy you and then take over.*

Muslim historians claim that the Arab conquest of Christian Egypt liberated the Coptic Christians from the oppression of the Orthodox Christian Byzantine Empire. But such historians fail to tell us that the Arab invasion of Egypt ended Christianity in that nation, changing the laws of Egypt to sharia, its language to Arabic, and its religion to Islam by the sword of terror. Now Muslims in Egypt claim to be the victims of Coptic Christians who want to rebel against Islam.

Positioning Muslims as victims not only justifies their violent attacks on non-Muslims. It also redirects Muslims' anger about their miserable lives under sharia law. They do live lives under oppression—from Islamic law. But the misery and horror of life under sharia must be blamed on the outside world if Islam is to survive. So the West must always be seen as exploiting Muslims, plotting against them, stripping them of their honor and pride.

As a child, I remember often seeing Israeli leaders portrayed in Arabic cartoons as monsters with the blood of Arab children dripping from their mouths. Western leaders were shown as puppeteers manipulating the poor Arabs and their puppet leaders.

Islamic schools today teach Arab children that the late Palestinian leader Yasser Arafat died by poisoning at the hands of Jews, so they call him "shahid," or martyr. The reality of Arafat's chronic health issues does not stop the Islamic propaganda.

This strategy of spreading paranoia and the victimhood mentality has worked miracles for Islam for fourteen hundred years. This same accusation was leveled at the time of Muhammad's death—supposedly the Prophet was poisoned by Jews. The tactics are the same, they just keep repeating, but the West never seems to learn from history.

Even acts of compassion and kindness by Jews and Christians, such as the distribution of free medicines to poor nations, or food aid in times of catastrophe, are often twisted around and portrayed as acts of intentional evil. When Israel went to help Haitian earthquake victims, it was reported on Arab television that the Israelis had really gone to Haiti not to help but to harvest the organs of the Haitian people. The Arab audience, who are constantly told lies and are also commanded by their religion to lie, believe and repeat such lies as true. Islamic culture has killed Muslims' human instinct to question slander. And the upshot is that Muslims are prevented from developing feelings of compassion or empathy toward the enemies of Allah.

The Biblical Revolution in Ethics vs. the Islamic Counter-Revolution

The Bible has given us an ethics revolution to live by, but with Islam humanity got a major setback. Today there is a global fight between the ethics of Islam and the ethics of the Bible. Western politicians tell us Islam is a religion of peace that does not represent an existential threat. That is a lie.

The flame of the Islamic rebellion against the Bible has been burning for fourteen hundred years. It is fueled by terrorism, but also by intentional misinformation, propaganda, and lies.

When I became Christian and heard for the first time that we human beings were made in the image of God, I wept. I was in awe at the honor, after being given shame and little value under Islam. The God of the Bible tells me that I am His child and that I am forgiven and saved. I am safe and blessed by Biblical ethics because the God I know from the Bible will never give us commandments that are hurtful to others or to ourselves. It was so freeing to adapt to the blessings of the Bible after suffering under the commandments of Islamic sharia. Those commandments have destroyed not only countless individual human psyches, but whole nations.

Biblical ethics were designed by the true, loving God to give us the best life possible, a happiness that is even beyond our imagination. Life, liberty, and the pursuit of happiness are ours to keep, but only if we keep on holding tight to our Bible.

CONCLUSION

"The sword of Mahomet, and the Koran, are the most fatal enemies of Civilization, Liberty, and Truth, which the world has ever known; an unmitigated cultural disaster parading as God's will."

—Sir William Muir (1819–1905), Scottish historian who specialized in the era of Muhammad and the early caliphate

When I started this book I had thought of about fourteen or fifteen differences in the moral values between the Bible and Islam. By now, I have more than fifty, and I'm still counting:

1. We Are All Sinners vs. They Are All Sinners
2. Life Is Sacred vs. Death Is Worship
3. Pleasing God vs. Pleasing Human Beings
4. Judge the Sin and Not the Sinner vs. Judge the Sinner, Not the Sin
5. Redemption from Sin vs. Immunity from Sin
6. Guided by the Holy Spirit vs. Manipulated by Human Terror
7. God the Redeemer vs. Allah the Humiliator

8. Healing of Spirit, Body, and Soul vs. No Healing Is Needed

9. Jesus came to Save Us vs. We Have to Save Allah and Muhammad

10. Jesus Died for Us vs. We Must Die for Allah

11. Confession of Sin vs. Concealment of Sin

12. At War with the Devil vs. at War with Flesh and Blood

13. The Truth Will Set You Free vs. Lying Is an Obligation

14. Trust vs. Distrust

15. Faith vs. Submission

16. Fear Not! vs. Fear as a Tool of Enforcement

17. Children of God vs. Enemies or Slaves of Allah

18. One Man and One Woman vs. One Man and a Harem

19. Transformation vs. Conformity

20. Changing Yourself vs. Changing Others

21. Fearing God vs. Fearing Man

22. Praising vs. Cursing

23. Personal Prayer vs. Exhibitionist Prayers

24. Prayers for All vs. Prayers Only for Muslims

25. Vengeance Is the Lord's vs. Vengeance Is Prescribed for Muslims

26. Forgiveness and Mercy vs. Reveling in Unforgiveness

27. Upholding Human Rights vs. Sacrificing Human Rights

28. Work Ethic vs. Wealth through Conquest

29. More than Conquerors vs. to Conquer Is to Prevail

30. God Loves Us All vs. Allah Hates Non-Muslims

31. Love Your Enemies vs. Hate Allah's Enemies

32. Covenant of Peace vs. Covenant of War

33. Self-Control vs. Controlling Others

34. The Wages of Sin Is Death vs. Die in Jihad to Be Forgiven
35. Pride Is a Sin vs. Allah Is Prideful
36. Humility vs. Pride
37. Envy Is a Sin vs. the Envious Can Put the Evil Eye on Those They Envy
38. Lust and Gluttony Are Sins vs. Lust and Gluttony Are Allah's Lure to Jihadists
39. Anger Is a Sin vs. Anger Is a Tool for Power
40. Self Reliance vs. Dependency/Reliance on Caliphate/ Government
41. Love Your Neighbor vs. Kill Your Non-Muslim Neighbor
42. Both Men and Women Shall Not Commit Adultery vs. Only Wives Have to Be Faithful
43. Stealing Is a Sin vs. Seizing Non-Muslims' Property Is a Right.
44. Thou Shalt Not Bear False Witness vs. Lying and Slander Are Obligatory in Defense of Islam
45. Thou Shalt Not Covet vs. Covet the Possessions of Allah's Enemies
46. The Bible vs. a Rebellion against the Bible
47. Constitutional Republics vs. Totalitarian Theocracy
48. Christianity Controls Sin vs. Islam Controls Governments
49. The Kingdom of God Is Not of This World vs. Allah and the State Are One
50. Government Serves the People vs. the People Serve the Government
51. An Ethics Revolution vs. a Counter-Ethics Revolution

It is clear: everything God tells us in the Bible that He loves, Islam has set out to destroy. Islamic values are backward, the opposite to what every Jew and Christian holds dear. Islam rejected the God of Abraham, condemned the Bible as false, and condemned Christians and Jews to a life of oppressive subordination—or death.

The Bible and Islam do not share the same God. The true God could not have provided His creation with two opposite sets of values in two very different books. One of these books was never from God, and, obviously, it is the Koran. The Koran represents a negative power, a dark and subversive force that relentlessly challenges the authority of the Bible and God Himself.

What differentiates sharia, Islamic law, from the Biblical commandments—and any other system of law—is Allah's delegation of his power to severely punish sins against him (and also to protect family honor). These crimes, such as apostasy, blasphemy, and adultery by women, are punished more harshly than murder and stealing.

As we have seen, Allah granted the caliphate divine totalitarian powers over both Muslims and non-Muslims. So telling a Muslim to give up on his ambition to live under an Islamic government that enforces sharia law is equal to telling him to give up on Allah.

But unfortunately, the West is under the illusion that there can be an Islam that does not aspire to live under a caliphate. And too many Christians and Jews have bought into the Islamic propaganda that Allah is the same as the God of the Bible, that Islam is an Abrahamic religion. That claim from the Koran is widely publicized by Muslims; other material in their holy book doesn't get the same publicity—as when Muhammad commands Muslims to kill the descendants of Abraham, the Jews, wherever they find them: "The Day of Judgment will not come about until Muslims fight the Jews, when the Jew will hide behind a rock or a tree, the rock and tree will say O Muslims, O Abdullah, there is a Jew behind me, come and kill him" (Bukhari 41:6985).

After centuries of hard work by Jews and Christians to build free societies and elevate humane values, Islam is hard at work dismantling those great achievements to replace them with totalitarian sharia law. Every Christian civilization in the Middle East has already been eradicated, and Islam is still fighting the Jews over the Biblical Holy Land. The light of the Bible in the Middle East was snuffed out by Islamic jihad. The black flag of Islamic conquests has been flying over the ruins of old Christendom for many centuries. The fervent Muslims' goal today is to finish the job by taking over the Bible-based culture of the West.

Attracted to the Light vs. Attracted to the Darkness

You would think that most human beings, under normal conditions, would be attracted to Biblical values, but unfortunately human nature is not as simple as that. There is a side to human nature that is attracted to Islamic values. I know that from experience. Islam gives some men and women an intoxicating amount of power over other human beings. It is not a coincidence that Adolf Hitler lamented belonging to the wrong religion, saying "You see, it's been our misfortune to have the wrong religion.... The Mohammedan religion... would have been more compatible to us than Christianity."[1] The Führer also complained, "Had Charles Martel not been victorious at Poitiers... then we should in all probability have been converted to Mohammedanism, that cult which glorifies the heroism and which opens up the seven Heavens to the bold warriors alone. Then the Germanic races would have conquered the world. Christianity alone prevented them from doing so."[2]

Hitler lamented the defeat of Islam in Europe, because he considered Islamic values to be the right tools he could have used to conquer the world. It is ironic that Europe, which lost millions of lives fighting Hitler, has allowed itself today to be overrun by millions of Muslim immigrants and refugees who openly and proudly say that they are in Europe to take over and to turn Buckingham Palace into a mosque.[3] European leadership and the Obama administration in the U.S. welcomed Muslim refugees, apparently unconcerned that Islamic terrorists were among them.[4]

Ironically Hitler's wish for the Islamization of Europe is being fulfilled today. Pleasing Muslims has become a top priority of politicians in Europe and America, who put it above pleasing and protecting Western citizens.

But if we are to continue to live our lives in the light of freedom and the other Biblical values that have made the West what it is, we must exercise constant vigilance against the values of darkness, oppression, and tyranny. Human nature does not always choose the light. Many men and women are attracted to the darkness.

For those who are not comfortable with the light of truth, Islam is their answer. Defenders of Islam are many and various. Islamic jihadists openly dedicate their lives and threaten the lives of others to expand Islam. But most Muslims are more discreet. Some choose to defend and support the jihadists, others finance them, and others simply look the other way, allowing jihad violence to go unchallenged. But the most dangerous kind of Muslims are those who deny that jihadist terror has anything to do with Islam. These apparently assimilated Muslims pretend that they are completely different from the violent jihadis, and yet they too want sharia in the West. All these different groups of Muslims appear very different from each other, but in fact they all work in perfect harmony, like an orchestra playing one tune. In their different ways they are all working to bring the West under submission to Islam.

Throwing a Lifeline to a Dying Islam

Islam is not as powerful as it looks, and Muslims are conscious of its weakness. Muslim leaders dread debating Christian leaders. This is because their religion is not based on reason but on violence. Thus they are not equipped to use dialogue and logic to win debates. Their Prophet and their books have convinced them that they can only win with terror.

Violence and terror—both in jihad against non-Muslim governments, and in the oppressive enforcement of sharia by Muslim governments—are Islam's tools for survival. Many Muslim leaders admit to that openly. Terror and fear can rob nations of their faith in the Bible, and the jihadis know that. They also know how to use Christians' love, goodness, and generosity against us.

It is unsettling to see how the secular leftists in the West, who do share Islam's rebellion against the Bible, are eager to flood America with un-vetted Muslim refugees. They are extending a lifeline to Islam; a religion that must feed itself by constantly invading new lands before it self-destructs.

Islam is a dying religion that spreads its poisonous fruits wherever it goes, but humanity keeps resuscitating it out of certain death. This is perhaps because Islam is very useful for totalitarian regimes. Islam provides weak governments with a legal and religious formula that enables totalitarian control and forces the submission of citizens. One of the reasons for Islam's fast expansion across the Middle East, in which whole nations were quickly converted, was its appeal to leaders who chose to compromise with the Devil to preserve or gain power over people.

The appeal of Islam to Western leftist politicians, who should know better, defies logic. Many Western political leaders often go out of their way to defend Islam and equate it with the Bible. Western countries compete to see who can take in more Muslim refugees, even at the risk of infiltration by ISIS terrorists. At the same time, Western citizens are intimidated, called racists and "Islamophobes" by their own leaders if they dare criticize Islam.[5] It is not clear why this is happening, but I hope it is not because Western politicians and media have any use for Islam and its sharia.

There are powerful secular and socialist forces that share Islam's vehement rebelliousness against the Bible and its values. But it is hard to understand why they ignore the warnings that history is full of regarding Islam. Turkey's reformist Muslim president Kemal Ataturk (1881–1938) warned the world about his country's religion when he said, "Islam, the absurd theology of an immoral Bedouin, is a rotting corpse which poisons our lives."

Despite the barbaric actions of ISIS, many Muslim leaders are telling us that ISIS and Islam are the same—and no reputable Western media outlet will report it. Adel Kalbani, for example, former imam of the Grand Mosque in Mecca, recently said, "ISIS has the same beliefs as we do."[6] Not even such an admission from Islamic authorities will convince the Left to end its support of Islam.

The inexplicable impulse that Westerners seem to have to coddle and excuse is a lifeline thrown out to a dysfunctional belief system that otherwise would be dying from its own internal contradictions.

How the West Can Beat Islam

To beat Islam, the West will have to get ready to use extraordinary measures for self-preservation and the protection of its citizens, freedoms, and Biblical values. Since Islam only respects power, the West must be ready to use its military power. But the West must also end the denial and wishful thinking. Western citizens must be told the truth about Islam.

There is a lot of talk about winning the ideological war, but no one defines it. The ideological war between the West and the Muslim world is all about proving that Biblical values are superior to Islamic values. The values of the Bible lead to peace, prosperity, life, liberty, and happiness. And Islamic values will take any society to Hell.

The West has no time for any more appeasement, especially with the millions of Muslims Western countries are taking in. The message should go out to the Muslim world that if they continue their policy of jihad the doors of immigration to the West will be closed. Muslims will only reevaluate their life under Islam when they have nowhere else to go. By taking them in, the West is leaving Islamic lands to ISIS and other brutal jihad groups, to rule and expand. Western media characterizes any suggestion of limiting Muslim immigration as xenophobic and racist, when in fact it is a necessary tool for winning the ideological war. One and a half billion Muslims are living under the slavery of Islam, and they will never truly rebel as long as they can simply leave for the West—where they will work to impose sharia on the rest of us.

Beating Islam is necessary. But it is not sufficient. Western culture is facing other problems. The West must revive its Biblical roots and values, which are the foundation of its culture. The threat to the West from Islam is exacerbated by a more serious threat inside the soul of Western civilization today: the erosion of Biblical values.

Most Americans understand that America was founded on Biblical values, but we have been doing very little, collectively, to stop the constant assault on Biblical values by the U.S. media and education system. The secularization of American society and government is well under way.

On its own Islam is not really all that powerful. Even Muslims believe their religion cannot succeed or even survive without the use of terror. Islam can only be as powerful as Western governments and citizens allow it to be—and their appeasement is making it very powerful.

A huge storm of Islamic darkness is sweeping across our planet today. Let us never take our Biblical values for granted or think that we could maintain Western morality while rejecting "In God We Trust," Biblically-based education, and the Ten Commandments. Our hope is the revival of Biblical values, our joy in the Lord, and holding on to our Bible. It's all we've got.

ACKNOWLEDGMENTS

I want to thank my children and their spouses, friends, and family for their love, patience, and support during the many months I was busy writing this book.

I especially want to thank my pastor and his wife, Jim and Alice Tolle, for their guidance and advice throughout this book project.

This was also made possible by a grant from the Middle East Forum. I am very appreciative of their kind support of my work for many years.

And last but not least, I am especially thankful for my publisher Regnery Publishing and their excellent and dedicated staff, especially my editor, the talented Elizabeth Kantor.

NOTES

INTRODUCTION

1. Raheem Kassam, "London's Islamist-Linked Mayor Tells U.S. Audience: Immigrants Shouldn't Assimilate," Breitbart, September 16, 2016, http://www.breitbart.com/london/2016/09/16/londons-muslim-mayor-tells-u-s-audience-immigrants-shouldnt-assimilate/.

2. Brian T. Kennedy, "Donald Trump and National Security," *Claremont Review of Books*, November 5, 2016, http://www.claremont.org/crb/basicpage/donald-trump-and-national-security/.

3. Nicole Lafond, "Gore, Current Silent as Cleric Affirms Death Penalty for Leaving Islam on Al-Jazeera," Daily Caller, February 12, 2013, http://dailycaller.com/2013/02/12/gore-current-silent-as-cleric-affirms-apostacy-death-penalty-on-al-jazeera/.

4. Christine Williams, "Canadian Imam: Islam and Democracy are 'Absolutely Incompatible,'" Jihad Watch, September 28, 2016,

https://www.jihadwatch.org/2016/09/canadian-imam-islam-and-
democracy-are-absolutely-incompatible.

1: MY TRANSFORMATION

1. See the Bukhari Hadith Collection at QuranExplorer.com, http://
   www.quranexplorer.com/hadith/english/index.html. Collections
   of hadiths—the words and deeds of Muhammad—are generally
   referred to by the names of their collectors, which I do
   parenthetically throughout the book.
2. IsraelFullTruth, "'Palestinians' Fake Funeral: Pallywood in Its
   Best," YouTube, September 9, 2014, https://www.youtube.com/
   watch?v=2DF8f2YAJq4.
3. Katie Pavlich, "Disgrace: Green Beret Who Defended Boy against
   Rape in Afghanistan Loses Appeal," TownHall, September 23,
   2015, http://townhall.com/tipsheet/katiepavlich/2015/09/23/army-
   to-green-beret-punished-for-defending-boy-from-an-afghan-rapist-
   nope-you-cant-come-back-n2055822.

2: THE SIN FACTOR

1. Quotations of the Bible throughout the book are from the King
   James Version.
2. Bill Warner, "Sharia Law for Non-Muslims Chapter 5—The
   Kafir," Political Islam, July 17, 2010, https://www.politicalislam.
   com/sharia-law-for-non-muslims-chapter-5-the-kafir/.
3. "Kafirs in the Trilogy," Center for the Study of Political Islam,
   http://cspipublishing.com/statistical/TrilogyStats/
   AmtTxtDevotedKafir.html.
4. Throughout the book, I use a number of different Koran
   translations, including: M. Pickthall, trans., *The Koran* (New York
   and Toronto: Alfred A. Knopf, 1992); Abdullah Yusuf Ali, trans.
   The Koran (Wordsworth Editions Limited, 2000); Muhammad

Muhsin Khan, trans., *The Noble Qur'an* (King Fahd Complex, 1998); Saheeh International, trans., *The Quran* (Abul-Qasim Publishing House, 1997). A helpful resource that compares six different English translations side by side is legacy.quran.com.

5. Ahmad ibn Naqib al-Misri, *Reliance of the Traveller*, trans. Nuh Ha Mim Keller (Beltsville, MD: Amana Publications, 1991). Parenthetical citations to *Reliance* throughout the book refer to this work.

6. This hadith is from the collection of Abu-Dawud, as quoted in Mansura Abubakar, "Kindness in Islam," Muslimah, July 7, 2012, https://9jamuslima.wordpress.com/2012/07/07/kindness-in-islam/.

7. Tim Arango, "A Century After Armenian Genocide, Turkey's Denial Only Deepens," *New York Times*, April 16, 2015, http://www.nytimes.com/2015/04/17/world/europe/turkeys-century-of-denial-about-an-armenian-genocide.html?_r=0.

8. "Fatwa No : 184937: Conceal His Sin, but Don't Let Him Be in Seclusion with,Her," August 8, 2012, http://www.islamweb.net/emainpage/index.php?page=showfatwa&Option=FatwaId&Id=184937.

9. "The Prophets Are Masoom (Free from Errors) with Regards to Conveying the Message," Quran Sunnah Educational Programs, http://qsep.com/modules.php?name=assunnah&d_op=viewarticle&aid=235.

10. My translation of a clip from Wafa Sultan, "War without Weapons," February 19, 2016, Youtube, https://www.youtube.com/watch?v=EaGnR4lBiAA.

3: HEALING, SALVATION, AND THE HOLY SPIRIT

1. From my search of the Koran at www.legacy.quran.com.

2. Sharia Unveiled, "Female Islamic Cleric Teaches That 'Enslaving and Raping Little Girls Is Permissible in Islam," YouTube, February 7, 2016, https://www.youtube.com/watch?v=6fo6vnx1BAQ.

3. From my search of the Koran at, www.legacy.quran.com.

4. L. Azuri, "Uproar over Drinking the Prophet's Urine," Sweetness & Light, June 13, 2007, http://sweetness-light.com/archive/uproar-over-fatwa-on-drinking-prophets-urine.

5. Walid Shoebat, "Camel Urine: A Mouthful a Day [Does Not] Keep the Doctor Away," April 18, 2012, http://shoebat.com/2012/04/18/camel-urine-a-mouthful-a-day-does-not-keep-the-doctor-away/.

6. Nick Sommarlad and Russell Myers, "Hate Preacher Accused of Radicalising 7/7 Bombers Now Recruiting Brit Jihadis for ISIS," Mirror, July 7, 2015, http://www.mirror.co.uk/news/uk-news/hate-preacher-accused-radicalising-77-6016094.

4: THE TRUTH WILL SET YOU FREE VS. LYING IS AN OBLIGATION

1. Sania Hamady, Temperament and Character of the Arabs (New York: Twayne Publishers, 1960), pp. 28, 85.

2. See http://corpus.quran.com/search.jsp?q=beat.

3. See http://legacy.quran.com/4.

4. See, for example, http://www.thereligionofpeace.com/pages/quran/wife-beating.aspx.

5. Title in Arabic (my translation): "Azhar Sheikh denies Apostasy Capital Punishment in Quran, but does not deny it to Egyptian apostates," YouTube, May 17, 2016, https://www.youtube.com/watch?v=PMFVNzqC8i4.

6. "Clip #2268—Egyptian Cleric Mahmoud Al-Masri Recommends Tricking Jews into Becoming Muslims," MEMRI, August 10, 2009, http://www.memritv.org/clip/en/2268.htm.

7. "Clip #1519—Egyptian Cleric Mahmoud Al-Masri Teaches Children It Is OK to Lie—to the Wife, to Jews in Times of War, and In Order to Reconcile between Two Muslims," MEMRI, July 21, 2007, http://www.memritv.org/clip/en/1519.htm.

8. Meron Rapoport, "In the Name of Truth," Haaretz, April 28, 2005, http://www.haaretz.com/in-the-name-of-truth-1.157189.

9. Imam Abu `Isa Muhammad at-Tirmidhi in the book of Faith Vol. 5, Book 38, Hadith 2640.

10. Khalid Muhammad Khalid, "Abu Bakr Has Come" (book one), in *Successors of the Messenger*, trans. Muhammad Mahdi al-Sharif, (Beirut: Dar al-Kotob al-Ilmiyah, 2005), p. 99.

11. "13th Hadith: Trust in God (Tawakkul)," Al-Islam, https://www.al-islam.org/forty-hadith-an-exposition-second-edition-imam-khomeini/thirteenth-hadith-trust-god-tawakkul.

12. This is my translation.

13. Al-Fudayl Ibn Iyyad, "Obligation to Believe in the Messenger, Obey Him and Follow His Sunnah, The," Sunnahonline.com, www.sunnahonline.com/library/beliefs-and-methodology/185-obligation-to-believe-in-the-messenger-obey-him-and-follow-his-sunnah-the.

14. Occidental Soapbox, "Islamic Crusades 2: Before Islam... Egypt, Iran, Iraq," YouTube, September 28, 2008, http://www.youtube.com/watch?v=GH4eekCNoDE.

15. Matthew Schauki, "Karawadi—Apostasy," YouTube, February 26, 2013, http://www.youtube.com/watch?v=tB9UdXAP82o.

16. Text of the "Cairo Declaration on Human Rights in Islam," August 5, 1990, available at the University of Minnesota Human Rights Library online, http://hrlibrary.umn.edu/instree/cairodeclaration.html.

17. Pamela Geller, "Media Lies about Rifqa Bary," *American Thinker*, August 25, 2009, http://www.americanthinker.com/articles/2009/08/media_lies_about_rifqa_bary.html.

5: FREEDOM IN THE BIBLE VS. FREEDOM IN ISLAM

1. Andrew G. Bostom, "Is Freedom 'Perfect Slavery'?," Front Page Magazine, March 3, 2006, http://archive.frontpagemag.com/readArticle.aspx?ARTID=5375.

2. Daniel Pipes, "Islamist Calls for Slavery's Legalization," Middle East Forum, October 15, 2014, http://www.danielpipes.org/blog/2003/11/saudi-religious-leader-calls-for-slaverys.

3. See, for example, https://www.youtube.com/watch?v=03r8VxqW9B0.

4. Tufail Ahmad, "India-Centric Jihadi Media Releases Urdu Book on Jihad Dedicated to Indian Jihadis; Book Quotes 11th Century Jurist Al-Sarakhsi as Arguing: 'One Who Rejects Jihad Is an Infidel,'" MEMRI, August 21, 2014, http://www.memri.org/report/en/0/0/0/0/0/0/8123.htm.

5. Hendrick Simoes, "US Personnel in Bahrain Prepare for Ramadan," *Stars and Stripes*, June 24, 2014, http://www.stripes.com/news/middle-east/us-personnel-in-bahrain-prepare-for-ramadan-1.290721. http://www.stripes.com/news/middle-east/us-personnel-in-bahrain-prepare-for-ramadan-1.290721.

6: THE BIBLICAL VALUES THAT CHANGED ME

1. Raymond Ibrahim, "Muslim Prayers of Hate," RaymondIbrahim.com, November 7, 2011, http://raymondibrahim.com/2011/11/07/muslim-prayers-of-hate/.

2. Ibid.

3. "Rafah Cleric Brandishes Knife in Friday Sermon, Calls upon Palestinians to Stab Jews," MEMRI, October 9, 2015, http://www.memritv.org/clip_transcript/en/5098.htm.

4. Jay Akbar, "Parents Forced to Watch ISIS Executioner Behead Their 14-Year-Old Son after He Missed Friday Prayers," *Daily Mail*, February 4, 2016, http://www.dailymail.co.uk/news/

article-3432393/Parents-forced-watch-ISIS-executioner-behead-14-year-old-son-missed-Friday-prayers.html.

5. "Complaint Says Crosses at Catholic School Offensive, Prevent Muslim Prayers," Beliefnet, http://www.beliefnet.com/columnists/news/2011/10/lawsuit-says-crosses-at-catholic-university-offensive-prevent-muslim-prayers.php.

6. Rich Calder, "Muslims Booted from Empire State Building for Praying: Suit," *New York Post*, March 18, 2014, http://nypost.com/2014/03/18/muslims-booted-from-empire-state-building-for-praying-suit/.

7. "Muslim Women Harassed For Praying In Public With A Hijab!! (SOCIAL EXPERIMENT)," YouTube, https://www.youtube.com/watch?v=exVTGCZnTII.

8. Pamela Geller, "Belgian Imams REFUSE to Pray for Victims of Brussels Attacks because It Is AGAINST ISLAMIC LAW," Geller Report, March 29, 2016, http://pamelageller.com/2016/03/belgian-imams-refuse-to-pray-for-victims-of-brussels-attacks-because-it-is-against-islamic-law.html/#sthash.NMV2FHr7.dpuf.

9. Michael Theodoulou, "Eye for an Eye: Iranian Man Sentenced to Have Drops of Acid Poured onto His Face for Blinding His Lover's Husband," *Daily Mail*, December 12, 2010, http://www.dailymail.co.uk/news/article-1337957/Eye-eye-Iranian-man-sentenced-drops-acid-poured-face-blinding-lovers-husband.html#ixzz4BFUwuCrT.

10. Roland Muller, "Honor and Shame in a Middle Eastern Setting," Nabataea, 2000, http://nabataea.net/h%26s.html.

11. "Search Results: Torture," legacy.quran.com, http://legacy.quran.com/search?q=torment&page=1.

12. Raymond Ibrahim, "Sodomy 'for the Sake of Islam,'" Gatestone Institute, July 12, 2012, http://www.gatestoneinstitute.org/3158/islam-sodomy.

13. Daniel Pipes, "Islamist Calls for Slavery's Legalization," Middle East Forum, November 7, 2003, http://www.danielpipes.org/blog/2003/11/saudi-religious-leader-calls-for-slaverys.

14. Vaxiavvval, "Spectacular, a Decent Muslim Scholar Says Islamics Are Lazy Idiots on Memri.TV," July 8, 2011, YouTube, https://www.youtube.com/watch?v=i0K7A_V7XHQ.

15. Abul A'la Maududi, *The Meaning of the Qur'an,* vol. 5, p. 66, note 51.

7: THE FRUITS OF THE SPIRIT VS. THE FRUITS OF ISLAM

1. Mansura Abubakar, "Kindness in Islam," Muslimah, July 7, 2012, https://9jamuslima.wordpress.com/2012/07/07/kindness-in-islam/.

2. Hisham Eladl, "Greatest Quotes by Sadat," YouTube, April 10, 2011, https://www.youtube.com/watch?v=b47NCdZYEGY.

3. Andrew Bostom, *The Legacy of Islamic Antisemitism* (Prometheus Books, May 30, 2008), p. 50.

4. Bill Warner, "Sharia Law for Non-Muslims Chapter 5—The Kafir," Political Islam, July 17, 2010, https://www.politicalislam.com/sharia-law-for-non-muslims-chapter-5-the-kafir/.

5. "Kafirs in the Trilogy," Center for the Study of Political Islam, http://cspipublishing.com/statistical/TrilogyStats/AmtTxtDevotedKafir.html.

6. FreedomPost.org, "Muslim Imam Preaches Non-Stop Killing of Kafirs 'Even if They Do Not Fight You,'" YouTube, March 16, 2016, "Islamhttps://www.youtube.com/watch?v=ovLiw_79XPI.

7. Kader Abdolah, *The House of the Mosque,* trans. Susan Massotty (Canongate, 2010), p. 336.

8. Daniel Pipes, review of *The Spirit of Allah* by Amir Taheri, Middle East Forum, January 30, 1986, http://www.danielpipes.org/24/the-spirit-of-allah.

9. Offer Binshtok, "The Root of the Conflict: The Highest Value in Islam Is Paradise. All Means Justify the Goal," apartheidsharia. com, October 29, 2015, http://www.apartheidsharia.com/the-root-of-the-conflict-the-highest-value-in-islam-is-paradise-all-means-justify-the-goal/.

10. Andrew J. Bostom, "Qaradawi and the Treason of the Intellectuals," *American Thinker*, February 22, 2011, http://www.americanthinker. com/articles/2011/02/qaradawi_and_the_treason_of_th.html.

11. "Statistical Islam Reference Library," Center for the Study of Political Islam," http://www.cspipublishing.com/statistical/charts. html.

12. "Leading Saudi Cleric Says IS and Saudi Arabia 'Follow the Same Thought," Middle East Eye, January 28, 2016, http://www. middleeasteye.net/news/top-saudi-cleric-says-and-saudi-arabia-follow-same-thought-626782255.

13. Mansura Abubakar, "Kindness in Islam," Muslimah, July 7, 2012, https://9jamuslima.wordpress.com/2012/07/07/kindness-in-islam/.

14. Mega Kovalan, "Saying Merry Christmas Is Worse than Murder: The Muslim View on Christmas," YouTube, November 7, 2014, https://www.youtube.com/watch?v=Qs5ZdmGNeR8.

15. Sarah Kaplan, "After Wishing Christians a Happy Easter, Beloved Glasgow Shopkeeper Is Allegedly Slain by Another Muslim," *Washington Post*, March 29, 2016, https://www.washingtonpost. com/news/morning-mix/wp/2016/03/29/after-wishing-christians-a-happy-easter-a-beloved-glasgow-shopkeeper-is-allegedly-slain-by-another-muslim/.

8: THE SEVEN DEADLY SINS

1. Raymond Ibrahim, "'Sex Jihad' Fatwa Permits Incest in Syria," Front Page Magazine, May 1, 2014, http://www.frontpagemag.

com/fpm/224606/sex-jihad-fatwa-permits-incest-syria-raymond-ibrahim.

2. El-Sayed Rachad el-Moussaoui, *The Great Names of Allah* (Chicago, Muhammad Islamic Foundation, 1993), pp. 125–27.

3. See, for example, Pamela Geller, "Geert Wilders Greeted with 'Islam Will Dominate the World,' 'Freedom Go to Hell,' 'Shariah for the Netherlands,'" Geller Report, October 16, 2009, http://pamelageller.com/2009/10/geert-wilders-greeted-with-islam-will-dominate-the-world.html/.

4. "Islam as an 'Arab Pride' Moment," Islam Speaks, June 29, 2014, https://irrationalislam.wordpress.com/2014/06/29/islam-as-an-arab-pride-movement/.

5. "Kuwaiti Man 'Marries' Four Women on the Same Day," *Deccan Chronicle*, June 25, 2016, http://www.deccanchronicle.com/lifestyle/viral-and-trending/250616/kuwaiti-man-marries-four-women-on-the-same-day.html.

6. *Sirah Rasul Allah*, p. 466.

7. Itamar Marcus and Nan Jacques Zilberdik, "Fatah Calls for 'Day of Rage' Tomorrow," Palestinian Media Watch, October 30, 2014, http://www.palwatch.org/main.aspx?fi=157&doc_id=12929.

8. Apeacet, "Privileged Hatred: Students for Justice in Palestine," YouTube, April 2, 2015, https://www.youtube.com/watch?v=rool4bFqg9o.

9. Amir Sulaiman, "Danger," Genius, http://genius.com/Amir-sulaiman-danger-lyrics.

10. Rehan Ahmad, "Food Waste in Ramadan: Trends and Counter-Measures," EcoMENA, November 21, 2015, http://www.ecomena.org/food-wastes-ramadan/.

9: A REBELLION AGAINST THE TEN COMMANDMENTS

1. Muqtedar Khan, "Sharia Is Based on Ten Commandments," On Faith, http://www.faithstreet.com/onfaith/2010/07/26/islamic-shariah-is-based-on-the-ten-commandments/4165.

2. Rich Swier, "Can Muslims Be Loyal to Anything Other than Allah?," Dr. Rich Swier's website, July 16, 2015, http://drrichswier.com/2015/07/16/can-muslims-be-loyal-to-anything-other-than-allah/.

3. "Islamists Target Egypt's Christians," IPT (Investigative Project on Terrorism) News, May 25, 2011, http://www.investigativeproject.org/2904/islamists-target-egypt-christians#.

4. Itamar Marcus and Nan Jacques Zilberdik, "Hamas: Killing Jews Is Worship of Allah," Palestinian Media Watch, November 27, 2012, http://palwatch.org/main.aspx?fi=157&doc_id=8091.

5. Tufail Ahmad, "India-Centric Jihadi Media Releases Urdu Book on Jihad Dedicated to Indian Jihadis; Book Quotes 11th Century Jurist Al-Sarakhsi as Arguing: 'One Who Rejects Jihad Is an Infidel,'" MEMRI (Middle East Research Institute), August 21, 2014, http://www.memri.org/report/en/0/0/0/0/0/0/8123.htm.

6. Itamar Marcus, "Fatah to Terrorist Alyan: 'Glory Kneels before You,'" Palestinian Media Watch, September 1, 2016, http://www.palwatch.org/main.aspx?fi=157&doc_id=18685.

7. Marc A. Thiessen, "A Horrifying Look into the Mind of the 9/11 Mastermind, in His Own Words," *Washington Post*, November 28, 2016, https://www.washingtonpost.com/opinions/a-horrifying-look-into-the-mind-of-911s-mastermind-in-his-own-words/2016/11/28/bf5827a8-b575-11e6-b8df-600bd9d38a02_story.html?utm_term=.4d49c953a0e6&wpisrc=nl_opinions&wpmm=1.

8. Phyllis Chesler, "Worldwide Trends in Honor Killings," *Middle East Quarterly*, Spring 2010, http://www.meforum.org/2646/worldwide-trends-in-honor-killings.

9. Tea Partiest, "Leading U.S. Imam and Professor: Muslims Can Take Property of 'Filthy' Christians and Jews," YouTube, December 11, 2015, https://www.youtube.com/watch?v=abW12CUkAeI.

10. "U.S. Imam: Muslims Can Take the Property of Christians and Jews," Consortium of Defense Analysts, November 9, 2013, https://cofda.wordpress.com/2013/11/09/u-s-imam-muslims-can-take-the-property-of-christians-and-jews/.

11. Pamela Geller, "Seized Documents Reveal Islamic State's Department of 'War Spoils' aka Booty," Geller Report, December 28, 2015, http://pamelageller.com/2015/12/seized-documents-reveal-islamic-states-department-of-war-spoils-aka-booty.html/#sthash.wBDhjZwJ.9D51GJxs.dpuf.

12. The Defender of Truth, "Sheikh Abu Ishaq al-Huwayni Gives Solution to Muslims," YouTube, June 18, 2011.

13. Leda Reynolds, "Pretend to Be Christians: ISIS Urges UK Jihadis to Cut Beards, Shun Mosques & Wear Crosses," *Express*, January 13, 2016, http://www.express.co.uk/news/world/632806/ISIS-guide-tells-UK-jihadis-lose-beard-ditch-mosque-and-wear-cross-before-killing.

10: MENTAL HEALTH IN THE BIBLE VS. MENTAL HEALTH IN ISLAM

1. "Saudi Family Therapist Khaled Al-Saqaby Gives Advice on Wife Beating as a Good Thing and Says: Women's Desire for Equality Causes Marital Strife," MEMRI (Middle East Research Institute), February 24, 2016, http://www.memri.org/clip/en/0/0/0/0/0/0/5444.htm.

2. "Quotable Quotes," Clarion Project, https://www.clarionproject.org/content/beaten-lightly-some-women-enjoy.

3. "TTP Commander Maulana Fazlullah Says Jihad Is 'Addiction,' Defends Polygamy, Urges Women Not to Marry Pakistani Soldiers: 'Don't Wed with Army Soldiers. . .; They are Apostates; Persuade

Your Husbands, Brothers, and Sons Categorically for Waging Jihad,'" MEMRI (Middle East Media Research Institute), March 7, 2012, http://www.memri.org/report/en/0/0/0/0/0/845/6151. htm.

4. See for example Munzari Mundhari, *Targhib wa-al-Tarhib min al-Hadith al-Sharif* (Beirut: Dar al-Kitab al-Arabi, 2005), http:// www.alkitab.com/7895.html.

5. Salman Al Awdah, "The Balance between Carrots and Sticks— Principle of Reward and Punishment, Materially and Morally— to Exaggerate in Both Directions—Serves as the Carrot and the Shrine of Intimidation—the Issues and Evidence in the Carrot and the Stick," Al Jazeera, http://aljazeera.net/programs/religiona ndlife/2008/5/11/%D8%A7%D9%84%D8%AF%D8%B9%D9 %88%D8%A9-%D8%A8%D9%8A%D9%86-%D8%A7%D9 %84%D8%AA%D8%B1%D8%BA%D9%8A%D8%A8- %D9%88%D8%A7%D9%84%D8%AA%D8%B1%D9%87% D9%8A%D8%A8.

6. Abu 'Amr alQa'idi, *A Course in the Art of Recruitment*, quoted in Brian Fishman and Abdullah Warius, "A Jihadist's Course in the Art of Recruitment," *CTC Sentinel*, https://www.ctc.usma. edu/wp-content/uploads/2010/06/Vol2Iss2-Art5.pdf.

7. Raymond Ibrahim, ed. and trans., *The Al Qaeda Reader* (Doubleday, 2007), 43.

8. Raymond Ibrahim, "The Two Faces of Al Azhar," Middle East Forum, July 20, 2016, http://www.meforum.org/blog/2016/07/ two-faces-of-alazhar.

9. https://www.youtube.com/watch?v=oCpRGFa8r9I.

10. Khurram Dara, "In a Boy's Hand, the Islamist Disease," *Wall Street Journal*, January 28, 2016, http://www.wsj.com/articles/ in-a-boys-hand-the-islamist-disease-1454022599.

11. "What Happens after Death? Life in the Grave," Islamic Insights, http://www.islamicinsights.com/religion/what-happens-after-death-life-in-the-grave.html.

12. "Top Ten Bizarre or Ridiculous Fatwas," ListVerse, February 25, 2010, http://listverse.com/2010/02/25/top-10-bizarre-or-ridiculous-fatwas/.

13. Burak Bekdil, "Turkish Clerics Weigh in on Father-Daughter Lust," Middle East Forum, January 12, 2016, http://www.meforum.org/5796/turkey-father-daughter-lust.

14. Macrina Cooper-White, "Religion & Mental Health: New Study Links Belief in 'Punitive God' to Mental Problems," Huffington Post, April 24, 2013, http://www.huffingtonpost.com/2013/04/24/religion-mental-health-angry-god-brain_n_3097025.html.

11: FAMILY

1. "Outbreeding the Enemy—Does It Work?," ATS (Above Top Secret), February 9, 2009, http://www.abovetopsecret.com/forum/thread434285/pg1.

2. "Jihad: The Forgotten Obligation," https://www.2600.com/news/mirrors/harkatmujahideen/www.harkatulmujahideen.org/jihad/o-jihad.htm.

3. https://www.youtube.com/watch?v=JE1aR-IDkOU.

4. "ISIS Member Executes His Own Mother in Public," Jews News, January 10, 2016, http://www.jewsnews.co.il/2016/01/10/isis-member-executes-his-own-mother-in-public.html.

5. Raymond Ibrahim, "'Sex Jihad' Fatwa Permits Incest in Syria," Front Page Magazine, May 1, 2014, http://www.frontpagemag.com/2014/raymond-ibrahim/sex-jihad-fatwa-permits-incest-in-syria/.

6. Ibid.

1. "Saudi Arabia: Panel of Scientists Admits Women Are Mammals, Yet 'Not Human,'" World News Daily Report, http://worldnewsdailyreport.com/saudi-arabia-panel-of-scientists-admits-women-are-mammals-yet-not-human/.

12: FEMINISM: BIBLICAL, SECULAR, AND ISLAMIC

1. Gabby Aossey, "Muslims Are the True Feminists," Huffington Post, May 10, 2016, http://www.huffingtonpost.com/gabby-aossey/muslims-are-the-true-feminists_b_9877692.html.
2. M. Muhsin Khan, trans. (Alexandria, VA: Al Saadawi Publications, 1996).
3. "Female Islamic Scholar Says Muslims Can Rape 'Non-Muslim Women,'" Conservative Videos, January 20, 2016, http://conservativevideos.com/female-islamic-scholar-says-muslims-can-rape-non-muslim-women/.
4. YouTube, October 6, 2014, https://www.youtube.com/watch?v=4sP0RWPhhCM.
5. "Watch: Muslim Imam Explains 'Sex after Death in Islam,'" Support Israel, http://i-supportisrael.blogspot.co.il/2016/01/watch-muslim-imam-explains-sex-after.html.
6. "Collective Feminist Activity Now Deemed Criminal in Iran," Clarion Project, August 11, 2016, http://www.clarionproject.org/news/collective-feminist-activity-now-deemed-criminal-iran.
7. Danusha V. Goska, "An Open Letter to Muslim Feminist Linda Sarsour: Let's Talk about ISIS Rape Victims," Front Page Magazine, August 17, 2015, http://www.frontpagemag.com/fpm/259811/open-letter-muslim-feminist-linda-sarsour-danusha-v-goska.
8. Carla Power, "Muslim Women Are Fighting to Redefine Islam as a Religion of Equality," Time, March 20, 2015, http://time.com/3751243/muslim-women-redefine-islam-feminism/.

9. Itamar Marcus and Nan Jacques Zilberdik, "Widespread Violence against Palestinian Women in Gaza," Palestinian Media Watch, April 6, 2015, http://palwatch.org/main.aspx?fi=157&doc_id=14431.

10. Raheem Kassam, "UK's First Female Sharia Judge: 'We Can't Ask Muslims Not to Have More than One Wife,'" Breitbart, July 2, 2015, http://www.breitbart.com/london/2015/07/02/uks-first-female-sharia-judge-we-cant-ask-muslims-not-to-have-more-than-one-wife/.

11. Taylor Wofford, "ISIS Is Using an All-Women Brigade to Enforce Sharia Law in Syria," *Newsweek*, July 30, 2014, http://www.newsweek.com/isis-using-all-women-brigade-enforce-sharia-law-syria-262074.

12. Joshua Partlow, "Taliban Kills 10 Medical Aid Workers in Northern Afghanistan," *Washington Post*, August 8, 2010, http://www.washingtonpost.com/wp-dyn/content/article/2010/08/07/AR2010080700822.html.

13. Eric Lieberman, "CNN Anchor Says Muslim Fencer More Deserving than Phelps of Carrying American Flag at the Olympics," Daily Caller, August 8, 2016, http://dailycaller.com/2016/08/08/cnn-anchor-says-muslim-fencer-more-deserving-than-phelps-of-carrying-american-flag-at-olympics/#ixzz4IYk7QGnc.

14. "Raped in Oslo," *Brussels Journal*, December 13, 2006, https://www.brusselsjournal.com/node/1754.

15. Theresa Corbin, "I'm a Feminist and I Converted to Islam," CNN, October 14, 2014, http://www.cnn.com/2014/10/14/opinion/muslim-convert-irpt/index.html?sr=fb101414feministislam1pstorygallphoto.

13: "MY KINGDOM IS NOT OF THIS WORLD" VS. ISLAM AND THE CALIPHATE ARE ONE

1. "Mawdudi—Islam Is a Form of Fascism," The 4 Freedoms Library, February 4, 2012, http://4freedoms.com/group/theology/forum/topics/mawdudi-panorama-and-the-mcb-islam-is-a-form-of-fascism.

2. Abu A 'la Mawdudi, *Jihad fi Sbilillah [Jihad in Islam]*, trans. Kurshid Ahmad (Birmingham, UK: Islamic Mission Dawah Center, 1997), p. 14.

3. Ibid., pp. 12–14.

4. Abul A'la Mawdudi, *Towards Understanding the Quran: English Version*, trans. Zafar Ishaq Ansari, vol. 3 (Leicester: The Islamic Foundation, 1990), surahs 7–9.

5. Mawdudi, *Jihad fi Sbilillah*, p. 154.

6. Adams, pp. 119–21.

7. Bob Unruh, "General: Muslim Brotherhood Inside Obama Administration," WND, January 9, 2014, http://www.wnd.com/2014/01/general-muslim-brotherhood-inside-obama-administration/.

8. F. Brinley Bruton, "Egyptian Teens Convicted of Blasphemy for Video Mocking ISIS," NBC News, March 14, 2016, http://www.nbcnews.com/news/world/egypt-should-quash-blasphemy-convictions-christian-teens-who-mocked-isis-n537781.

14: ISLAM: A REBELLION AGAINST THE BIBLE

1. Abul A'la Maududi, Towards Understanding Islam, http://www.azquotes.com/quote/1034764.

2. W. E. H. Lecky, *History of European Morals* (New York: Appleton, 1905), vol. 1, pp. 28–29, https://www.probe.org/the-social-and-historical-impact-of-christianity/.

3. W. Montgomery Watt and M. V. McDonald, trans. *The History of al-Tabari: Muhammad at Mecca* (Albany, NY: State University of New York Press, 1988), vol. 6, 93–95; Sam Shamoun, "Muhammad and the Meccans: Who Antagonized Whom? Examining Muslims' Justification for Muhammad's Atrocities," Answering Islam, http://www.answering-islam.org/Shamoun/antagonizing.htm.

4. "Top 100 Facts about Islam That Christians Must Learn," The Interactive Bible, http://www.bible.ca/islam/islam-encyclopedia-westerners-need-to-know-list.htm.

5. "Quotations on Islam from Notable Non-Muslims," WikiIslam, http://wikiislam.net/wiki/Quotations_on_Islam_from_Notable_Non-Muslims#Theodore_Roosevelt.

6. Bosch Fawstin, "The Muslim World Is a World Where the Bad Guy Won," Front Page Magazine, May 2, 2013, http://www.frontpagemag.com/fpm/188241/muslim-world-world-where-bad-guy-won-bosch-fawstin.

7. Mary Chastain, "Counter Jihad: Islamic Revolution in America," Breitbart, March 17, 2016, http://www.breitbart.com/big-government/2016/03/17/counter-jihad-islamic-revolution-in-america/.

CONCLUSION

1. Albert Speer, *Inside the Third Reich: Memoirs* (New York: Simon & Schuster, 1970), p. 96.

2. Adolf Hitler, *Hitler's Table Talk, 1941–1944: His Private Conversations*, trans. Norman Cameron, (1953), p. 667.

3. Jasper Hamill, "ISIS Will Turn Buckingham Palace into a Mosque, Jihadis Vow after Dodging Twitter Ban," *Mirror*, January 29, 2015, updated January 30, 2015, http://www.mirror.co.uk/news/

technology-science/technology/isis-turn-buckingham-palace-mosque-5049243.

4. Peter Henn, "Angela Merkel ADMITS Groups of Terrorists Are. in Stream of Migrants Heading into Europe," *Express*, July 11, 2016, http://www.express.co.uk/news/world/688368/Merkel-admits-jihadists-migrant-groups.

5. Brendan O'Neill, "Stop Smearing Critics of Islam as Islamophobes," Reason.com, March 17, 2015, http://reason.com/archives/2015/03/17/stop-smearing-critics-of-islam-as-islamo.

6. Pamela Geller, "Former Imam of the Grand Mosque in Mecca, Adel Kalbani: 'ISIS Has the Same Beliefs As We Do,'" Geller Report, January 29, 2016, http://pamelageller.com/2016/01/former-imam-of-the-grand-mosque-in-mecca-adel-kalbani-isis-has-the-same-beliefs-as-we-do.html/.